The Prayer Book Guide
to Christian Education

Third Edition
Revised Common Lectionary

Sharon Ely Pearson and Robyn Szoke

Morehouse Publishing
NEW YORK · HARRISBURG · DENVER

Morehouse Publishing, 4775 Linglestown Road, Harrisburg, PA 17112
Morehouse Publishing, 445 Fifth Avenue, New York, NY 10016
Morehouse Publishing is an imprint of Church Publishing Incorporated.

Cover design by Jennifer Glosser

Library of Congress Cataloging-in-Publication Data
Pearson, Sharon Ely.
The new prayer book guide to Christian education : Revised Common Lectionary / Sharon Ely Pearson and Robyn Szoke. -- 3rd ed.
    p. cm.
Includes bibliographical references and index.
ISBN 978-0-8192-2337-1 (pbk. : alk. paper) 1. Christian education--Textbooks--Anglican. 2. Episcopal Church.--Book of common prayer (1979) 3. Church calendar--Study and teaching. I. Szoke, Robyn. II. Title.
 BX5875.N48 2009
 268'.8373--dc22
                        2009001102

Printed in the United States of America

09 10 11 12 13 14   10 9 8 7 6 5 4 3 2 1

Table of Contents

Part II: The Revised Common Lectionary for Christian Education

Year C

Part III: Keys to Teaching and Learning

Acknowledgements

Sharon is grateful to her godparents, Barbara Alley and Irving Haase, and her parents, Clifford and Trinette Ely, as well as all those who have supported her life of faith from childhood through today. Robyn is especially grateful to her mother, Lela Grigonis, and her daughter, Christina Luo, for the deep understanding and importance of living our faith generation to generation.

We would like to thank the Domestic and Foreign Missionary Society of the Episcopal Church, which holds copyright to this and earlier editions, for its generous support of this revised and expanded third edition of an Episcopal Church classic.

The companionship of Christian educators, friends and colleagues who have walked the seasons of the Church year in story, song and reflection in so many ways helped form the Christians we are today. To all those faithful mentors, young and old alike, we dedicate this book. Together we share in the goal to broaden and deepen our understanding of being a people of God in the 21st century. It is in that spirit of education and memory that we offer this text as a way to build upon the vision of education offered by The Reverend Canon Joseph Russell. He danced with *The Book of Common Prayer* in one hand and encouraged all of us to join him. Let the dance continue.

Sharon Ely Pearson
Robyn Szoke
Feast of the Annunciation 2009

Foreword

It has often been said that if you want to know what the Episcopal Church believes theologically, you need to listen to the Episcopal Church at prayer. The Book of Common Prayer, with its rites, prayers, catechism, calendar (commemorations, lectionary, and wealth of tradition), carries the weight of theological understanding for the church.

If the prayer book is the cornerstone of Anglican theology, then it makes sense to see the prayer book as the cornerstone for Christian education in the Episcopal congregation. It was with this understanding in mind that a group gathered in 1982 at the invitation of Judith Carlson, the Children's Ministries Officer at the Episcopal Church Center at the time, who served as contributor and editor. Members of a special task force were Nancy Rayfield, Ruth Cheney, Wilm Smiley, Richard Bower, and Joseph Russell. Their task was to uncover the treasure of educational objectives and ideas within the Book of Common Prayer. With a foreword by Presiding Bishop John Allin, the first edition of *The Prayer Book Guide to Christian Education* was thus born, becoming a resource found on many Christian educators' bookshelves.

In 1996, Joseph Russell was asked to produce a new edition of this text, to update and strengthen certain sections of the first part of the original book concerning the seasons of the church year The second part of the original book provided brief outlines of the lessons and psalms, and collects of the three-year lectionary. Since this treatment of the lectionary had become available in several other sources, an entirely new format directed more specifically at the church educator and taking into account the renewal of the Catechumenate and the centrality of baptism was added. With this third version, we now provide the lessons from the Revised Common Lectionary.

Understanding that teaching and worshipping together involves team planning and coordination that has a life of its own, we will continue to share new insights and ideas to accompany using the prayer book in Christian education through a website: www.prayerbookguide.com. Add your thoughts, questions, and ideas as together we build up the Body of Christ through worship and learning.

To paraphrase Joseph P. Russell's statement in the edition that precedes this one, "With deep appreciation to the committee who produced the original, *The New Prayer Book Guide to Christian Education* is offered to the church with the prayer that the faith of the church can be embodied in the life of the congregation as it gathers week by week around God's word and sacrament."

Sharon Ely Pearson
Robyn Szoke

Introduction

OUR HERITAGE AND TEXTBOOK

There are many ways of being Christian, commonly called denominations. To be an Episcopalian is one such way of being Christian. It is unique among the denominations because its identity and its heritage are found in the Book of Common Prayer. The Book of Common Prayer is a manual for worship. As such, it is both the statement of what we believe and our call to ministry. It offers a flexible format for present-day worshiping communities, yet links us securely to our history and traditions; it is a handbook of faith in action. The Book of Common Prayer is a primary textbook for Christian formation in the Episcopal Church.

In 1994, the Episcopal Church published *Called to Teach and Learn: A Catechetical Guide for the Episcopal Church*[1] in order to lift up a vision of Christian formation and to provide guidelines for planning and implementing Christian formation in various contexts. It provided guidelines that could shape the life of an entire congregation in dynamic ways. *Called to Teach and Learn* did so by defining each member of the community as both a teacher and a learner. Using its approach forms Christians in a way that leads to ministry and mission shaped by the Baptismal Covenant. This approach to Christian formation found its nascence in the writings of third century (C.E.) theologian Tertullian. He wrote, "Christians are fashioned (made), not born" [*Apologeticus*, XVIII.4[2]]. Our goal as Christian educators is to make Christians. This includes preparation for baptism and deepening the life and faith of the already baptized. The process whereby Christians are made is known as Catechesis. Catechesis comes from the Greek root of a verb meaning, "to cause to sound in the ear," or "to echo." We "sound" the biblical story and the stories of the

---

1 *Called to Teach and Learn: A Catechetical Guide for the Episcopal Church*. New York: The Domestic and Foreign Missionary Society PECUSA, 1994).
2 Bardenhewer, Otto. 1908. *Patrology: The Lives and Works of the Fathers of the Church*. Freiburg in Breisgau and St. Louis: B. Herder. English translation by Thomas J. Shahan.

tradition in the ears of the learners. Most of all, we "sound" the Word that is Jesus into the lives of the learners. Jesus' authority came from his living the Word. Consequently, Catechesis is a lifelong apprenticeship in the tradition of Jesus Christ.

In its broadest sense, Catechesis is everything and anything happening anywhere that helps the Christian community grow in its life in Jesus Christ and in witness to God. Catechesis can be seen and understood as three intentional, interrelated, lifelong processes: formation, education, and instruction/training.[3]

According to *Called to Teach and Learn*, formation "is the participation in and practice of the Christian life of Faith . . . it is the means by which a community's worldview and value system are transmitted,"[4] whether via enculturation, assimilation, or inculturation. Our faith (how we perceive our lives), our character (our identity and behavior), and our consciousness (our awareness and predispositions to particular experiences) result from such practices.

Areas of formation in which the whole congregation and individual can be impacted are:

- *Participation in the communal rites of the church*—ritual worship that is carefully planned and executed is at the heart of who we are as a community.
- *The environment*—we shape our space and our space shapes us.
- *The ordering of time*—Our church calendar is based on a story just as our character and consciousness is shaped by our personal story.
- *The organization of our life*—Together our lives contribute to God's reign. Activities and programs sponsored by the church equip us for ministry in daily life and work.
- *Communal interactions*—Life in the congregation should be a sign to the world of what life in God's reign looks like.
- *Role models*—Those persons, past and present, whom we raise up to be examples of some aspect of Christian life.
- *Disciplines*—We learn to pray by the practice of prayer. We learn to care for others by the practice of caring. We learn to be a Christian by experience.
- *Language*—As Christians we need to be intentional about how we talk and write. When we listen and do not object to sexist or racist remarks, we encourage their continuance and contribute to the oppression of others. When we neglect feminine images of God, we make our God too small.

---

3 The following descriptions and definitions are taken from Called to Teach and Learn and Discovering Called to Teach and Learn, both published by The Episcopal Church and available at http://www.episcopalchurch.org/48931_49323_ENG_HTM.htm.
4 *Called to Teach and Learn*, p. 21.

Instruction/training is the process of discovering the necessary content about the Christian life and faith to make critical reflection and faithful formation possible. Instruction in Christian knowledge concerns learning about:

- The Bible and how to interpret its meaning in our lives today;
- Christian theology and ethics—skill in theological thinking and ethical decision-making;
- The spiritual life—the discernment of God's will and ways of prayer;
- Christian service and ministry—bringing Christ's message to the world through our words and actions in the local community and beyond.

The part of Catechesis with which this text largely concerns itself is Christian education. Christian education includes our whole congregational life—everything that we do as a community. It includes preaching and teaching, listening and learning, and the intergenerational sharing in liturgy. It is critical reflection through gospel eyes. Consequently, it is important to remember that the church is not so much an educational program as it is an educational community.

Education is a process that intends to produce change, to aid us to reform and renew our personal and communal lives, to bring them into line with more Christ-like lives. It is how we continually examine and reflect upon how faithfully we are engaging in formation. Scripture, tradition, and reason inform the educational process.

FAITH DEVELOPMENT AND THE BOOK OF COMMON PRAYER

The 1979 Book of Common Prayer is very clear with regards to the purpose of education and formation. In fact, its purpose is directly prayed for every Sunday during the celebration of the Holy Eucharist. It is found in all of the post-communion prayers, as well as in the catechism section on ministry. It is even found in the promises we make every time our worship includes a baptism. We pray, as we believe, that each baptized member—no matter what age or stage—is called to engage in an active ministry and mission, to be "sent out to do the work God has given us to do." That calling is the purpose of education and formation.

Two fundamental theological principles for ministry that we find in the 1979 Book of Common Prayer provide evidence for this. Both are foundational to any education or formation process that a congregation develops—no matter the chosen curriculum, resource, or focus. The principles lead us to educating for ministry. The first principle is that "all baptized persons are called to minister in Christ's name, to identify their gifts with the help of the church, and to serve Christ's mission at all times and in all places." The second principle is that all baptized persons are called to sustain their ministries through commitment to life-long Christian formation, as a part of the baptismal commitment—"to continue in the apostles' teaching."

To achieve the precepts of these fundamental principles, an understanding of the faith development of individuals and communities—of congregations—is necessary. As it did with the disciples, faith development moves from unbelief to belief, from fear to courage, and from faith to action. An understanding of such development is necessary because it will ground any educational offering in a way that will allow that offering to support the individual and community in spiritual growth, in the development of knowledge, and, above all, in the way they live out God's mission and ministry.

Historically, there are many ways to describe the faith development of individuals and communities, the pilgrimage that deepens our understanding of God's love for us. For example, Teresa of Avila used the analogy of a journey through the interior crystal castle of the soul. Each of the castle's rooms holds its own challenges of faith, its own new experiences, and its own ways through which to relate to God. The ultimate goal of traveling deeper into the castle is to come closer to God. As another example, John Bunyan used the analogy of an adventure during which a person travels across many different kinds of terrain. There are places of danger and risk, as well as of places of security and comfort. James Fowler, who has been one of the leading researchers and writers in the area of faith development over the past thirty years, has described faith development in stages. These stages are similar to those in other areas of human development, e.g. cognitive development and moral development.

Today, many Americans feel uncomfortable with the idea of moving from one stage of faith to another, however. Stages have been misunderstood to be boxes with a definite hierarchical sequence. Perceived in this way, they do not usually allow for chaotic, organic, and less hierarchically structured human situations. Consequently, Heinz Streib, professor of Faith Development at Bielefeld University, writes of styles of faith rather than stages, while Sam Keen, former professor of philosophy and religion at Boston University and Princeton Seminary, chooses the idea of dimensions to describe faith development. Recently, Adrienne Thompson, a spiritual director and author from New Zealand, suggested the notion of zones of faith. Zones are less rigid and more fluidly interconnected and can overlap.

We might think of faith development as a journey through rooms, terrains, stages, styles, dimensions, zones, spaces, or places of faith. The reality is that, for many people, their experience of faith changes from childhood to adulthood and again (perhaps many times) during adulthood. For Episcopalians, the key to understanding these changes is found in the 1979 Book of Common Prayer.

The Book of Common Prayer is purposefully designed in content and context as a framework for the faith journey. Consider the movement of the Easter Vigil, which contains the history of salvation, along with prayers of birth and death, sacrifice and salvation, exodus and exile, along with a vision of new life found in the community of faith that knows it is the living body of Christ. Each liturgical expression offers an opportunity to teach and learn. The discovery of the faith journey actualized in liturgy allows faith development to intersect with mission and ministry, both individually and collectively.

When planning a Christian education offering, the congregational leadership for Christian education needs to determine the ways they will discern the development of the members of their congregation. In order to do this, the congregational leadership should observe how the people engage in ministry and mission, i.e., how they put their faith in action. There are four main ways to do this:

Prayer: The first way the congregational leadership can observe engagement in ministry and mission is look at practices of prayer, which include weekly worship with the congregational community, daily offices and devotions, and microcommunities of intercessory prayer. For example, how often do the members of a congregation share in the Daily Devotions found in the Book of Common Prayer? The four brief Daily Devotions for Individuals and Families are designed to offer a framework for deepening one's faith development by blending praise and scripture. Furthermore, when prayed daily, they become integrated with the cycles of prayer found in our liturgical seasons.

Study: The second way to observe a congregation's engagement in ministry and mission is to look at participation in Bible studies, retreat and reflection opportunities, and seasonal studies (for example Advent events) and the percentage of people who are comfortable sharing the Biblical story. The Collect for the second Sunday in Advent sums up beautifully our call to study and learn as well as what we should be handing over from generation to generation: "Blessed Lord, who called all Holy Scriptures to be written for our learning, help us to hear them, to read, mark, learn and inwardly digest them that through patience and the comfort of Your Holy Word we may embrace and forever hold fast the hope of everlasting life which You have given us in our Savior, Jesus Christ." We say, Amen.

Hospitality: The third way to observe engagement in ministry and mission is to look at the way the congregation demonstrates the hospitality of God, including providing ministry to children and youth, pastoral care, incorporation of newcomers into the faith community, and facilitating ecumenical and interfaith projects. The elements necessary for these ministries are all found in the 1979 Book of Common Prayer. For example, in our Liturgy for Baptism, we use the words "seek" and "serve," "persevere," "continue," "proclaim," and "strive." The Prayers of the People remind us of the levels of community, which we need to serve. Furthermore, in the Exhortation as well as in the act of Contrition and Absolution we share every Sunday, we are called to examine our lives, to perceive where we have offended God or another. This reflection is designed to lead from confession to forgiveness, forgiveness to reconciliation, and an understanding of the depth of love we receive from God and then give to others.

Stewardship: The fourth way to observe a congregation's engagement in ministry and mission is to look at the way that giving time, talent, and treasure supports mission in the community, in the nation, and in the world. The Pastoral Offices found in the 1979 Book of Common Prayer provide a liturgical structure that enables one to come closer to God and one another in community. Thus, from birth through death, there are spiritual milestones that deepen one's sense of belonging in community. This, in turn, encourages the giving of time, talent, and treasure. These Offices are direct applications of the teaching of Jesus applied to human needs and conditions.

WHO ARE THE EDUCATORS OF CHRISTIANS?

At the ordination of a bishop the candidate is asked, "Will you boldly proclaim and interpret the Gospel of Christ, enlightening the minds and stirring up the conscience of your people?" This responsibility is not solely the bishop's. Priests who are charged by the canons "to be diligent in instruction" also share it. At the ordination of a priest, the candidate hears these words that define his or her role in the church: "Now you are called to work as a pastor, priest, and teacher, together with your bishop and fellow presbyters, and to take your share in the councils of the Church."

The directions for Holy Baptism declare that parents and godparents are to be "instructed in their duties to help the new Christians grow in the knowledge and love of God." During the service the entire faith community is asked, "Will you do all in your power to support these persons in their life in Christ?" Then together they accept both personal and corporate responsibility for Christian nurture by affirming and renewing the Baptismal Covenant and by welcoming and receiving the newly baptized into the household of God.

Very clearly, Christian education is a network of mutual responsibility for a ministry in which all persons, both laity and clergy, share. It happens locally, within a congregation as well as within a family. Growth and learning take place throughout our lives, with possibilities as limitless as God's grace. Teachers and learners become interchangeable as people of all ages discover together to what they are called and to whom they belong.

We are shaped in conscious and in subliminal ways by the liturgy of the church. Faith is formed by the worship experiences shared over a lifetime. That is one reason why the worship experience of the congregation is so crucial. The familiar expression "actions speak louder than words" is true in worship as well. When children, youth, and adults hear God's word proclaimed with power and conviction, they are formed by a community of faith and belief. When they feel a coldness and distance in worship, no number of programs and educational opportunities can cancel out or replace their experience of congregational worship. We must see the liturgy of the church as consistent with what we believe, as well as what we teach and proclaim, so that everyone in the faith, young and old, experiences welcome, care, inclusion, and love.

How liturgy is developed as well as how it is a shared praxis has a crucial impact on Christian education. Worship and education must be coordinated and drawn together at every possible juncture. This will take extra time and care, but if educators, musicians, clergy, lay ministers, and others gather around God's word as it unfolds week by week in the lectionary, the stimulation of shared insights will enhance liturgical preparation and lesson planning. Liturgists and educators find themselves as members of a team rather than as isolated individuals struggling for relevance in a lonely pursuit of truth.

Who Can Use This Book?

This companion guide to the Book of Common Prayer is intended to gather in one place information and counsel for living, learning, and engaging the questions of everyday life through the cycle of the church year. Therefore, this book is not just for those who have responsibility for planning or teaching in the church, but for all who share in the life of the Christian community:

- Teachers and directors of education;
- Individuals and families who study, teach, and pray in the home;
- Clergy and lay leaders;
- Lay readers and chalice bearers;
- Altar guild members and sacristans;
- Organists and music directors;
- Writers of church bulletins and newsletters;
- Inquirers of all ages;
- Individuals and families who study and pray at home;
- Families who home-school;
- Summer camp directors;
- Retreat leaders.

This guide is for use along with the Bible and *The Hymnal 1982,* as well as other resources such as *Lesser Feasts and Fasts* and our many supplemental hymnals: *Lift Every Voice and Sing; Wonder, Love and Praise; Voices Found;* and *My Heart Sings Out,* a hymnal for children. *The Book of Occasional Services* and *Changes* also offer opportunities for prayer and education in the midst of our daily life, transitions, and milestones. Some of the material may already be familiar, but other resources, including those in the list of "Suggested References and Resources," offer more detailed information when needed. It is hoped that from this raw material, programs meeting particular needs can be molded according to local creativity and imagination.

THE CHURCH YEAR: FRAMEWORK FOR CHRISTIAN LIVING

We live by many calendars—social, seasonal, civil, personal. The rhythm of our experiences and commitments shapes each of us and provides a context in which we can search for meaning in our personal lives, in our relationships with God and others, through our work and play, in joy and pain, in our very living and dying. The church year gives us as Christians this same opportunity. At every point the focus is upon what God has done in Christ for all people in all ages, including our own day. In remembering and celebrating our Christian heritage we are not only drawn into the salvation story, but realize we as a people of God are part of the Story, to encounter and ponder, to proclaim and show forth Jesus Christ, who is "the same yesterday and today and forever" (Hebrews 13:8).

Season by season, feast or ordinary day, the church year is like a bright jewel turning in the sunlight whose facets reflect light and hold it for a time so that we may see more clearly within the unity the many splendors, joyful and contemplative, of what it means to share Christ's life on earth. Each repetition of season and feast holds the possibility of our seeing something new, a fresh surprise that can illuminate our understanding and bring us to deeper faith and commitment. The church year gives us, as it has given Christian people throughout the ages, a way to live in Christ so that every year becomes the Year of Our Lord. So we mark our calendars Anno Domini, and with "those in every generation in whom Christ has been honored" we "pray that we may have grace to glorify Christ in our own day."

The liturgical year, with its calendar of seasons and commemorations, was really the first curriculum of the church. The familiar pattern of Advent/Christmas/Epiphany and Lent/Holy Week/Easter evolved out of the need of the early church to guide candidates for baptism through the essential narratives and teachings that would form their understanding of God in Christ over the rest of their lives. The Christian calendar, moreover, was developed in part out of the calendar of temple and synagogue as those institutions existed in Jesus' time. Thus the roots of education that are based in lectionary and worship go very deep in our heritage.

WAYS TO USE THIS GUIDE

The many components of the Book of Common Prayer are outlined chronologically in this book, from Advent through the Season after Pentecost, to help you adapt and use them in your own home or congregational setting. Part I provides an overview of the entire season; the headings described on the following pages are used in each chapter in this first section. Part II proceeds through the lectionary texts of the season Sunday by Sunday, according to years A, B, and C. This section gives a summary of the Old and New Testament readings, as well as the appointed psalm, collect, and gospel of the Day. Part III offers additional resources for furthering exploration and support in planning educational opportunities to reinforce the lectionary themes.

A website, www.prayerbookguide.com, will offer up-to-date resources, links, and ideas in order to ensure this text remains a current and living document. Updates are posted for reflections for the Sunday in light of current events, as well as questions for conversation in Indaba groups or other settings.

Definition of the Season

Here the season is defined theologically as well as in time and history.

- Mark the season on your calendar and then look at the ways your schedule of vacations, holiday times, and events unfold in your life, in the life of the congregation, in the community in which you live, and in the world. Observe those events in relationship to the liturgical calendar.
- Think about researching how the liturgical season has been observed in history and how it still has meaning for us today.

Holy Days in the Season

The major saints' and holy days to be commemorated during the season are listed in this section.

- Review the complete list of saints' and holy days provided in the calendar at the beginning of the Book of Common Prayer, or
- See *Lesser Feasts and Fasts* (reissued after each General Convention) for prayers, lessons, and biographical information concerning saints in the church calendar. This book introduces the church of today to the great Christians of yesterday. Sam Portaro's *Brightest and Best: A Companion to*

the Lesser Feasts and Fasts gives further reflections on our saints. Paging through these books is like looking through an old family album. Ask yourself, "Who were these people and why are they remembered by the Christian family today?"

Themes of the Season

This section describes the meaning of the season reflected in the biblical texts specified for Sundays and holy days and in the traditions associated with the season.

- Choose a theme as a starting point. Introduce it for study and application.
- In seasons with several related themes, emphasize one theme this year, another the next.
- Find out where in your community the theme of the season is being expressed today. Where can the theme be discovered in your daily newspaper? A bulletin board of clippings, a journal, church website link or blog could emphasize the theme in your congregation.

Great Words of the Season

Here we see at a glance different words that express various aspects of the themes of the season.

- Look for the story behind a word.
- Create a litany, prayer, or a poem using the words.
- Feature a "Word of the Week" in the church bulletin, website, or on a poster, or invent crossword puzzles or word games.
- Ask, "What experience have you had of (word)?" Explain the word as if to someone from another country, giving examples.
- Illustrate a word visually with banners, dioramas, or mobiles or liturgically through stoles and altar frontals.

The Season Through the Eyes of a Child (Ages 0–12)

This section will provide you with a variety of ways to invite children to grow in their faith, by sharing theological themes that use simple language and concepts.

Often children can understand visually or in actions what they cannot express in abstract words. It is important for adults to learn ways to provide children with the opportunity to respond.

After sharing the biblical story, whether at church or at home, give children time to respond through artistic expression, music response, prayer, and even dance and movement. Let them make their own pictures; let them act out ideas spontaneously. Ask yourself, "In terms of experiences known to these children, how can this idea be explained?" Ask yourself, "If I am five or ten years old, in terms of reflection upon my own experiences, how can I share this idea of God or family or time or faith with a child?"

CHARACTERISTICS OF THE YOUNG CHILD AND FAITH

Young children naturally embody the gifts of wonder, contemplation, and joy. The young child's heart is naturally open to God, and in fact their first knowledge and awareness of God comes through their parent's proclamation of love. Developing a healthy environment is as important as the content to be learned. Their prayer is often their work, their play. They are active learners who need sensory-motor or practical application of their new learning.

Provide direct experiences for them, include them in prayers, and ritual and symbol. Do not hesitate to include the young child in the richness of the liturgical experience of the seasons. Observe them closely as they engage in the biblical story, the stories of the church, and the stories of their faith journey, and they will lead you closer to God.

CHARACTERISTICS OF THE OLDER CHILD AND FAITH

The older child begins to master concepts of time and understanding of history. This is a key time to emphasize the historical narratives found in Scripture, maps, geography, and an awareness of faith developing through time. The liturgical seasons can take on new meaning, in regards to life and prayer, and even faith growth.

They have a definite view of right and wrong, which encourages us to share the Scripture lessons of justice. Social interaction is also so important at this time; inclusion in a vital community is necessary for their sense of belonging.

Seasonal Worship Sentence for Young Children

A brief sentence of Scripture accompanied by hand motions that can be used in worship or as an opening prayer in the learning setting.

The Season Through the Eyes of Youth (Ages 12–18)

Youth are in the process of identity formation, including that of their faith. There is no better time to connect them to the life and death of Christ. This is the time for them to discover how relationships are incarnational, developed in the presence of Christ in their lives. Their search for Truth can be met through an understanding of the love of Christ and a desire to imitate it.

Icons, prayer labyrinths, prayer beads, Bible study, and complex images of God are all appropriate for this age. Adolescents are drawn to the holiness of life as God reaches for them; therefore experiences need to be provided for them that set them in the context of knowing they can make a difference in the world by being in Christ.

This is also an important time to connect them to ways to respond to injustices in the world, giving them the opportunities to learn and put their faith into action beyond their own culture, community, and core beliefs.

CHARACTERISTICS OF FAITH DEVELOPMENT WITH YOUTH

As youth work hard at their own identity, their music, their dress, and their actions exemplify their searching, while at the same time there is an emphasis upon awe, wonder, and other experiences that are beyond the mundane, everyday life that connect the individual to something transcendent and/or of ultimate importance. For the adolescent, there is a lure of the transcendent that happens during this stage of physical development.

Youth often experience a degree of turmoil in their lives as they challenge the beliefs and systems of their childhood as well as their elders. It is the call of the church to affirm God's forgiveness and to appropriate the strength God provides to overcome the problems and live a healthy Christian life.

Youth workers use a variety of names to identify the present youth of this generation: Mosaics, Millennials, Net Generation (N-Gen), Navigators, the Y. The use of media and global concepts, as well as being service-oriented, are critical characteristics to be aware of in ministry with youth. They are seeking a practical, pragmatic, everyday faith they can grasp that will help them to make sense of the world around them, and one of the strongest characteristics they possess is hope.

The Season Through the Eyes of Daily Life

Ministry is about vocation, the vocation of all baptized persons. Even today some Christians still hesitate to call what they do—at home, at school, in the office or the factory, on the farm, in retirement—ministry. All of these can be places of service if what is done is done with mindfulness and compassion following the example set by Jesus of Nazareth.

As the faith community gathers each week to be fed by word and sacrament, it is sent "out to do the work that you have given us to do, to love and serve you as faithful witnesses of Christ our Lord" (BCP 366). Educators are called to assist in helping make the Sunday to Monday connection by helping the baptized grow in personal prayer, reflect on God's action in daily life, and be a more faithful steward of God's gifts to us and of God's creation. Being more intentional about daily life and work as the context for loving and serving God as well as practicing a way of life that manifests this understanding is at the core of the Baptismal Covenant.

- How can one's life become one of thanksgiving to the One who came that we might have life in all its fullness?
- What is the relationship between one's individual vocation and the Christian community? The biblical story and one's daily life?
- How might one's ministry become evangelistic in response to the day's readings? The Evangelical Lutheran Church of America maintains a weekly resource for personal reflection on the Sunday readings that connect faith and daily life. Daily Discipleship has a key "attitude word" for discipleship and a focus question for each Sunday to be reflected upon throughout the week: http://www.elca.org/Growing-In-Faith.aspx.

A. Wayne Schwab in *When the Members are the Missionaries: An Extraordinary Calling for Ordinary People* (Essex, NY: Member Mission Press, 2002) offers six principles for guiding the planning of worship that recognize the ministry and mission of its members:

- Liturgy should express the way we live rather than be a separate exercise apart from life.
- The connections between liturgy and real life should be easy to discern.
- Adapt the worship to the specific characteristics of the place of worship.
- Find ways to express the specific daily missions of the worshipers.
- Find ways for the laity to share their own journeys in faith during worship.
- Make sure the laity are prominent and visible in leading worship in order to demonstrate their mission in church life.

The Season Through the Eyes of Our Global Community

The Baptismal Covenant calls each Christian to "strive for justice and peace among all people, and respect the dignity of every human being." Prophets like Amos and Micah constantly warned the people that social justice and compassion were at the heart of offering worship and praise to God. Because issues of social justice can be controversial, educators and preachers all too often steer clear of focusing on them even when they occur in the lectionary texts. If we are to be faithful to Torah, to the gospel, and to the Baptismal Covenant, themes of social justice need to stand at the center of preaching and teaching.

- Let the lectionary and the Bible shape congregational life. If social justice issues are seen to be a natural outgrowth of biblical concerns for mission and ministry, some of the controversial sting will be removed.

- General social issues that naturally arise could easily become specific and timely for a local educational event and/or an action group.
- Focus panel discussion on issues of social justice or global concerns.
- Sponsor a field trip or guest speaker to offer closer involvement with an issue.

The church's call "to know Christ and make him known" is central to the 1979 Book of Common Prayer and shapes the beliefs and faith life of those who use it. Our focus on mission extends into our global community. As members of the Episcopal Church, we are a part of the global community of the Anglican Communion and have engaged in mission throughout the world. The word "mission" appears in the current prayer book much more frequently than in any earlier version, thus our praying strengthens our call to mission and lifts our eyes to the world. Many of the liturgical prayers focus on mission, including the Collect "Of a Missionary" and prayers and thanksgivings for the mission of the church. We believe that our prayers shape our believing, thus many congregations participate in mission in many different ways. One way is to begin to look out into the world, and see a global vision for Christ's mission:

- Establish a mission committee that keeps before the clergy and congregation the mission imperative and looks for opportunity for cross-cultural ministry within the parish's locale.
- Develop education opportunities for seeing the liturgical seasons from a global perspective.
- Learn about their companion Diocese and/or congregation, and develop a mission relationship with them.
- Develop relationships to work in mission to accomplish the Millennium Development Goals (MDGs) and to fight domestic poverty.
- Throughout the year commemorate the Feast Days of the many missionaries who have helped spread the gospel using *Lesser Feasts and Fasts* as a primary resource.

Symbols and Traditions of the Season

Symbols represent something with which they are identified, and have meaning when that connection is recognized. Symbols help us to learn about and understand people of other cultures, and to share in their seasonal traditions:

- Use symbols in creative activities. Symbols can be created from all sorts of materials.
- In studying liturgies, identify the symbols and the symbolic actions for clues to learning.

- Find out why some traditions have a long history, while others developed recently. Look at the infinite variety of local variations.
- Traditions are preserved by being practiced. Look for the roots of traditions in your family and in your community.

Great Bible Stories for the Season

Bible stories are often found in the season's lectionary and reflect its themes. As noted above under "The Season Through the Eyes of a Child," stories that appear in lectionary texts will be pointed out under the section on the readings (or Propers) for that Sunday.

- Stories naturally engage the attention of child and adult alike. Tell the Bible stories that appear in the lectionary texts and are identified in the outline of the Propers for each Sunday.
- Choose your own form of telling the story: paraphrasing, using objects, PowerPoint, video, or other illustrations, adding music, doing it as a skit or other dramatization such as choral reading or a silent tableau, or even by using puppets.
- Choose one character in the reading with whom to identify. "What does it feel like to be that person?" "How would you act or respond?"
- To study the stories of the Bible, read from more than one translation and refer to Bible commentaries.
- Ask questions to aid in your reflection on a Bible passage: What is the writer trying to say?
- What was the context or situation in which it was written?
- Where do you see or hear God in the story? Christ? The Holy Spirit?
- How is God speaking to us today?
- Where are you in the story?
- What will be different for you after hearing this story?

Great Hymns of the Season

Hymns from *The Hymnal 1982* and other hymnals are included as a reminder of the importance of music and hymnody in our worship and education. *The Hymnal 1982* is, in addition to the Bible and the Book of Common Prayer, the church's third major resource book for Christian education.

- Sing familiar songs as well as new ones: singing is an enjoyable way for children and adults to learn about a season.
- Reflect on the words of the hymns, as expressions of the church's faith.

- Study the hymns that are imbedded in the New Testament. For example, Philippians 2:6–11 is considered by many scholars to be a fragment of an early Christian hymn or creed. Trace the biblical origins of hymns. How do the hymns reflect the biblical texts?
- Look at the worship bulletin for the day and discuss why particular hymns were chosen. Ask your church organist or music director to join the discussion.
- Learn the stories that lie behind the hymns. For example, the familiar hymn "Amazing Grace" came out of the painful conversion experience of John Newton, an eighteenth-century slave trader who accepted Christ and later became a priest who worked for the abolition of slavery in the British Empire. The text takes on a whole new meaning with that story in mind!
- Use *The Episcopal Musician's Handbook* for more complete references and information about hymns.
- Nancy Roth has written several books of meditations to coincide with each year of the lectionary: *A Closer Walk*—Year A, *Awake, My Soul*—Year B, and *New Every Morning*—Year C.
- Introduce canticles alongside hymns for worship and study. Canticles are songs or chants, other than psalms, with words taken from a biblical text. For example, "The Song of Mary" (BCP 119) is taken from Luke 1:47–55.
- Also consider music from Taizé, Iona, and other religious communities.
- Consider how young children are ready to learn the refrain of hymns, as well as use hand motions to kinesthetically represent words or concepts.

The Season in the Book of Common Prayer

This section looks at the season in the context of the Prayer Book and links themes of the season with prayers and services found in the Book of Common Prayer. The Book of Common Prayer can be supplemented with *The Book of Occasional Services*, which is issued in succeeding editions after each General Convention and contains a wide variety of services used on an "occasional" basis, such as house blessings and prayers for catechumens. *Enriching Our Worship* and *Changes* are other supplemental texts to the Book of Common Prayer.

- Read the services at home, or use them for study. A discussion might consider the form, historical usage, and significant personal impressions of the services. Note how their symbols and biblical images and ideas express the season's meaning.
- Participate in corporate worship whenever possible. Liturgy is doing. For example, participate in the Reconciliation of a Penitent and then reflect

on the experience by asking, "What have I discovered about sin and reconciliation as a result of my experience of this service?"

- Families might want to have a house blessing, share a blessing of a pet, or even use the prayers for daily devotions.

Living the Season at Home and Church

This section offers ideas for home and family worship, devotions, and activities. These ideas are intended to help people of all ages participate actively in learning about and expressing the themes of each season.

THE SUNDAYS OF THE SEASON

The second section of this book gives an overview of each Sunday, according to Years A, B, or C. The following headings are offered to help you gain a quick overview of the lectionary texts for each Sunday in the season.

Theme of the Lections

During the great seasons of the church year, the theme will usually be reflected in all three readings and the appointed psalm. During the Season after Pentecost (often referred to as "Ordinary Time"), two themes may be listed. This is because both the gospel of the year (Matthew in Year A, Mark in Year B, and Luke in Year C) and several epistles are read semi-continuously during these months, and therefore any thematic relationship between the gospel and epistle lections is coincidental. The psalm is a meditative response to the first reading. In this section, a summary of each lesson will be given, as well as the themes expressed in the Collect for the day, providing another way of expressing the theme through banners, bulletin covers, or artistic renditions of the focus text.

Key Words, Ideas, and Concepts to Explore

As "Great Words" are offered seasonally, so words, ideas, and concepts that unfold in each week's lectionary readings are outlined as well. Here you may want to focus in on one idea, such as the "mountain of the Lord" or "the second coming" in Advent.

Stories to Tell

If a Bible story is a part of one of the readings, it is mentioned here.

Christian Practice and Liturgical Tradition

Sometimes a biblical text lies behind a particular practice or tradition of the church. An appreciation for history and heritage is enhanced when we begin to see the biblical sources for the worship and life of the church.

Formation in Baptismal Discipleship

In this final section, attention is drawn to how the texts need to be embodied in the life of the congregation so that children, youth, and adults are truly formed in the faith. We are formed through our participation in and practice of the Christian life, so that the values and beliefs of the church become our own. In this section, we move from "head to heart."

Lesser Feasts and Fasts

When a "saint's day" is on the church's calendar during the week, it will be noted on the preceding Sunday's lectionary readings page.

PART I:
THE CALENDAR OF THE CHURCH YEAR

The Seasons of the Church Year

ADVENT

Definition

Advent means "coming" in Latin. Advent is the first season of the Western Christian year. It has four Sundays; the first is the Sunday nearest November 30. The last day of Advent is always December 24, the day before Christmas. In Greek, Advent is translated from *parousia*, commonly used in reference to the Second Coming of the Messiah.

Holy Days in Advent

- St. Andrew the Apostle (November 30)
- St. Thomas the Apostle (December 21)

Advent Themes

A season of preparation, to prepare the way of the Lord:
- For the Messiah (Savior) promised by God and foretold by the prophets;
- For the expected coming of the baby Jesus, born of Mary at Bethlehem;
- For Christ, the Prince of Peace, who is coming again at the close of this age (called *Eschaton*) to rule as Lord over the promised kingdom (or reign) of God;
- For each of us to pray the Lord's Prayer with conviction: "*your* kingdom come, *your* will be done." The constant question to ask is: If Jesus revealed God's will and kingdom, how do we as individuals and the church witness to that reality?

Great Words of Advent

Angels (messengers of God)	Light of the world
Annunciation	Longing
Anticipation	Redemption
Apocalypse	Maranatha! Come, Lord Jesus!
Coming	Messiah
Deliverance	Peace
Eschatology (end times)	Preparation
Expectation	Promise
Fulfillment	Prophet
Hope	Reconciliation
Judgment	Waiting
Kingdom of God	

Advent Through the Eyes of a Child

In Advent, we, along with our family and all who are the church:

- Wait for the birth of the baby Jesus, who is a gift God gave to us and to all people because God loves us so much and has made us one big family;
- Prepare for the time that Jesus will come again to earth, and God will be in all and make all things new;
- Ask what we can give to others to celebrate the fact that in Jesus, God loves us so much his promise to be with us always is complete;
- Tell the stories of hope and promise, and wonder how the light breaks through the darkness;
- Examine an Advent wreath, a circle of evergreen with three purple or blue candles and one pink one, one to be lit each Sunday. Say special prayers (such as the Collect for each Sunday of Advent) when lighting each candle, or read a verse of Scripture.
- Remember that Jesus will come again in glory and loving power to make all things new;
- Understand Advent by experiences of waiting, hope, promises, and love in our lives now.

Advent Worship Sentence for Young Children

"Come down to dwell with us, Lord Jesus. Open our hearts to receive you."

Suggested hand motions: Arms outstretched above head; hands brought down, arms crossed over heart on word "heart" and then opened wide at 45-degree angle.

Advent Through the Eyes of Youth

In Advent we advertise that we have faith in the birth of Jesus as well as faith that Christ will come again. We in the church:

- Wait with joy! Prepare for the birth of Christ by giving the gift of yourself.
- Hold on to the promise that Christ will come again by having an "alternative gift fair" after or between worship services during Advent. Invite members to "buy" their Christmas presents there, filling out a simple order form and writing one check when they are done, choosing to make donations to local agencies or world wide relief agency efforts such as Heifer Project International, Church World Service, and Episcopal Relief and Development. When purchasing, give them gift cards to fill out.
- Learn and share the Advent stories each week. Week 1: the prophets; Week 2: Mary; Week 3: Joseph; Week 4: The time when Christ will come again.
- Pray, ask, and respond: Who are the people in our world who need the message of God's love? What are our hopes for how people today can receive the message of God's love? How do we help others know God's love?

Advent Through the Eyes of Daily Life

Advent is a time of preparation, of patience, of remembering what grounds and sustains us. The function of Advent is to remind us who God is and who we are meant to be, as well. Advent is about the riches of emptiness. God coming as an infant without retinue or riches is the metaphor of a humility that requires us to remember how really small we are in the universe. In our secular culture, a tone of wanting more, spending more, and accumulating riches on earth surround us. As Christians, we long for our society to live up to God's vision, for the kingdom to come in its fullness outside of materialism. The cry of Advent, "Wake up! Be alert! Watch for his coming" is difficult amidst the busyness of the season. We can practice some simple, but not easy, disciplines. We can fast from the media to become more alert to the still small voice of God. We can focus on the giving of ourselves to God. Plan to spend time apart from the busyness of the season each day so you can be alert to God in the silent, the small, and the simple.

Advent Through the Eyes of Our Global Community

Advent is a time of concern for God's judgment, particularly in reference to the coming kingdom. The power of this theme of judgment brings about a realization of the sinfulness of the present age. As Christians, we believe it is Jesus who bears this judgment through his life, death, and resurrection, revealing the reign of God to the church in every generation. Our Eucharistic Prayer reminds us that Christ will come again. This is the hope for Advent and this is the hope we find in the Lord's Prayer.

The Lord's Prayer leads us to pray that God's will (not ours) be done, "on earth as in heaven." As we pray, "thy Kingdom come," how do these familiar words call us into a reality of the real presence of Christ in our lives as we look at our own response in our own time? How do these familiar words call us into judgment?

The Collects of the Advent season give us a natural way of reflecting on this incarnational judgment. They remind us how we are living in the reality of Christ's presence that allows us to approach ethical, social justice, and global issues:

THE FIRST SUNDAY IN ADVENT

"Give us grace to cast away the works of darkness" (BCP 211).
- In personal ethics—things we do as individuals that we are ashamed of when we hold our actions up to the light of Christ;
- In business and political ethics—looking at business practices that fail to measure up to the demands of the coming kingdom.

THE SECOND AND THIRD SUNDAYS IN ADVENT

". . . who sent your messengers the prophets to preach repentance and prepare the way for our salvation" (BCP 211).

Social issues raised by Amos and Isaiah provide an outline of contemporary issues:
- Corruption in public affairs;
- Oppression of peoples, especially the poor, through selfish, self-indulgent lifestyles;
- Failing to carry out justice for the good of the people, and to care for the poor, the widow, the orphan, and the disadvantaged;
- Practicing empty formalism in religion, concentrating on self-fulfillment rather than the word of the Lord, listening to false prophets who mislead the people;
- Relying on military power for security;
- Seeking wealth by acquiring lands and acquisitions to the detriment of others (corporate ethical responsibility);
- For freedom from want, from oppression, and from war (Isaiah 9:1–7);
- When has religion been used for unjust actions?

THE FOURTH SUNDAY IN ADVENT

". . . Jesus Christ, at his coming, may find in us a mansion prepared for himself . . ." (BCP 212):
- Whatever we do personally and publicly will be done in a way that prepares the world for the coming of Christ.

Symbols and Traditions of Advent

- Color—dark "royal" purple or Sarum blue (from the Medieval Sarum Rite) symbolizes preparation, penitence, and royalty
- Advent wreath—a green wreath with candles (purple or blue to coincide with your church practice), one for each of the four Sundays
- The third Sunday of Advent, known as Gaudette ("Rejoice," from an ancient antiphon based on Philippians 4:4) Sunday, has an especially joyous emphasis, heightening the eager sense of anticipation as Advent moves toward its longed-for fulfillment. Often the candle in the Advent wreath for this third Sunday will be the joyful color of rose or pink.
- Jesse tree—a tree with symbols of Old Testament prophecies of Jesus' coming; compare the Jesse tree to your own family tree or one about your parish
- Empty crèche—awaiting the Christ child
- Advent calendar—to count the days to Christmas
- Light contrasted with darkness—Jesus is the Light of the world; at the time of Christmas, the days begin to get longer
- The Gloria and other "glorious hymns"—omitted as we solemnly prepare for Christ's coming
- The "O Antiphons"—study the hymn "O come, O come, Emmanuel" with concordance and Bible
- An Advent Festival of Lessons and Carols—a traditional English service, found in *The Book of Occasional Services*

Great Bible Stories for Advent

THE MESSIANIC PROPHECIES IN ISAIAH

- The Lord's sign to the House of David (Isaiah 7:10–17)
- The stem of Jesse and the peaceable kingdom (Isaiah 11:1–10)
- Comfort, O comfort my people (Isaiah 40:1–11)
- A light to the Gentiles (Isaiah 42:6–7)

ELIZABETH

- Mary visiting her cousin (Luke 1:39–56)
- The birth of John the Baptist is promised (Luke 1:5–25)

JOHN THE BAPTIST

- Baptizing in the river Jordan (Matthew 3:1–12; Mark 1:1–8; Luke 3:7-18)
- Messengers sent from John (Matthew 11:2–11)

MARY AND JOSEPH
- The Annunciation (Luke 1:26–56)
- Joseph's dream (Matthew 1:18–25)

Great Hymns of Advent

FROM *THE HYMNAL 1982*
- Advent hymns 53–76, including:
- Come, thou long-expected Jesus (Hymn 66)
- O come, O come, Emmanuel (Hymn 56)

FROM *WONDER, LOVE AND PRAISE*
- Advent hymns 721–726, including:
- People, Look East (Hymn 724)

FROM *LIFT EVERY VOICE AND SING*
- Advent hymns 2–20, including:
- We're Marching to Zion (Hymn 12)

FROM *VOICES FOUND*
- Advent hymns 31–34, including:
- Comfort ye my people (Hymn 32)
- Jesus, name above all names (Hymn 81)
- God, creator, source of healing (Hymn 93)
- Jesus calls us (Hymn 128)

FROM *MY HEART SINGS OUT*
- Advent hymns 58–63, including:
- Stay awake, be ready (Hymn 62)
- Prepare ye the way (Hymn 63)

Advent in the Book of Common Prayer

PRAYERS AND THANKSGIVINGS
- Eucharistic Prayer B emphasizes the Incarnation (BCP 367–369)
- Collects 6 and 7 (BCP 395) conclude the Prayers of the People with Advent themes

CANTICLES

In keeping with Advent's contemplative mood, the Kyrie eleison or Trisagion is sung in place of the more joyous Gloria in excelsis.

- Canticle 9: The First Song of Isaiah (Ecce, Deus, BCP 86)
- Canticle 3 or 15: The Song of Mary (Magnificat, BCP 50 or 91) especially on the Fourth Sunday of Advent
- Canticle 4 or 16: The Song of Zechariah (Benedictus Dominus Deus, BCP 50 or 92) especially on the Second or Third Sundays of Advent
- Canticle 11: The Third Song of Isaiah (Surge, illuminare, BCP 87)

A SERVICE WITH ADVENT THEMES

- Order of Worship for the Evening (BCP 109–114)

Living the Advent Season at Home and Church

- Make an Advent calendar.
- Start a collection of food, clothes, or toys in preparation for sharing Christmas love with someone who is needy.
- Try some creative writing (a poem, prayer, or story) on an Advent theme—hope or waiting or light, for example. Mary was waiting (Luke 1:26–38); what is it that you are waiting for? Or discuss why hope is an Advent theme and what a message of hope might be for you.
- Make an Advent capsule (like a time capsule) to tell the children and adults in your family (or congregation) twenty-five years from this Advent what is important to you today. Include news items that may be offered with the Prayers of the People.
- Express through the visual arts (banners, murals, paintings, PowerPoint) some of the prophecies about the expected Messiah. What do they tell us about Jesus and the kingdom of God?
- Talk about the dreams you may have as you contemplate the coming of the fullness of God's reign. Share the beautiful poetry of hope in passages such as Revelation 21:1–6. What imagery and poetry could we use to describe God's intentions for the coming day based on what we know of Jesus and the great men and women of the Bible who pointed to God's way?
- Plan and keep an Advent discipline, perhaps daily Bible reading and reflection with shared prayer time.

CHRISTMAS

Definition

December 25 is the feast day on which we celebrate the birth of our Lord Jesus Christ. Our word "Christmas" comes from the old English "Christmasse" (Christ's Mass). In ancient calendars the feast was set close to the winter solstice, when the sun returned light to the world.

Holy Days in the Christmas Season

- St. Stephen, Deacon and Martyr (December 26), Symbols: stones and a palm branch
- St. John, Apostle and Evangelist (December 27), Symbol: an eagle
- The Holy Innocents (December 28), Symbols: crown with stars representing martyrdom
- The Holy Name of Our Lord Jesus Christ (January 1) tells of the naming of Jesus in accordance with the divine plan (Luke 2:21). Jesus means "the Lord saves," and in remembering his name we remember what God's love has done for us.

Christmas Themes

Christ is born!

- In the birth of Jesus, God gave us the greatest gift by becoming a human being and dwelling among us. Jesus is truly God and truly human—the Incarnation is God's plan for reconciling and redeeming his people.
- It is important to emphasize at Christmas that the great celebration is more than a remembrance of the birth of the baby Jesus. It is a joyful proclamation of the Incarnation. God is known in the flesh of human life. People who knew Jesus realized with awe and wonder that to be with Jesus was to be with God. They knew God in their flesh and blood relationship with Jesus. The good news of Christmas is that through the power of the Holy Spirit, we can still know God in the flesh of human life and relationship. God is not a distant creative power. God is as close as the love that binds one to another in a way that points beyond the human encounter to the divine revelation.
- In Christ we, who are made in the image of God, behold the dignity of our human nature. Because Christ came to bring salvation (healing, "salving"), we have hope and assurance of sharing his life both now and always.

Great Words of Christmas

Angels	Nativity
Annunciation	New light
Celebration	Reconciliation
Fulfillment	Redeemer
Incarnation	Savior
Judge	

Christmas Through the Eyes of a Child

At Christmas, we who are the church:

- Welcome Jesus and joyfully celebrate his birth; the church is often filled with greens and trees and lights. Something wonderful has happened and it is time to celebrate. Children love celebrations.
- Give thanks for God's greatest gift of love to us, the Son, Jesus Christ. The child offers thanks and praise, clapping hands, shouting for joy; whole family worship is vital during Christmas.
- Proclaim the messianic prophecies that have been fulfilled, by cutting out or sharing Christmas card verses or making prayer cards of the fulfillment of the prophecies.
- Respond to the Light that has come into the world never ever to leave again. Light a candle at dinner to be reminded of Christ's presence within the household.
- Give to others in response to the gift that has been given to us.
- Treasure our children in their open-hearted response to the birth of Jesus.

This is the time to blend family traditions—meals, visits, and activities—with an awareness of the birth of Jesus. The traditional crèche and manger need to have a prominent place for children to touch and re-enact the story of the birth of Jesus. Child-friendly pageants and Christmas plays that invite the children into telling and being a part of the story are critical, as well as doing something as a family such as serving at a soup kitchen or gathering up clothes that no longer fit to give to those in need, to teach and demonstrate ways to bring the light of Christ into the darkness.

Music is important; singing the beloved Christmas carols that announce the birth of Christ will offer the child a way to proclaim how the love of God breaks into the world in the birth of Jesus.

Christmas Worship Sentence for Young Children

"Rejoice, rejoice! God has come to be a child like us. Rejoice, rejoice!"

Suggested hand motions: Arms are raised from the side of the body, crossing arms and sweeping them open again and holding them outstretched. Repeat. Arms brought down, hands touch chest. Rejoice motion repeated twice.

Christmas Through the Eyes of Youth

The church is called to demonstrate how:

- The birth of Jesus changes the whole world. This is the time for families to talk about God, for parents to share their faith with their teens and in particular to talk about their faith in regards to family traditions, that is, Christ's presence through the way the family marks the change in seasons.
- To invite the spirituality of teens to be offered for the whole family, to lead family morning prayers around the Christmas tree, or to have them help make an abundance of food for dinner and share part of their meal with a shut-in or invite friends and/or those in need to the dinner table.
- To welcome all to the joy of the birth of Christ, encourage youth to invite friends to attend worship service, to sit at dinner table, and to gather for sharing of gifts at the tree. Some of the sharing of gifts could include special reflections on gifts of faith, gifts of courage, gifts of sports, or intellectual gifts.
- Put faith into action: Invite youth into the question, "Where is there need for peace in our country? In our world?" What can one do? Jesus came to offer peace to all people, how can each one of us make a difference? Choose a particular project to complete during the Christmas and Epiphany seasons.

Christmas Through the Eyes of Daily Life

Christmas is to be celebrated for twelve days. Reflect on how we can live the joy of Jesus' birth this and every day, knowing that the Spirit of Christ dwells in us and guides us so that we may be his witnesses in all that we say and do. How do you live your life, knowing that God's Word lives among us?

Christmas Through the Eyes of Our Global Community

Christmas is the perfect time to offer opportunities for seeing the season of Christmas from the perspective of children from around the world. While the tradition of the 1979 prayer book centers us on the incarnation, it is vitally important that we look at the state of children from a global perspective. Holy Innocents (December 28) is often overlooked; this is a time to learn of those places where children are persecuted and the places where children have no hope.

- Expand the vision of mission during Christmas to respond to those who are most vulnerable, which includes the children of our world. The United Nations as well as the Children's Defense Fund offer current statistics and initiatives that a congregation can learn from and discuss as a way to discern possible mission initiatives for the New Year.
- An excellent opportunity for the season of Christmas is to look at the ways that cultures affect the interpretation of prayers and season. Learning how Christmas is celebrated around the world and comparing these traditions to one's own opens new insights into our own culture and practices.
- Christmas pageants are traditional events in many congregations. Develop the pageant with a mission focus, a way to reveal interpretations of the nativity from a variety of cultures.
- Consider a historical perspective, such as the Boar's Head Festival of Twelfth Night, that brings the Christmas story from the Medieval Anglican time.

Symbols and Traditions of Christmas

- Color—white for festival and joy
- Angels—they rejoiced at Jesus' birth
- Candles—Jesus is the Light of the world
- Chrismons—symbols about Jesus that are used as tree ornaments, such as stars, candles, mangers, crosses, and shepherds' crooks
- Crèche (manger scene)—to celebrate the uniqueness of each season, the three magi (wise men) are not placed in the crèche until the Feast of the Epiphany
- Evergreen garlands and wreaths (holly, laurel, mistletoe) for everlasting life
- Gifts—to share and show love as God has done
- St. Nicholas (Santa Claus)
- Sheep and shepherds
- Star

Great Bible Stories for Christmas

- The birth and childhood of Jesus (Luke 2:1–40)
- The flight into Egypt (Matthew 2:1–15)

Great Hymns of Christmas

FROM *THE HYMNAL 1982*

- Christmas hymns 77–115, including:
- Break forth, O beauteous heavenly light (Hymn 91)
- What child is this (Hymn 115)
- All glory be to God on high (metrical setting of the Gloria in excelsis) (Hymn 421)

FROM *WONDER, LOVE AND PRAISE*

- People, look East (Hymn 724)

FROM *LIFT EVERY VOICE AND SING*

- Christmas hymns 21–27, including:
- Go, tell it on the mountain (Hymn 21)
- Rise up, shepherd, and follow (Hymn 24)

FROM *VOICES FOUND*

- Mary borned a baby (Hymn 37)

FROM *MY HEART SINGS OUT*

- Christmas hymns 64–70, including:
- Jesus our brother, kind and good (Hymn 65)
- The Virgin Mary had a baby boy (Hymn 67)

Christmas in the Book of Common Prayer

PRAYERS AND THANKSGIVINGS

- Eucharistic Prayer B with its reference to the Incarnation is especially appropriate (BCP 367–69).

CANTICLES

- Canticle 6 or 20: The Song of Angels (Gloria in excelsis, BCP 52/94)
- Canticle 3 or 15: The Song of Mary (Magnificat, BCP 50/91)

SERVICES WITH CHRISTMAS THEMES

- The service of A Thanksgiving for the Birth or Adoption of a Child (BCP 439–445) expresses the wonder of birth and new life. Note the phrase "whoever receives a little child in the name of Christ receives Christ himself" (BCP 443), which reinforces the incarnational theme.

- A Festival of Lessons and Carols is a traditional English Christmas service (see *The Book of Occasional Services*). This can be held during Advent and later during Christmastide (the twelve days of Christmas) to remind us of the significance and relatedness of the two seasons.

Living the Christmas Season at Home and Church

- Families and congregations develop their own traditions for celebrating Jesus' birth. These often include gifts for others, such as clothing, toys, food, or money for persons in need. Gift-giving reflects the joy of God's gift to us; gifts are expressions of God's love shared between people.
- Put the Christ child into the manger in your home crèche. Add sheep and shepherds (but not the magi, yet!).
- Neighborhood caroling expresses the call to proclaim the gospel to the world.
- Small, trimmed Christmas trees can be made and shared with people who are ill or homebound.
- The *posada* (meaning "inn" in Spanish) is a Latin American tradition in which a procession with figures of Mary and Joseph goes from house to house (or room to room in a home or church) looking for a place of shelter. Sometimes the procession begins nine days before Christmas, which can give it Advent's flavor of expectation. When the "inn" is reached, the innkeeper asks a series of questions before he lets them enter: "Who is knocking?"; "Where have you come from?"; "What do you want here?" After entering the "inn," the figures are brought to the manger. On Christmas Eve the figure of the Christ Child is added, and a celebration with singing and dancing and feasting may follow. The *posada* dramatizes acceptance of the Christ Child into our lives and hearts.
- Candles can be made and burned during the Christmas season, perhaps every night until Twelfth Night. Doorways and walks can be lined with *luminarias*, according to a custom begun in the southwestern United States. These candles, placed on a bed of sand inside white or brown paper bags, give off an amber glow. Fold down the top of an ordinary small grocery bag about two inches to make it stay open. Place a votive candle firmly into the two-inch bed of sand at the bottom of the bag. Lighted at dusk and placed two or three feet apart along lawns or steps, the candles will burn gently for several hours and snuff out when they burn down to the sand base.

- Make a *Christingle*—an orange decorated with a lighted candle, raisins, and nuts. The orange represents the world, a red ribbon tied around the equator is the Blood of Christ, and the raisins and nuts are the fruits of the earth. The candle is the Light of the World. This Moravian custom might be shared as a gift or lighted from the Christ candle at church or at home. There is a special liturgy associated with the Christingle, with prayers offered for children around the world. Christingles could be lit at the end of a service and carried, symbolically, out into the world.

EPIPHANY

Definition

The Feast of the Epiphany, or Manifestation (revelation) of Christ to the Gentiles, is observed on January 6. Epiphany comes from a Greek word meaning "showing forth, appearance, manifestation, revelation." The Feast of the Epiphany proclaims the good news that Jesus revealed God to all humanity.

At Christmas the church celebrates the birth of Jesus, when God entered fully into the human experience. The Feast of the Epiphany takes the Christmas proclamation a step further, when the divine revelation in Jesus was revealed to the world as the magi came from the east.

The eve of the Feast of the Epiphany (Twelfth Night) marks the end of the Christmas celebration. The Epiphany, January 6, is followed by a period of "Sundays after the Epiphany"; the length of the Epiphany season varies in length from four to nine Sundays, depending on the date of Easter that year. The Last Sunday of Epiphany is celebrated as Transfiguration Sunday.

Holy Days Following the Feast of the Epiphany

- The Baptism of our Lord (The First Sunday after the Epiphany)
- The Confession of St. Peter the Apostle (January 18) (begins the Week of Prayer for Christian Unity)
- The Conversion of St. Paul the Apostle (January 25) (ends the Week of Prayer for Christian Unity)
- The Presentation of Our Lord Jesus Christ in the Temple, or Candlemas (February 2)
- St. Matthias the Apostle (February 24)

Epiphany Themes

- Manifestation (revelation) of Christ to the whole world. When we see Christ we are seeing God.
- Epiphany is a time for remembering the recognition of Jesus as God by many people, among them the magi, John the Baptist, Jesus' disciples, and Christians in every age, including our own.
- Epiphany is a time for rededicating ourselves to our own ministries and our missionary task—to continue the spread of Jesus' light in the world.
- In Epiphany we remember Christ's baptism and our own. Just as the disciples were called, we received our calling or vocation as Christians through our baptism. The theme of discipleship is the initial focus in the readings for the Sundays after the Epiphany.
- Epiphany is a time for remembering the signs of Jesus that revealed his presence to the people, as in the first miracle at Cana and in the healing miracles. Healing and the anointing of the sick are important themes of the Sundays after the Epiphany.

Great Words of Epiphany

Apostle	Magi (wise men)
Baptism	Ministry
Calling	Miracle
Conversion	Mission
Covenant	Outreach
Disciple	Revelation
Discipleship	Shining star
Gifts and treasures	Showing forth
Light	Sign

Epiphany Through the Eyes of a Child

What Jesus did and said helps us to know who God is and what God is doing for us:

- On the night of Jesus' birth, the giant comet star let the world know that God is with us; magi from far away saw the star and journeyed to visit Jesus;
- Jesus called his friends to be with him and to help him in his work;
- Jesus said and did amazing and wonderful things that no one else could do. He healed many people to show how much God loved them;
- Jesus, the gift of love, came for all the people of the world;

- Jesus is like a light, helping us to see better;
- We are a part of Jesus, and in Jesus we are baptized into God's family, the church;
- The wonder and mystery of the magi invite us to wonder about the mystery. Jesus, who are you really?

Look out into the night sky and look up at the stars and wonder at the gift of Jesus and what the magi discovered when they offered their gifts to Jesus. Make a poster of "What I Love" or "Gifts to Give." This is also a great time to make a "Tape of Joy": record children reading, sharing poems, or singing songs of joy to give to those who are homebound.

Epiphany Worship Sentence for Young Children

"Rejoice, rejoice! God has come to be a child like us. Rejoice, rejoice!"

Suggested hand motions: Arms are raised from the side of the body, crossing arms and sweeping them open again and holding them outstretched. Repeat. Arms brought down, hands touch chest. Rejoice motion repeated twice.

Epiphany Through the Eyes of Youth

The church is called to reveal Jesus to the world, and to re-affirm baptismal vows by strengthening the ways to seek Christ in all persons, and to continue in the apostles' teachings, breaking of bread, and the prayers.

- Epiphany is a time to celebrate the mystery of the visit of the magi to the infant Jesus.
- Epiphany is the sudden realization or comprehension of the essence or meaning of something sacred.
- *Theophany*, an appearance of God and Christ to humanity
- *Heirophany*, a manifestation of the sacred
- The Second Sunday of Epiphany is a time to reaffirm baptismal promises.

Invite the youth to read God's Word every morning; use the lectionary and follow the stories for the season of Epiphany. As they read the stories have them note when there is an Epiphany, Theophany, or Hierophany in the story.

Hold a First Night gathering at the church to celebrate New Years Eve. Invite the youth to bring in their favorite music to share, favorite foods to share, organize the gathering, and end in prayers. This is a wonderful season to take each sentence of the Baptismal Covenant and invite the teens to determine how to put it into action, not only for themselves, but for the community.

Encourage teens to invite a missionary to visit and share stories. Learn about your companion diocese connections to learn how Christ is made manifest and revealed in other cultures. The Anglican and Global Relations Office provides resources and guidelines for establishing partnerships in mission and companionship: http://www.episcopalchurch.org/79704_22087_ENG_HTM.htm.

Epiphany Through the Eyes of Daily Life

Epiphany is a time to bless the homes of Christians with holy water, incense, and prayers, that those who abide in the home may be empowered to live lives that are an epiphany of God's coming among us in Jesus, into whose body we have been incorporated at our baptism. (See *The Book of Occasional Services*.)

Epiphany Through the Eyes of Our Global Community

EPIPHANY 1: THE BAPTISM OF OUR LORD

The Collect for this day asks: "Grant that all who are baptized into his name may keep the covenant they have made" (BCP 214). The Baptismal Covenant calls Christians to strive for justice and peace among all people, and to respect the dignity of every human being (BCP 305).

EPIPHANY 6

The Collect for this Sunday affirms that, "in keeping your commandments we may please [God] both in will and deed" (BCP 216). Six of the Ten Commandments, which summarize the 613 commandments of the Torah, remind us that to honor God is to love others as we love ourselves. Many of the commandments of the Torah deal with proper treatment of the poor, the stranger, and the disadvantaged in society, as well as ethical business practices.

Jesus' "new Law" outlined in the Sermon on the Mount calls the Christian to an even higher standard:

- Reconciliation in all relationships, including sexual ones;
- Truthfulness in business, personal, and political matters;
- Justice and respect for human rights;
- Love for all people, even those perceived to be enemies.

LAST SUNDAY OF THE EPIPHANY

In 1997, the General Convention of the Episcopal Church designated this Sunday as World Mission Sunday to increase awareness of and participation in the wider global mission of the church.

Symbols and Traditions of Epiphany

- Colors—white, the festival color, for the Feast of the Epiphany and the days up to and including the next Sunday, which is the Feast of the Baptism of our Lord; green for the weeks after the Epiphany, the color of the ongoing life of the church.
- The "Feast of Lights" emphasizes the theme of the Light of the World, the True Light. Candlelight services are often held in cathedrals and parish churches on the Feast of the Epiphany.
- Baptisms are celebrated on the feast of Jesus' baptism, the First Sunday after the Epiphany.
- The magi or three wise men—Matthew's gospel (Matthew 2:1–12) tells of magi (people who studied the movement of the stars to interpret their meaning) who came from the east, following a special star and bringing gifts to the child Jesus. They were Gentiles, not Jews, and they worshiped him. The story of the magi that we know is grounded in legends that came out of the Middle Ages and described them as kings named Melchior, Caspar, and Balthazar.
- The gifts of the magi (as described in Matthew):
  - Gold for royalty, wealth, and the kingship of Christ;
  - Frankincense, made of gum from an Asian and African tree. It may be burned to produce aromatic smoke used in worship, and symbolizes divinity and prayer;
  - Myrrh, a bitter resin used in ancient times to anoint bodies before burial; a symbol of suffering and death, foretelling Christ's giving of self through death.
- A single star recalls the manifestation of Christ to the world.
- Candlemas (from Candle Mass), on February 2, takes its name from the candles carried at the celebration of the Presentation of Christ in the Temple (see *The Book of Occasional Services*). It celebrates a ritual of Jewish law related to first-born sons that Joseph and Mary carried out (Luke 2:21–40). Luke's gospel tells how Simeon and Anna, devout Jews, honored the infant Jesus as the promised Messiah.

Great Bible Stories for the Season of Epiphany

- The Story of Moses and the burning bush (Exodus 3:1–10) provides a story of God's revelation to Moses and later to the Hebrew people with both words and actions.

- The three traditional stories associated with the Epiphany:
  - The visit of the magi (Matthew 2:1–12)
  - The baptism of Jesus (Matthew 3:13–17; Mark 1:9-11; Luke 3:21–22; John 1:29–34)
  - The marriage in Cana (John 2:1–11)
- The calling of the disciples:
  - The first disciples (Matthew 4:18–22; Mark 1:16–20; Luke 5:1–11; John 1:35–51 and 21:1–8)
  - Names of the Twelve (Matthew 10:1–4; Mark 3:13–19; Luke 6:12–16)
  - Matthew (Matthew 9:9–13; Mark 2:13–17; Luke 5:27–32)
  - Philip (John 1:43–51)

Great Hymns of the Season of Epiphany

FROM *THE HYMNAL 1982*

- Epiphany hymns 116–139, including:
- We three kings of Orient are (Hymn 128)
- What star is this, with beams so bright (Hymn 124)
- The Church's mission hymns 528–544, including:
- In Christ there is no east or west (Hymn 529)
- God is working his purpose out (Hymn 534)
- O Zion, haste (Hymn 539)
- Jesus calls us (Hymn 550)
- They cast their nets (Hymn 661)

FROM *WONDER, LOVE AND PRAISE*

- Heal me, hands of Jesus (Hymn 773)
- We all are one in mission (Hymn 778)
- Lord, you give the great commission (Hymn 780)
- We are marching in the light of God (Siyahamb´ ekukhanyen´ kwenkhos´ Marcharemos en la luz de Dios) (Hymn 787)
- Peace before us (Hymn 791)
- Holy God, you raise up prophets (Martin Luther King, Jr.) (Hymn 792)
- Put down your nets and follow me (Hymn 807)

FROM *LIFT EVERY VOICE AND SING*

- Hear am I, send me (Hymn 126)
- Take me to the water (Hymn 134)
- I have decided to follow jesus (Hymn 136)

- Wade in the water (Hymn 143)
- This little light of mine (Hymn 160)
- He's got the whole world in his hands (Hymn 217)

FROM *VOICES FOUND*

- Spirit of God (Hymn 58)
- Give me oil in my lamp (Hymn 61)
- We stand within the circle (Hymn 77)

FROM *MY HEART SINGS OUT*

- Epiphany hymns 71–81, including:
- When Jesus saw the fishermen (Hymn 76)
- I, the Lord of sea and sky (Hymn 77)
- What does it mean to follow Jesus? (Hymn 89)
- Child of blessing, child of promise (Hymn 119)

Epiphany in the Book of Common Prayer

PRAYERS AND THANKSGIVINGS

- Eucharistic Prayer B (BCP 367–369)
- Thanksgiving for the Mission of the Church (BCP 838)
- Collect for the Mission of the Church (BCP 257)
- Collect: Of a Missionary (BCP 247)
- Thanksgiving for the Gift of a Child (BCP 841)

SERVICES WITH EPIPHANY THEMES

- Holy Baptism (BCP 299–310)
- Confirmation (BCP 413–419)
- A Form of Commitment to Christian Service (BCP 420–421)
- Ordination—Bishop, Priest, Deacon (BCP 512–551)
- Celebration of a New Ministry (BCP 559–564)
- An Order of Worship for the Evening (BCP 109–114) expresses the theme of light

Living the Epiphany Season at Home and Church

- Be particularly aware of baptisms on the feast of the Baptism of our Lord on the First Sunday after the Epiphany. We all celebrate birthdays; in the church it is appropriate to celebrate and talk about the anniversary of our baptism. (Those who were baptized as infants may need to ask their parents or godparents about their baptisms.) If there are baptisms on this Sunday, make gifts for those to be baptized (such as a baptismal candle or baptismal day memory booklet). Discuss and plan ways that everyone in the faith community can support the newly baptized.

- Have a procession of the three kings, robed and bearing their gifts to the crèche as part of the liturgy on the Feast of the Epiphany.
- Move the sheep and shepherds away from the crèche; bring the figures of the magi to the Christ Child.
- A parish party could include an Epiphany cake, caroling, and a visit from the three kings bearing gifts. The magi are an important focus among many Latin American and Spanish-speaking groups. In Spain, Costa Rica, and Puerto Rico, children fill their shoes with hay for the magi's camels, later finding presents in their place given by the kings, a reminder of the gifts to the Christ Child.

LENT

Definition

"Lent" comes from the Anglo-Saxon word *lencton*—the time of year when the days grow long. The season begins on Ash Wednesday and ends with the Easter Triduum that includes Maundy Thursday through Easter Sunday, covering forty days (excluding Sundays). Since every Sunday is a "little Easter" celebrating the Resurrection, Sundays remain feast days even during the solemn Lenten season. The five Lenten Sundays are followed by the Sunday of the Passion (Palm Sunday), which ushers in Holy Week.

In the early church, Lent was the time of preparation for the Easter baptism of converts to the faith. Persons who were to receive the sacrament of baptism—"new birth," "death to sin"—were expected to fast and prepare during these weeks. As noted below, the Bible readings appointed for the five Sundays in Lent provide a short course in the meaning of baptism.

Holy Days in Lent

Because Lent is determined by the movable date of Easter Day, it is necessary to check the Calendar of the Church Year (BCP 19–33) or *Lesser Feasts and Fasts* for the holy days, lesser feasts, or other special observances that occur during Lent in a particular year.

Lenten Themes

- Baptism—The major theme of the season is the meaning of baptism, which reflects the origins and continuing focus of the season. Lent is a time of preparation for baptism at the Easter Vigil; in the early church, this was the only time baptisms occurred. Candidates for baptism were led through the stories of the Bible that helped them examine the nature of the life they were about to enter. Through the experience of fasting, self-denial, and acknowledgment of their need to repent and turn to God, they began to live out Paul's vision of offering oneself to God: *I appeal to you therefore, brothers and sisters, by the mercies of God, to present your bodies as a living sacrifice, holy and acceptable to God, which is your spiritual worship* (Romans 12:1).
- Fasting—The forty weekdays of Lent represent the days of fasting and temptation that Jesus spent in the wilderness. Self-denial is an opportunity for discipline, the sacrifice of our will to the purpose of God.
- Reconciliation—Lent is a time for reconciliation with God, self, and others.
- Discipleship—During the Lenten season we consider the nature of the ministry of Jesus and what it means to be a disciple.

Great Words of Lent

Atonement	Overcoming temptation
Calvary	Penitence
Catechesis (teaching the faith)	Pilgrimage
Catechumenate	Preparation
Catechumens	Redemption
Contrition	Return to God
Conversion	Sacrifice
Cross	Salvation
Crucifix	Self-denial
Fasting	Social justice
Humility	Reconciliation
Meditation	Wilderness

Lent Through the Eyes of a Child

Lent is:

- A time for forgiveness; looking at the things we have done that are wrong, asking God's and other people's forgiveness; and making a promise not to do them again;

- A time for giving up the things that keep us from being loving people;
- A time for doing extra things that will help us grow closer to God;
- A time to be more aware of what it means to love as God loves *us*;
- A time to ask God to help us to be more loving, remembering that God is always ready to strengthen us;
- A time to think about our baptism and what it means to be a child of God. Pull out the family photo album and review the pictures and stories of baptism.

Children, ask adults to help us take away the barriers that prevent us from coming closer to God. Parents, help your child read the Bible every day. Invite them to reflect on the stories, particularly inviting reflection on the life of Jesus as he approaches the cross.

DETERMINE A MISSION PROJECT FOR THE LENTEN SEASON
- Invite the children to participate in an ingathering by encouraging their participation to save or set aside a bit of their allowance every week during Lent.
- Engage in activities that call for the children to save their allowance, giving it to a higher purpose.

CHOOSE RESOURCES FOR STUDY DURING THE SEASON OF LENT
- Mark the forty days by having a "cross" box. Each day the child can choose a cross that has a "good deed" written on it. Place the crosses on each day of a calendar that is posted for the child's use.
- Share the Biblical stories of the "stations of the cross" (see *Book of Occasional Services*). Have the children create their own stations, by telling the story, writing the story in their own words.

Lenten Worship Sentence for Young Children

"Lent is a time to prepare for Easter. Let us get ready for new life!"

Suggested hand motions: Both hands make the sign of the cross, then a quick raising of the arms straight up. (Alternative: Arms are folded on chest, and body is slightly bowed at the waist. Then the quick arm sweep, ending with arms above the head.)

Lent Through the Eyes of Youth

Communicating passion during the Passion, the church is called to:
- Recognize Christ in the poor, the stranger at the gate;

- Follow the Creed as rule of life;
- Faithfully follow daily practices that imitate Christ for the sake of others;
- Explore the Penitential Order and how we can be reconciled within our families, our schools, our communities, our church.

Traditionally many congregations encourage youth to participate in their "Shrove Tuesday" or pancake supper event, to demonstrate the need to use up all the milk, eggs, and fat substances before Lenten fasting begins. Hold an educational program along with the supper about the tradition of cleaning out the family pantry before the Lenten fast begins. Suggest that with the money saved from not eating extravagant foods during Lent, contributions can be made to local or global initiatives. Share information from Episcopal Relief and Development, church mission experiences, or through contemplative Bible study, and reflection how Lenten fasting can help others while deepening our awareness of the riches we already have.

Demonstrating an outward and visible sign of Lenten participation:

- Encourage the youth to lead a Lenten ingathering that serves the poor either in the church community or local areas.
- Invite the youth to serve at soup kitchens, at shelters, at the Salvation Army, or any other program or institution that serves the poor and hungry and homeless.
- Invite the youth to define evil, reflect upon the ways they see evil in the world, and describe how the mission and ministry of the church responds.
- Hold overnight or day "retreats" for youth that include contemplation, reflection, and action, with a focus beginning with the first Sunday of Lent.

Lent Through the Eyes of Daily Life

ASH WEDNESDAY

In the liturgy for Ash Wednesday there is a litany of confession, particularly in regard to our decisions that impact our environment and relationships with others.

We confess to you, Lord,

- All our past unfaithfulness: the pride, hypocrisy, and impatience of our lives;
- Our self-indulgent appetites and ways, and our exploitation of other people;
- Our anger at our own frustration, and our envy of those more fortunate than ourselves;
- Our intemperate love of worldly goods and comforts, and our dishonesty in daily life and work;
- Our negligence in prayer and worship, and our failure to commend the faith that is in us.

The season of Lent is marked by self-examination and repentence culminating in the Rite of Reconciliation; by prayer and meditating on Holy Scripture; by fasting (not eating between sunrise and sunset on Fridays to remind us what food we need most for life); and by acts of self-denial, best understood as acts or positive practices that enhance an every-growing and loving relationship with God. However, the main emphasis during Lent is for each person to prepare for the renewal of baptismal vows and covenant at the Easter Vigil.

Lent Through the Eyes of Our Global Community

ASH WEDNESDAY

Ethical issues are raised in the Litany of Penitence (BCP 267–269):
- Exploitation of other people
- Dishonesty in daily life and work
- Indifference to injustice, human need, suffering, and cruelty
- Prejudice and contempt toward those who differ from us
- Waste and pollution of God's creation

As we explore more fully the Baptismal Covenant and the covenant of the Torah, we become increasingly aware of how far we have strayed from God's ways.

THE FIRST SUNDAY IN LENT

"ONE Sunday" is part of the Episcopal Church's ongoing commitment to fight extreme poverty and achieve the Millennium Development Goals (MDGs). It is designated as a day for prayer for fulfillment of the eight goals. "As Christians around the world begin their Lenten journeys with commitments to acts of personal devotion, prayer, and almsgiving, congregational celebration of 'ONE Sunday' provides an opportunity to deepen our commitment to actively participate in God's mission of healing the world." —Presiding Bishop Katharine Jefferts Schori

THE SECOND SUNDAY IN LENT

God's mercy for us calls for mercy from us:
- Criminal justice issues
- Death penalty
- Treatment of refugees and displaced persons

Symbols and Traditions of Lent

- Color—purple, for penitence and royalty, or rough linen or a similar material, unbleached, raw, plain, and austere, to reflect the mood of Lent

48

(based upon the sackcloth of Old Testament mourning). For some, the Salisbury tradition of using sackcloth during Lent is taken from the Jewish custom of putting on sackcloth as a sign of humiliation (1 Kings 21:27–29) and repentance (Matthew 11:21 and Luke 10:13).

- Ashes—prepared from the previous year's palms for Ash Wednesday to symbolize our mortality and sorrow for our sins. The people of the Hebrew Scriptures put ashes on their foreheads as a sign of penitence. Job (Job 42:6) and the King of Nineveh (Jonah 3:6) repented in ashes, wearing sackcloth.
- Alleluias, joyful canticles, the Gloria in excelsis—omitted from worship and replaced with songs and responses that are more in keeping with Lent's contemplative mood.
- Vestments and hangings—more austere and solemn; flowers may be omitted from the altar.
- Shrove Tuesday—the day before Lent begins on Ash Wednesday. On this day it used to be the custom to use up all milk, eggs, and fat in a household since these were not allowed in the strict fasting of Lent. The ingredients were made into pancakes, a meal which came to symbolize preparation for the discipline of Lent. "Shrove" comes from the verb "to shrive" (to confess and receive absolution), referring to the ancient practice of confessing sins and receiving absolution in order to begin and keep a holy Lent. Other names for this day include Carnival, meaning "farewell to meat," and Mardi Gras, meaning "Fat Tuesday." Some congregations offer a carnival-type event as a part of their Shrove Tuesday preparation for Lent.
- The cross—symbol of Christ and his sacrifice, love, salvation, redemption, atonement, and victory.
- Retreat time—during Lent, time is set aside for teaching and learning, spiritual growth, fasting and self-denial, meditation, and retreats.
- Conversion and repentance—as a preparation for baptism or the renewal of baptismal vows at Easter.
- Stations of the Cross—began in the Holy Land as a series of devotions along the *Via Dolorosa* (Way of Sorrow) and later spread to parish churches, where the faithful stop to pray and reflect along a way that outlines Jesus' passion.
- Refreshment Sunday (also Mid-Lent Sunday)—the fourth Sunday in Lent when the gospel speaks of Jesus feeding the five thousand, and Lenten discipline was relaxed to remind Christians of the true Bread, Jesus, who gives life to the world. The English often interrupted the Lenten fast with simnel cake which was very rich and sweet.

- Mothering Sunday—In England children away from home at school or work were permitted to go home to visit their mothers and/or to visit their cathedral or mother church on this fourth Sunday of Lent. Today, many cathedrals and "mother" churches invite all who had been baptized there to return "home" to worship.
- Preparation for baptism—historically a period to prepare for the baptisms and confirmations that traditionally occur at the Vigil of Easter.

Great Bible Stories for Lent

- The Story of the Creation and Fall (Genesis, Chapters 2–3)
- The Flood—God's Promise to Noah (Genesis, Chapters 6–9)
- God's Call to Abraham (Genesis 12:1–8)
- Abraham's Test with his Son, Isaac (Genesis 22:1–19)
- The Joseph Saga (Genesis, Chapters 30–50)
- David and Bathsheba (2 Samuel, Chapter 11)
- The Story of Jonah (Jonah, Chapters 1–4)
- The Temptations of Jesus (Matthew 4:1–11, Mark 1:12–13, Luke 4:1–13)
- Parable of the Prodigal Son (Luke 15:11–32)
- Zacchaeus (Luke 19:1–10)
- Feeding of the Five Thousand (John 6:4–15)

Great Hymns of Lent

FROM *THE HYMNAL 1982*

- Lenten hymns 140 to 152, including:
- Forty days and forty nights (Hymn 150)
- The glory of these forty days (Hymn 143)
- I sing the almighty power of God (Hymn 398)
- The God of Abraham praise (Hymn 401)
- O love, how deep (Hymn 448)
- There's a wideness in God's mercy (Hymn 470)

FROM *WONDER, LOVE AND PRAISE*

- Lenten hymns 727–729
- All who hunger gather gladly (Hymn 761)
- Taste and see (Hymn 764)
- Sh´ma Yisrael (Hear, O Israel) (Hymn 818)

FROM *LIFT EVERY VOICE AND SING*

- How great thou art (Hymn 60)
- I love to tell the story (Hymn 64)
- In the garden (Hymn 69)
- Steal away (Hymn 103)
- We are climbing Jacob's ladder (Hymn 220)

FROM *VOICES FOUND*

- All who hunger gather gladly (Hymn 87)

FROM *MY HEART SINGS OUT*

- Lenten hymns 82–89
- God it was who said to Abraham (Hymn 85)
- We are on our way (Hymn 96)
- It rained on the earth forty days (Hymn 97)
- God of the sparrow, God of the whale (Hymn 129)
- All night, all day (Hymn 158)

Lent in the Book of Common Prayer

SERVICES WITH LENTEN THEMES

- The Daily Office (BCP 37–135) reflects the discipline of prayer and the regular reading of the Bible
- Reconciliation of a Penitent (BCP 447–452)
- A Penitential Order (BCP 319–321/351–353)
- The Great Litany (BCP 148–155)
- Burial of the Dead (BCP 469/491)
- The Holy Eucharist (BCP 323/355)

CANTICLES

- Kyrie eleison or Trisagion is sung in place of the Gloria in excelsis at the Eucharist
- Canticle 14 (BCP 90): A Song of Penitence
- Canticle 10 (BCP 86): The Second Song of Isaiah

Living the Lenten Season at Home and Church

- Write and illustrate Litanies of Penitence by children and/or adults.
- Dramatize the gospel lessons and other readings that are especially rich in

Lent and lend themselves to participation by a large group. Think about using recorded "radio plays" or sound effects, or about using PowerPoint, pantomime, puppets, or shadow plays, as well as choral readings and dramatic presentations.

- A study or review of our faith as Episcopalians might focus upon An Outline of the Faith (BCP S45–862).
- "Bury the Alleluia" is a medieval Christian tradition. Make an "Alleluia" as a painting, small banner, plaque (possibilities are numerous). Wrap it in plastic or cloth to protect it, put it in a box, and bury it on the last Sunday before Lent. On Easter Day dig it up and display it, singing, "Jesus Christ is risen today! Alleluia!"
- Jesus the True Bread is part of the Collect of Lent's fourth Sunday. Sponsor a day for family bread baking, or a day of baking bread for a Eucharist (perhaps for Easter Day). Fancy breads can be frozen for an Easter feast.
- A Lenten pilgrimage can offer opportunities for reading and reflection done either all at one time or for a shorter time each week. It can be done at home or at designated quiet areas in the church building. Instructions may include bringing a Bible, paper, and pencil; a simple guide sheet will help the "pilgrims" begin. Brief suggested readings might be the epistles or other readings for Lent, one for each "station," with a short commentary and questions to aid in reflection. "Pilgrims" move at their own pace, using the guide sheet to meet their own schedule and needs. Perhaps the last "station" will be the altar rail, reading an account of the Easter story or some other passage that points toward the climax for which Lent is a preparation.
- The labyrinth is also a metaphor for taking a pilgrimage. Research where an outdoor, canvas, or floor labyrinth might be located in your community. Or use a finger or table labyrinth for individual use: http://www.labyrinthsociety.org.
- Remembering our heritage, some selections that might be studied are:
  - The Lord's Prayer (BCP 97);
  - The Apostles' Creed (BCP 96);
  - The Ten Commandments (BCP 350);
  - The names of the books of the Bible;
  - The Twenty-third Psalm (BCP 612-613);
  - A Table Blessing (BCP 835);
  - A Collect for the Renewal of Life (BCP 99);
  - Antiphon of the Song of Simeon (BCP 134): "Guide us waking, O Lord ...";
  - A prayer: "Keep watch, dear Lord, with those who work ..." (BCP 134).

HOLY WEEK

Definition

In Holy Week the church dramatizes the events leading up to and including the suffering and death of Jesus on the cross. Holy Week begins with the Sunday of the Passion, or Palm Sunday, and the joyous triumphal entry into Jerusalem, and ends with the Triduum (*Triduum Sacrum*, meaning in Latin "the sacred three days"), which begins with the celebration of the Eucharist on Maundy Thursday and ends with the vespers of Easter Sunday evening.

The name Maundy Thursday comes from the Latin *mandatum* or "command," from the words attributed to Jesus in the gospel of John: "I give you a new commandment, that you love one another. Just as I have loved you, you also should love one another" (John 13:34). Good Friday commemorates the crucifixion of our Lord. It is known as "Good" because of the new life brought about by Christ's victory of the cross.

Holy Days in Holy Week

Each day of Holy Week is considered a "red letter" feast day, has its own lections that can be found in the Book of Common Prayer. Many churches offer special services each noonday or evening to commemorate this last day of Jesus' life. Specific liturgies are held on Thursday (Maundy Thursday) and Friday (Good Friday) as noted below.

Holy Week Themes

The principal theme of Holy Week is Jesus' passion: "No one has greater love than this, to lay down one's life for one's friends" (John 15:13). Jesus gives his life to save us from sin and death.

The language of sacrifice is difficult to understand. The New Testament draws heavily on the sacrificial practices of the temple in describing the unique role of Jesus in bringing salvation through the cross. Paschal lambs were sacrificed at Passover, and Jesus' death on the cross was seen in the light of that temple practice. He is the true paschal Lamb offered, finally, for the sins of the whole world. Without that background of temple practice, some of the language about Jesus' death and its significance will not be clear. It may be helpful, therefore, to take time this week to study the temple in the days of Jesus.

During Holy Week it is also important to see the cross from the perspective of the love that God has for us. Jesus' death on the cross shows us how much God loves us, for in the words of St. Paul, "For I am convinced that neither death, nor life, nor angels, nor rulers, nor things present, nor things to come, nor powers, nor height, nor death, nor anything else in all creation, will be able to seperate us from the love of God in Christ Jesus our Lord" (Romans 8:38–39). It is because we share Christ's victory over sin and death that we face the cross with feelings of sadness and remorse, but also with deep thankfulness for what we have been given. Good Friday is about triumph.

The tension between suffering and glorious triumph is set immediately before us on Palm Sunday, when joyful hosannas ring out even as the sense of foreboding grows. Jesus enters Jerusalem proclaimed as a king, riding toward a destiny of suffering and death amid the shouts of those who soon will turn against him.

Maundy Thursday recalls the Last Supper, when Jesus commanded his disciples and us to do two things—the two things he did in the Upper Room. He broke bread with them, saying, "Do this in remembrance of me" (Luke 22:19); in the Eucharist we have the promise of his presence with us always. When he washed the disciples' feet, he commanded them to follow his example to love and humbly serve one another: "I give you a new commandment, that you love one another" (John 13:34).

Holy Saturday is a time for reflecting upon Jesus' death and burial and what it means for our lives. It is the calm after the storm as we await the sunrise.

Great Words of Holy Week

Atonement	Lash
Broken	Last Supper
Bread	Night watch
Calvary	Passion
Crown of thorns	Redemption
Crucifix	Remembrance
Crucifixion	Suffering
Cup of wine	Gethsemane
Denial of Peter	Golgotha
Footwashing	Hosanna
Holy	Tomb (sepulcher)
Mysteries	Trial before Pilate
Humility	Way of the cross

Holy Week Through the Eyes of a Child

- When Jesus rode into Jerusalem on the back of a donkey, the people who greeted him expected a powerful hero. They did not understand that Jesus' power was not physical strength, but the power of love.
- Jesus showed us that we are to remember him and follow his example of caring for and serving others. We remember him in the gift of bread and wine that mysteriously becomes the body and blood of Christ. It is the time when we know he is present with us.
- At the time of the Last Supper, we see Jesus' example of humbly serving others in love in his washing of the disciples' feet.
- Jesus proclaimed God's forgiveness from the cross as he was dying. He forgave Peter, who had denied him, and those who caused his death, and he will forgive us for all that we do that hurts others. That's why Good Friday is good.
- As God was with Jesus in his suffering, he is with us when we suffer.

Talking about death and grief with children is critical to their faith, however, and even though it is Holy Week and not yet Easter it is necessary to give the proclamation, "Christ has died and Christ has risen from the dead." Children will be thinking bunny rabbits, Easter eggs and baskets, and time home from school, and this is the time to instill in them through prayer and practice the importance of Holy Week in their faith. For example, you might want to do a "foot washing" at home in a special way after sharing the story of Jesus and the Last Supper. You might encourage the children to participate in a "Good Friday" service. Talk about how sad the disciples and Mary the Mother of Jesus must have been to see Jesus die, but there was a promise Jesus needed to complete. Attend an Easter Vigil service and remind them of the story of our salvation, from Old Testament times to the present. The children may want to act out the Good Friday/Easter story in much the same way they enjoy the Christmas story.

Holy Week Through the Eyes of Youth

The church is called to proclaim that Christ before his death invited us to remember how much God loves us, so much so that bread and wine mysteriously become what we share at Eucharist when we eat and drink of his flesh and blood, and that through his death new life would be offered for all humanity.

- The idea of an omniscient deity sending his only son to earth to die for the sins of humankind, only to be resurrected from the dead, can be difficult to grasp.

- We may fear that we will lose our awareness of a connection with God, or even that we have "lost" God or that our connection with him is invalid. We must be willing to let go of former experiences, no matter how powerful, and continually redefine what it means to be a follower of God at every stage, to be in new life.
- It is not easy to speak about God with friends; many of them see the church as a reality that judges youth, that opposes their desire for happiness and love. It is a constant Good Friday struggle.

Holy Week is the time to stay current and connected to the youth. Consider with the youth ways in which twenty-first century discipleship calls us to go to the cross. What are the crosses youth will need to bear in the twenty-first century? Practice noticing all kinds of people and responding to them as Christ is in them.

Holy Week Though the Eyes of Daily Life

During Holy Week some communities gather each day to meditate on Jesus' final days before his death on the cross. Begin the journey with Jesus, following his path to Jerusalem through prayer with others or in solitude. As Jesus washing the feet of his disciples, we are called to follow his example as we humbly care for one another, especially the poor and unloved. At the Lord's table we remember Jesus' sacrifice of his life, even as we are called to offer ourselves in love for the life of the world. Plant the cross on your heart, so that in its power and love you can continue to be Christ's representative in the world at work, school, and play.

Holy Week Through the Eyes of Our Global Community

Two collects heard during Holy Week set the focus for social justice:
- Palm Sunday: "Mercifully grant that we may walk in the way of his suffering" (BCP 272).
- Monday in Holy Week: "Almighty God, whose most dear Son went not up to joy but first he suffered pain, and entered not into glory before he was crucified: Mercifully grant that we, walking in the way of the cross, may find it none other than the way of life and peace" (BCP 220).

These collects remind us that we are called:
- To identify with the suffering peoples of the nation and the world and not to remain aloof;
- To have compassion for "all sorts and conditions" of people (BCP 814).

Symbols and Traditions of Holy Week

- Color—red (crimson); or purple as in Lent.
- Palms—fronds for the procession on Palm Sunday. The people in Jerusalem waved them joyously as we might wave flags in a parade. As the rubric on page 270 of the prayer book points out, branches can be from local trees or shrubs.
- Donkey—the "colt of an ass" on which Jesus rode into Jerusalem; symbol of humility.
- Bowl and towel—reminders of Jesus' act of washing the disciples' feet; symbols of service and humility.
- Rooster—reminder of Peter's denial of Jesus before the cock crowed.
- Tenebrae—a monastic office of readings and music based on the Lamentations of Jeremiah, kept on Wednesday night of Holy Week in some parishes. The most conspicuous feature of Tenebrae is the gradual extinguishing of candles until only a single candle, a symbol of Christ, remains. Toward the end of the liturgy, the candle is hidden, symbolizing the apparent victory of evil. At the very end, after the singing of Psalm 51, a loud noise is made symbolizing the earthquake at the time of the resurrection, the hidden candle is restored to its place, and the congregation departs. (See *The Book of Occasional Services.*)
- Silencing of the organ—some congregations silence the organ from the Maundy Thursday liturgy until the Gloria at the Easter Vigil.
- Stripping of the altar—traditionally the altar is stripped and washed and the sanctuary is cleared after the Eucharist on Maundy Thursday. No hangings remain until the Easter Vigil.
- Watch on Maundy Thursday—after the stripping of the altar an all-night watch is kept, usually with the reserved sacrament, just as Jesus prayed in the garden of Gethsemane.
- Crown of thorns—a Good Friday symbol (from Matthew 27:29 and John 19:2) because the soldiers mocked Jesus as a king, dressing him in a purple robe and placing a crown of thorns on his head.
- Crucifix—the image of the crucified Jesus upon the cross is a Good Friday symbol of suffering.
- Dogwood—according to legend, the dogwood, with its cross-shaped blossom marked as though with nail prints, may have been the tree used to build the cross.
- Lamb—Jesus, called the Lamb of God, was sacrificed like a Passover lamb: "Christ our Passover is sacrificed for us" (BCP 364).

- Sand dollar—a legendary symbol of Good Friday because of the five wounds of Jesus which appear to be depicted on it: four nail marks and the mark of the soldier's spear (John 19:34).
- Holy Saturday—as noted in the rubric for that day, this is the only day in the church year on which there is no communion, only a Liturgy of the Word (BCP 283) to ponder as we await the third day.

Great Bible Stories for Holy Week

Story	Matthew	Mark	Luke	John
Triumphal entry into Jerusalem	21:1–11	11:1–11	19:28–40	12:12–19
Anointing in Bethany	26:6–13	14:3–9		12:1–8
Cleansing of the Temple		11:15–19	19:45–46	
Conspiracy against Jesus	26:1–5	14:1–2	19:47–48; 22:1–2	11:45–53
Betrayal by Judas	26:14–16, 20–25, 47–50	14:10–11, 17–22, 43–46	22:3–6, 21–23, 47–48	13:1–2, 18–30, 18:1–5
Footwashing				13:3–17
The Lord's Supper	26:26–29	14:22–25	22:14–23	
Peter's denial	26:31–35, 69–75	14:26–31, 66–72	22:31–34, 54–62	13:26–38; 18:15–18, 25–27
Jesus in Gethsemane	26:36–46	14:32–42	22:39–46	18:1
Jesus arrested	26:47–56	14:43–52	22:47–53	18:2–12
Jesus before Caiaphas	26:57–68	14:53–65	22:54, 63–71	18:13–14, 19–24
Jesus before Pilate	27:1–2, 11–14	15:1–5	23:1–5	18:28–38a
Jesus before Herod			23:6–12	
Jesus sentenced to die	27:15–26	15:6–15	23:13–25	18:38b–19:16
Jesus mocked	27:27–31	15:16–20		19:2–3
Jesus' crucifixion and death	27:33–56	15:22–41	23:33–49	19:18–30
Jesus' burial	27:57–61	15:42–47	23:50–56	19:31–42
The guard at the tomb	27:62–66			

Great Hymns of Holy Week

FROM *THE HYMNAL 1982*

- Holy Week hymns 153–173, including:
- The Liturgy of the Psalms: Processional (Hymn 154)

FROM *WONDER, LOVE AND PRAISE*

- Holy Week hymns 728–737, including:
- Mantos y palmas esparciendo (Filled with excitement) (Hymn 728)
- Three holy days enfold us now (Hymn 731)
- Bless the Lord my soul (Hymn 825)
- O Lord hear my pray'r (Hymn 127)
- Ubi caritas (Hymn 831)

FROM *LIFT EVERY VOICE AND SING*

- Holy Week hymns 28–39, including:
- He never said a mumbalin' word (Hymn 33)
- Were you there? (Hymn 37)

FROM *VOICES FOUND*

- Holy Week hymns 40–44

FROM *MY HEART SINGS OUT*

- Holy Week hymns 90–94, including:
- A new commandment (Hymn 92)
- Brother, sister, let me serve you (Hymn 94)

Holy Week in the Book of Common Prayer

SERVICES WITH HOLY WEEK THEMES

- Palm Sunday (BCP 270–273)
- Maundy Thursday (BCP 274–275)
- Good Friday (BCP 276–282)
- Holy Saturday (BCP 283)
- The Reconciliation of a Penitent (BCP 447–452)
- Ministration to the Sick (BCP 453–461)
- The Burial of the Dead (BCP 491–505)

Living Holy Week at Home and Church

- Make dioramas or arrange several rooms as scenes from the main events of Holy Week to clarify our understanding of the happenings they portray. A guided tour or narration can explain the scenes to visitors adding experiential activities such as waving palm branches in procession or washing each other's feet.

- Make a crown of thorns by soaking stems of a plant with thorns until they are pliable enough to shape. Wire or tie the ends together to hold the shape as the stems dry out. Use the symbol in worship or in a place of meditation.

- Make a large wooden cross to be used as the rubric for the Good Friday liturgy indicates (BCP 281).

- Produce a video that could give the details of Jesus' way to Calvary as a television news reporter might describe them.

- Construct the front page of a local newspaper, with various articles, interviews, and stories about the events unfolding.

- Make a list of every adjective you can think of that might describe the feelings of those who were witnesses to the Holy Week events. Share times when you have had similar feelings.

- Using gestures in silence, act out a Holy Week hymn, such as "Alone thou goest forth, O Lord" (Hymn 164).

- Bend large nails or palms to make small crosses for Holy Week devotions.

- Study the various kinds of crosses throughout Christian history to make examples for display.

- Encourage parents to participate in the services of the Triduum (Maundy Thursday through Easter Sunday) and the Easter Vigil. Children can be deeply touched by the music and rites of the services.

- Organize all-night prayer vigils with one-hour shifts, starting with the end of the Maundy Thursday service and ending with the Easter Vigil. Here again, children can be involved even if they simply sit with parents and read a book. They will remember the quiet and the commitment evidenced in such moments of devotion.

EASTER

Definition

Easter is a festival season of fifty days whose first day is Easter Day, the Sunday of the Resurrection, and whose last day is the Day of Pentecost. Easter begins after sundown on Holy Saturday. The celebration of Easter is initiated with the Easter Vigil, which can be observed after sundown but ideally is kept just before sunrise, so that the proclamation of Jesus' resurrection comes with the dawn of the new day. The Easter season includes the events of Christ's resurrection and ascension and the coming of the Holy Spirit on the Day of Pentecost.

- Easter Day is the principal feast of the church year.
- The word "Easter" comes from *Eostre*, a Teutonic goddess whose name is associated with springtime, growth, and fertility. In most languages the name of the day is *Pascha*, which means "Passover."
- Pentecost (from the Greek, meaning "fiftieth day") is the Christian feast that comes fifty days after Easter. The time between Easter and Pentecost is known as the Great Fifty Days.

Holy Days in Easter

It is necessary to check the Calendar of the Church Year (BCP 15–33) for the holy days, lesser feasts, or other special observances that occur during the Easter season in a particular year.

Easter Themes

The resurrection means that Christ has overcome death and in his victory has opened to us everlasting life. Nothing can separate us from the love of God (Romans 8:38–39). New life—the Lord's new life in which we share—is the message of this season.

- As the sacrament of new life, baptism is an Easter theme; as baptized Christians we take time during Easter to ponder the meaning of membership in Christ's body, the church. We look at events in the church's life—the sacraments, the accounts of resurrection, and the post-resurrection appearances of Jesus—to discover their meaning and what they tell us about how we as a community are to live the life of the Risen Lord.
- The word from the ancient tradition of the church to describe the Easter season is *Mystagogia*. This is the time when the "mysteries" of the sacraments, particularly baptism and Eucharist, are revealed to the recently baptized.

- After the Lord is glorified in the ascension, he is present in a new way to the church in the gift of the Holy Spirit at Pentecost.
- Like the two who walked the Emmaus road with Jesus, we can know Christ in the sharing of the word and in the breaking of bread at the Eucharist.

Great Words of Easter

Alleluia	New life (renewal)
Christ is risen!	Newly baptized
Empty tomb	Paschal Mystery
Everlasting life	Promise
Hope	Reconciliation
Joy	Resurrection
Love	Victory

Easter Through the Eyes of a Child

- Jesus is risen from the dead! Easter has brought us everlasting life because of Jesus' resurrection. The Alleluias are said and sung.
- God's love is stronger than anything, even death. Because of God's love, we do not have to be afraid of death.
- Easter is about new life, coming from what we thought was death and bringing unexpected possibilities and surprises. Easter eggs, Easter chicks, Easter flowers all remind us of the new life in Christ.
- We received new life at our baptism, and during Easter we think about what that baptism means in our lives. Reflect with the children on the ways we keep our baptismal promises:
  - *How do we keep the promises we make?*
  - *How do we show our love for God?*
  - *How do we show love for each other?*
- Make an alleluia banner for the table, and talk about why Jesus' resurrection would make us so happy. Take a walk and look at all the new life you begin to spot during the walk. Read stories of transformation and new life, such as *The Very Hungry Caterpillar* by Eric Carle. Name the baptismal promises and reflect on them with pictures of how you live each of them out with your family and friends, at home and at school.

Easter Worship Sentence for Young Children

Leader: "Alleluia! Christ is risen!"
Suggested hand motions: Arms at side; large arms-sweep, crossing arms in front of body; arms end in upraised position.

Response: "The Lord is risen indeed! Alleluia!"
Suggested hand motions: Arms are outstretched above head and then lowered quickly and raised again in a large sweep that crosses arms in front of body. Arms end in upraised position.

Easter Through the Eyes of Youth

- Mary Magdalene returns to the tomb on Easter morning, distraught that Jesus' body has been removed. After encountering two angels, she turns to the person she believes is the gardener and pleads with him to tell her where the body of her Lord has been taken. He responds by calling out her name, revealing to Mary that he is, in fact, Jesus. Jesus Christ has risen today!
- As the testimonies of Mary and the disciples led many to believe, so can the testimony or witness of the teens as to Christ in their lives affect others.
- Easter Action: This is the time to encourage youth to Easter reflection and action. Reflect upon the individual baptismal promises found in the Easter Vigil service, and invite the youth to respond to new ways that they can serve within the congregation:
  - Take Easter flowers to shut-ins;
  - Become part of a Lay Eucharistic Visiting Team;
  - Color Easter eggs for the young children and engage them in an Easter egg hunt;
  - Invite someone to church who does not have a "home" church;

Above all give youth an opportunity to witness to the fact that they believe Jesus has risen from the dead.

- Go: "Where does God need us to go—in school, in our neighborhood, town, and beyond?"
- Visit: "Who are the friendless, lonely, outcast people in our lives and how do we connect with them?"
- Listen: "Who are the people that no one pays attention to?"
- Care: "Why, God, are your people suffering?"
- Ask: "What can we do for needy people near and far?"
- Pray: "God, open our eyes and ears and hearts. Who will help us to live for others?"

- Invite: "Who will go with us? Which adults and teens can we invite to follow, to encounter and to become Christ today?"

Easter Through the Eyes of Daily Life

On this day the Lord has acted! On the first day of the week God began creation, transforming darkness into light. On this, the "eighth day" of the week, Jesus Christ was raised from the dead. We celebrate this new creation in the waters of baptism and in the feast of victory. Reflect on your baptism and how you live out the promises in every facet of your life. Throughout this season we hear stories of the men and women who recognized who Jesus really is, after failing to do so during his earthly life. We are enlightened by their visions and their visits with the Risen Christ as they proclaim that our Lord is alive and is life for the world. As we begin the great fifty days of Easter filled with hope and joy, be prepared to go forth to share the news that Christ is risen!

Easter Through the Eyes of Our Global Community

The Collects for Easter petition the living power of Jesus to open up new life to all. Our prayers and action can reflect God's desire of reconciliation for all. During the Easter season, direct attention is placed in prayer to alleviate the extreme poverty of the world. The Christ-centeredness of the Millennium Development Goals (MDGs) is an example of how making a commitment to others is a commitment to Jesus (John 10:10). For the sake of the poor and suffering of the world, our conversion (turning our lives around) at the individual, congregational, diocesan, national, and global levels can make a difference (Luke 18:18–23). Focus on one MDG for the whole liturgical cycle so that during the Easter season, a particular geographic area can be chosen to learn about the people, worship, and need in that area of the world or domestically. The Easter season can be a time to build direct relationships with another location in the Anglican Communion. Enter into mission with another, to help alleviate extreme poverty.

The Collect for the Third Sunday of Easter asks God to "open the eyes of our faith, that we may behold him in all his redeeming work" (BCP 224). It reminds us that:

- The actions of the church and of individual Christians must be judged as to whether they are redeeming or demeaning works.
- The healing ministry of the church involves the healing of society as well as individuals.

The lections for the Fifth Sunday of Easter, Year B tell the story of Philip baptizing an Ethiopian eunuch, which is a reminder that no one is excluded in the church. A eunuch was considered unclean, but Philip did not hesitate to baptize him (Acts 8:26–40).

Symbols and Traditions of Easter

- Color—white for festival and joy.
- The paschal candle—the darkness of death giving way to light and life, symbolizing Jesus' passing over from death into life. Also symbolizes the light of Creation, the pillar of fire that led the Israelites through the wilderness, the fire of Pentecost. *Pascha* is Greek for "Passover." The paschal candle is lit from Easter through the Day of Pentecost. The year's date is carved into the candle to show that the Good News of Easter is for every age, including today.
- The Exsultet is a song of praise and joy sung at the lighting of the paschal candle at the beginning of the Easter Vigil (BCP 286).
- The Easter Vigil captures all of the powerful story imagery of Easter—which is why this service is so important in the life of the congregation. In planning the vigil, keep children as well as adults in mind. The readings (as few as two or as many as nine) can be offered by storytellers, as dramatic readings, or in dramatic presentations. Have the congregation move from a place of sharing the great stories of the faith to another place for baptism, and finally to the Holy Table for the proclamation of the resurrection and the celebration of the Holy Eucharist.
- A customary Easter greeting that Christians have used for centuries:
  Leader: "Alleluia! Christ is risen!"
  Response: "The Lord is risen indeed! Alleluia!"
- Baptisms and confirmations have traditionally occurred in this season of initiation. Ideally these sacraments take place at the Great Vigil of Easter.
- Feasting—breaking the fast of Lent with a feast is a sign of celebration and symbolizes the joy of the Christian community at Easter.
- The empty cross—a sign of the victory of Easter.
- Alleluias and the Gloria—joyful acclamations from the Easter community.
- Butterfly—symbolizes resurrection or new life from a cocoon.
- Egg—the Easter symbol from which new life emerges.
- Pomegranate—a regal symbol, filled with red seeds that further symbolize life and fertility and the open tomb.
- Ear of corn—as it bursts open we see the fertile new life within.
- Easter lily—symbol of purity and of beautiful new life.
- Each Sunday is a "little Easter," reminding us as Christians of the

resurrection, since it was on the first day of the week that Jesus rose from the dead. The joy of each weekly remembrance of the resurrection is always maintained, even during penitential seasons.

Great Bible Stories for Easter

OLD TESTAMENT SAVING ACTS OF GOD

- Noah's Ark and the Flood (Promise of Deliverance): Genesis 6:5–8:22
- The Passover: Exodus 12
- The Valley of Dry Bones: Ezekiel 37
- Jonah and the Whale: Jonah 1–2:10

NEW TESTAMENT PARABLES OF THE KINGDOM

- The grain of wheat: John 12:23–26
- The talents: Matthew 25:14–30, Luke 19:22–27
- The lost sheep: Luke 15:1–7
- The lost coin: Luke 15:8–10
- The prodigal son: Luke 15:11–32

POST-RESURRECTION APPEARANCES OF JESUS

- The road to Emmaus: Luke 24:13–35
- Thomas: John 20:24–29
- Bribing the soldiers: Matthew 28:11–15
- Command to baptize: Matthew 28:16–20
- Peter's confession: Matthew 16:9–20
- Jerusalem appearance: Luke 24:36–53
- Mary Magdalene and the disciples: John 20:11–29

Great Hymns of Easter

FROM *THE HYMNAL 1982*

- Easter hymns 174–213, including:
- Hail, thee, festival day! (Hymn 175, Easter version)
- He is risen, he is risen! (Hymn 180)
- That Easter day (Hymn 193)
- Come, ye faithful, raise the strain (Hymn 199)
- Jesus Christ is risen today (Hymn 207)
- The strife is o'er, the battle done (Hymn 208)

FROM *WONDER, LOVE AND PRAISE*
- Peace before us (Hymn 791)
- Christ is risen from the dead (Hymn 816)
- Laudate dominum (Hymn 829)

FROM *LIFT EVERY VOICE AND SING*
- Easter hymns 40–43

FROM *VOICES FOUND*
- Easter hymns 45–50, including:
- That Easter morn (Hymn 45)

FROM *MY HEART SINGS OUT*
- Easter hymns 95–104, including:
- Crashing waters at creation (Hymn 95)
- Sing, O people (Hymn 101)

Easter in the Book of Common Prayer

SERVICES WITH EASTER THEMES
- The Great Vigil of Easter (BCP 285–295)
- The Burial of the Dead (BCP 491–505; note especially the rubric on BCP 507)

CANTICLES
- Invitatory: Christ our Passover (BCP 46, 83)
- Canticle 7 or 21: We Praise Thee or You are God (BCP 52, 95)
- Canticle 8: The Song of Moses (BCP 85)
- Canticle 9: The First Song of Isaiah (BCP 86)
- Canticle 18: A Song to the Lamb (BCP 93)

PRAYERS AND THANKSGIVINGS
- The Collect for Sundays reminds us of the Easter nature of every Sunday as a weekly remembrance of Christ's resurrection (BCP 56, 69).
- The Committal in the Burial Services reflects our confidence in the resurrection faith of Easter (BCP 485, 501).

Living the Easter Season at Home and Church

- Banners with the many symbols of Easter add to our mood of celebration and joy.

- Remember the "gardener" who met Mary on that morning of the third day (John 20:15). Make a garden by the church or tend the church yard. Planting seeds or bulbs or trees reminds us of Easter's new life. Assemble window boxes or perhaps "dish gardens" to be given to those who are homebound.
- Make a simple sculpture with wire and pliers to depict the joy of Easter, resurrection, and new life.
- An egg tree (decorated Easter eggs that have been "blown" and tied to a tree branch) can be used for a table centerpiece or classroom or home decoration.
- Eggshell mosaics can illustrate an Easter story or symbols. Wash eggshells and arrange eggshell pieces on poster paper with white glue to make a design or picture. Use plain or colored shells, adding color if desired, either before or after gluing. Mosaics could also be used to make Easter cards or boxes for decorative gift containers.
- Use a digital camera to take photographs or cut pictures from magazines that can be made into collages, posters, or booklets to illustrate experiences of death and resurrection in our lives. An assignment to capture such Easter experiences could make photographers of any age alert to everyday events that express this season. A "live" or taped narration or musical background could accompany the presentation.
- Easter cards can be made by hand or with computers, using any sort of lettering or drawings. Make potato-print stamps with Easter symbols on them by marking the design on the cut end of half a potato and scraping the background away, then placing the "stamp" on a sponge pad of poster paint or food coloring. Yarn, ribbon, string, leaves, or small flowers glued onto construction paper can also convey an Easter message.
- A triptych (made like a three-sided stained glass window) illustrating Palm Sunday, Good Friday, and Easter could be used in worship or a home meditation corner.
- Symbols of new life—eggs, butterflies, ears of corn, lilies, empty crosses— can be created in a great variety of sizes from all sorts of materials and recycled scraps. Hang them in spots all over church or home for an Easter celebration.
- Make kites with Easter symbols on them and enjoy flying them, remembering their symbolism of freedom and release.

ASCENSION DAY

Definition

The Feast of the Ascension is celebrated forty days after Easter Sunday (therefore always on a Thursday) and recalls our Lord's exaltation by being taken gloriously up into heaven. After Jesus' crucifixion and resurrection, Scripture tells us, he was seen for forty days before he ascended into heaven to be "seated at the right hand of God the Father." After Jesus' ascension, the disciples awaited the promised Spirit in Jerusalem.

Ascension Themes

- The ascension is the third event in the cycle of crucifixion-resurrection-ascension in which our Lord's life on earth culminates with his being raised to live and reign gloriously with God forever.
- The ascended Christ is Lord of all, and we are charged by Christ to be witnesses, evangelizing the world in his name: individuals, institutions, communities, and nations.
- In his ascension Christ has taken our human nature into heaven, where as our advocate, he intercedes for us continually.

Great Words of the Ascension

Christ is Lord	Fulfillment
Crown of life	Intercessor
Evangelize	King of glory
Exaltation of human nature	Witness

The Ascension Through the Eyes of a Child

The concept of Jesus saying goodbye to the disciples and ascending to God in heaven is an opportunity to offer to the child the importance of how we live our lives on earth. Some examples are:

- Jesus is Lord in heaven, but he is also Lord in our hearts.
- We do not have to be afraid of dying because Jesus has gone ahead to prepare a place for us in heaven with those who love God.
- We know and feel real things we cannot see, like our parents' and friends' love.
- The disciples needed to say goodbye to Jesus, and as Jesus left them, they turned to be closer to each other, to learn more about Jesus and to let others know about the Jesus who awaits them in heaven.

- Gather pictures of the ascension.
  - Imagine with the children how the disciples felt when Jesus left.
  - What did Jesus expect of the disciples upon his leaving?
  - Wonder with them: what does it feel like to say goodbye?
- Learn "The Lord's Prayer" (BCP), "Prayer of Humble Access" (BCP), or "post-communion prayer" (BCP).
- Share listening exercises. Encourage them to be still and silent and listen to God, as they listen to their mom, dad, or other caretaker.

The Ascension Through the Eyes of Youth

As Jesus leaves the disciples to go to prepare a place for them, he leaves them with each other, to continue to reflect on his teaching and to heal, and to teach, pray, and put into practice all that he taught them. How are we called to do the same in our own life? This is a wonderful opportunity to engage the youth in spiritual practices:

- Anglican Rosary, keeping the prayers, "Lord's Prayer";
- Labyrinth, reflection on the journey the disciples felt;
- Practice a variety of Bible study methods:
  - Aural Method;
  - Lectio Divina;
  - Contemplative.

Adolescents are in a time of tremendous transition in growth, in learning, and in responsibility. The disciples faced a time of tremendous transition when Jesus ascended. Consider the characteristics needed for transition:

- Hope;
- Vision for life;
- Rule of life;
- Focus;
- Willingness to learn, grow, take risks, and assume responsibility for failure and success;
- An attitude of gratitude.

Symbols and Traditions of Ascension Day

- Color—white, for festival and joy.
- Crown—symbol of the reign of our Lord Jesus Christ.

Great Bible Stories for the Ascension

- The accounts of the ascension of Jesus: Matthew 28:16–20; Mark 16:19; Luke 24:50–53; Acts 1:9–11
- Jesus' farewell discourse (he prepares our place): John 14:1–11

Great Hymns of the Ascension

FROM *THE HYMNAL 1982*

- Ascension hymns 214–222, including:
- Hail thee, festival day! (Hymn 216, Ascension version)
- The head that once was crowned with thorns (Hymn 483)

FROM *WONDER, LOVE AND PRAISE*

- Lord, you give the great commission (Hymn 780)

FROM *LIFT EVERY VOICE AND SING*

- The Right Hand of God (Hymn 61)
- Jesus, We Want to Meet (Hymn 81)
- Blessed Assurance (Hymn 184)

FROM *VOICES FOUND*

- At the name of Jesus (Hymn 135)

FROM *MY HEART SINGS OUT*

- Clap your hands (Hymn 113)
- We see the Lord (Hymn 114)

THE DAY OF PENTECOST

Definition

The Feast of Pentecost celebrates the day that the Holy Spirit came to the disciples as they were gathered together in Jerusalem. The Book of Acts tells us that the Holy Spirit was like the rush of a mighty wind, with tongues of flame like fire that rested on each person. After Easter, Pentecost is the second most important feast of the church.

"Pentecost" is from the Greek, meaning "fiftieth day." It was the Greek name for the Hebrew Feast of Weeks, which fell on the fiftieth day after Passover. Christians took this name because this was the same day that the Spirit descended upon the apostles. The Feast of Weeks celebrated the calling of the Hebrews into a covenant relationship with God at Mt. Sinai. With the coming of the Holy Spirit, the church realized a new covenant proclaimed by the prophet Jeremiah years before: "I will put my law within them, and I will write it on their hearts" (Jeremiah 31:33).

The Feast of Pentecost has also been known as Whitsunday. This name probably came from the white robes worn on the day of baptism (White-Sunday).

Pentecost Themes

- Christ the Lord, crucified, risen, and ascended, is present to the church through his Holy Spirit.
- Pentecost is the great and glorious climax of the Easter season, when the Holy Spirit gives power to the church through the apostles to spread the gospel to the ends of the earth.
- Pentecost is the fulfillment of Christ's promise that God would send the Spirit to be with us always and to give power to God's people (John 14:16).
- Pentecost is the birthday of the church, of the new covenant with God given to all believers.
- The author of Luke and Acts saw history as divided into three periods: the time of Israel and the prophets (with John the Baptist as the last prophet); the time of Jesus' earthly ministry; and the time of the church, which began at Pentecost and in which we are living now. Pentecost is the first event of the church's history.

Great Words of Pentecost

Apostles	Enthusiasm (Greek: filled with the Spirit)
Breath (sign of life)	Evangelism
Dove	Gift of speech
Empowered by the Spirit	

Pentecost Through the Eyes of a Child

- God promises to be with us always.
- We are strengthened from within by the Holy Spirit, whose power, like a strong wind, we can feel even though we cannot see it.
- The Holy Spirit gives us Gifts we need to strengthen in our relationship to God: "Understanding," "Proclamation," "Prophecy," "Love of God," "Knowledge," "Wisdom," "Fear of God."
- Now the church will continue to grow and learn more about Jesus, even after his death and resurrection.

Mission, building and re-building the church (what some call "congregational development"), with and for children is critical during the season of Pentecost. This is the time the children will wonder: What are the adventures of the early church? How was the early church built? The travels of St. Paul with maps and cities where Paul founded churches, as well as the travels of St. Peter, St. James, and St. John can be inspiring for children as they enjoy the concept of building something new.

Talk about the parts of a church—illustrate through either two- or three-dimensional models the parts of the church, and indicate transept, font, stained glass windows, organ or piano, altar, as well as pulpit and lectern. Young children have a tremendous capacity to engage in the concept of building, creating something new. This is a terrific opportunity to focus them by either having them put together models, either pasting it on paper or using three-dimensional blocks and wood and miniatures of what they see every Sunday.

Pentecost Worship Sentence for Young Children

"The Holy Spirit makes us one people in the name of the Lord."

Suggested hand motions: Arms outstretched above head, then lowered; hands touch shoulders and then take hands of people on either side.

Pentecost Through the Eyes of Youth

Spiritual gifts are given by the Holy Spirit to reveal the ways that Christians form the body of Christ and the way the variety of gifts are used within the body. These gifts are given for the purpose of:
- Equipping believers to share the good news: Matthew 10:19, 20; Luke 4:18; 1 Corinthians 2:13;
- Authenticating (proving) the gospel message: Hebrews 2:3, 4;
- Equipping believers to serve other believers: 1 Corinthians 12:7; 14:26.

Developing an authentic faith in the understanding of "God as Three" (Creator, Redeemer, Sustainer) is a vital part of youth spirituality. Youth are developing their identity, and part of that identity is formed through the gifts God has given them, including gifts of the spirit.

Questions to consider with youth:
- What will be and what will we leave to the next generation?
- Are we building our lives on firm foundations, building something that will endure?

- Are we living our lives in a way that opens up space for the Spirit in the midst of a world that wants to forget God, or even rejects him in the name of a falsely conceived freedom?

Pentecost is a perfect time to invite the youth to reflect upon the gifts that God has given them—not only the gifts they see in themselves, but the gifts they see in each other. Retreats can be most helpful to give the young people some time to remember the gifts the Spirit gave to the disciples, and the gifts that the Spirit gives to them.

Parents, teachers, and youth leaders are challenged during the time of Pentecost to create safe space where the teens can share their stories, witness to the spirit in their life. Using resources such as "Authority of Generations" (available at http://www.episcopalchurch.org/documents/authority_of_generations(1).pdf) invites the young people to share their sacred story with others.

We are also called to provide opportunities for the youth to "baptize their culture." Demonstrate the ways they see the spirit in school activities, in relationships, in their music, in their DVDs, in their study of other religions and cultures.

Pentecost Through the Eyes of Daily Life

On the fiftieth day of Easter we celebrate the Holy Spirit as the power of God among us that heals, forgives, inspires, and unites. Images of wind and fire describe the Spirit poured out on disciples of all nations. In the one Spirit we were baptized into one body, and at the Lord's table the Spirit unites us for witness in the world. The Spirit calls us to follow in the way and in the pattern and in the shape of the life of Jesus.

Pentecost Through the Eyes of Our Global Community

The Day of Pentecost opened the way of eternal life to every race and nation. On this day it is appropriate to study racism, sexism, and all other attitudes and actions that deny God's love for all people. It is common to see in the gift of the Spirit at Pentecost a sign that reveals God's purposes to heal and restore creation, including overcoming the disorder and confusion of languages that was told to have happened at Babel.

The Spirit of God crosses over the boundaries of language and culture to create a new people of God, a human family renewed and made whole. Consider the global perspective of how the church has made its journey from the time of Paul to today and how the message of Christ has spread throughout the world in its many forms and traditions.

Symbols and Traditions of Pentecost

- Colors—red, for the tongues of flame that signify the Holy Spirit.
- Descending dove—indicates the presence of divinity and the power of God working in people (see Matthew 3:16).
- Tongues of fire—an ancient symbol for divine presence.
- Lessons read in other languages at the Eucharist—remind us of the variety of languages spoken on Pentecost.
- Mighty wind—felt and heard by the apostles; a symbol of the spirit (in Hebrew, Greek, and Latin, the words for "wind" and "spirit" are the same).
- Pentecost vigil—held at night or early in the morning using the Order of Worship for the Evening (BCP 109–114; see BCP 227, 896). The readings are the same for all three years of the lectionary.
- Baptisms and confirmations—traditionally part of both the Pentecost Vigil and principal services, since Pentecost is one of the five "especially appropriate" days for baptism (BCP 312).
- The Easter Alleluias—used at worship on this final day of the Easter season.
- Wearing red clothing at worship services—to signify the tongues of fire of the Holy Spirit.

Great Bible Stories for Pentecost

- Tower of Babel—confusion of languages (Genesis 11:1–9)
- Mount Sinai (Exodus 19, 20)
- The Spirit resting on the seventy elders of Israel in the wilderness with Moses (Numbers 11:24–30)
- Elijah and Elisha (2 Kings 2:1–15)
- Nicodemus (John 3:1–21)
- The Pentecost experience (Acts 2)

Great Hymns of Pentecost

FROM *THE HYMNAL 1982*

- Pentecost hymns 223–230, including:
- Hail thee, festival day (Hymn 225, Pentecost version)
- Come thou Holy Spirit bright (Hymns 226, 227)
- Breathe on me, breath of God (Hymn 508)
- Like the murmur of a dove's song (Hymn 513)

FROM *WONDER, LOVE AND PRAISE*

- Loving Spirit (Hymn 742)
- There's a sweet, sweet Spirit in this place (Hymn 752)
- If you believe and I believe (Hymn 806)
- Veni sancte spiritus (Hymn 832)

FROM *LIFT EVERY VOICE AND SING*

- Ev'ry time I feel the Spirit (Hymn 114)
- Spirit of the living God (Hymn 115)
- I'm goin'-a sing when the Spirit says sing (Hymn 117)
- Sweet, sweet Spirit (Hymn 120)

FROM *VOICES FOUND*

- Pentecost hymns 51–63, including:
- Breath of God (Hymn 59)
- Give me oil in my lamp (Hymn 61)
- O fiery Spirit (Hymn 62)

FROM *MY HEART SINGS OUT*

- Pentecost hymns 105–112, including:
- We are all children of the Lord (Hymn 105)
- I am the church (Hymn 109)

Pentecost in the Book of Common Prayer

PRAYERS AND THANKSGIVINGS

- Eucharistic Prayer D (BCP 372–376, from the Liturgy of St. Basil)
- Collect "For the Unity of the Church" (BCP 255)
- Collects II (BCP 256) and III (BCP 256–257) pray for the Spirit's help in choosing suitable persons for ordained ministry and for the vocation of all Christians.

SERVICES WITH PENTECOST THEMES

- Vigil of Pentecost (see BCP 227). The vigil begins with the Order of Worship for the Evening (BCP 109–114). Instead of the *Phos hilaron* we may substitute the Gloria in excelsis and a series of readings listed on pages 896, 906–907, or 917 of the Book of Common Prayer. The service concludes with the Holy Eucharist.
- Ordination rites (BCP 512–555).
- The Dedication and Consecration of a Church (BCP 567–574).

Living Pentecost at Home and Church

- Have a birthday party for the church with balloons and banners and a birthday cake, perhaps with doves or flames of fire on it. Think of red food–strawberries, punch. (Refrain from releasing balloons outdoors as they have a negative environmental impact.)
- Make a gift for everyone attending the Pentecost service. Cut tongues of fire from red, orange, and yellow felt to pin on the shoulder.
- Have a celebration involving wind: make and use kites and pinwheels, fans, wind chimes, wind socks, mobiles that move in the breeze, toy sailboats for races, parachutes, scarves that trail in the wind, a model windmill.

TRINITY SUNDAY

Definition

Trinity Sunday is the first Sunday after Pentecost. It has been part of the Church Year since 1334, when it was designated in commemoration of the doctrine of the Trinity, the belief that God is revealed to us in three persons existing in a mutual relationship of love. It is the total revelation of God: God the Father as Creator; God the Son as Redeemer; God the Holy Spirit as Sanctifier and Comforter. Our understanding of the Trinity arises from the biblical, creedal, and doctrinal statements that emerged from the creative struggles of theologians in the church to understand and talk about the nature of God.

Trinity Themes

- The Nicene and Apostles' creeds express our faith in God revealed to us as a Trinity of persons: God the Father, God the Son, and God the Holy Spirit.
- After the crucifixion-resurrection-ascension cycle of our Lord's life and the descent of the Holy Spirit on the apostles at Pentecost, the church celebrates the full revelation of God in the three persons of the Trinity.

Great Words of Trinity Sunday

Community	One-in-three
Creator	Persons
God the Father	Redeemer
God the Son	Sanctifier
God the Holy Spirit	Three-in-one
Mutual indwelling	Unity

Trinity Through the Eyes of a Child

We know God when:

- We see God's creation all around us;
- We learn of God's love for everyone from Jesus' life and teaching;
- We feel the power and strength of God's Spirit within us;
- We know God's love in the community of the church.

Children see the sign of the cross people make before and after prayer, they also see an outward and visible proclamation that we rely on the gift of the Holy Trinity to be a part of our lives.

Rublev's *Icon of the Trinity* (http://www.wellsprings.org/uk/rublevs_icon/rublev.htm) is a wonderful way to encourage children to see the work of the Holy Trinity. Invite a conversation:

Six hundred years ago not many people went to school. Not many kids learned how to read and write. And if you didn't know how to read and write, then you wouldn't be able to read a Bible. So to help people understand God six hundred years ago, church ministers used to paint pictures so that people who couldn't read and write could still learn about God. What we can learn about God from this picture? How many people are in this picture? All three people have exactly the same circle, the same "halo" around their heads. That's the glow of God. Now, these three people are wearing four colors—green; brown; blue; gold. Six hundred years ago, blue was the color people painted God. Blue was God's color. Three people, all with circle halos around their heads. All wearing blue, the color of God. So, the painter of this picture was saying that these three people are God.

What are the three people holding? They are all holding a long stick. Exactly the same length. Look at their hands. What hand is holding the stick? All three right hands are holding the stick. Now look at their other hands; all the left hands have two fingers pointing down. We can see that the painter is saying that these people are the same; same halos; same blue, the color for God; same way of holding a staff in the same right hand; same way of pointing their fingers. Three people, who are God, who are all exactly the same.

Yet as well as being exactly the same, these three people are also different. One person has green, the side closest to us. Green is the color of spring, the color of things that grow; that green person is the Holy Spirit of God—who wants you, and this church, to be green and grow. One person has brown. Brown is the color of dirt. That brown person is Jesus, who came to earth, put his feet on the ground, felt dirt between his feet. One person is gold. That person is God the Father; gold because of beauty and God who created a beautiful earth. The painter is using a picture to tell us about God. That God is three persons: Spirit in green to help us grow; Jesus in brown walking in dirt; the Father in gold who created this beautiful earth.

Invite children to respond either through prayer, art, or song, such as creating their own icon.

Trinity Sunday Worship Sentence for Young Children

"God is the Creator, Redeemer, and Sanctifier."

Suggested hand motions: Arms outstretched above head (Creator); hands over heart (Redeemer); and with the fingers of one hand, make the sign of the cross on the forehead (sanctifier).

Trinity Sunday Through the Eyes of Youth

Understanding the inner life of the Trinity as relational and dynamic is one of the best ways to emphasize the Trinity to teens. The main teaching point is to focus on the meaning of relationship. There is a triune relationship between the Father, the Son, and the Holy Spirit; the Creator, the Redeemer, and the Sanctifier. What other Trinitarian relationships exist within the Triune God?

American individualism is engrained in our culture. In terms of development, teens want to be deeply connected to their peers, so the challenge by the radical Christian truth that the personal exists only in community with the Triune God and with one another is actually an easier concept to teach and to develop belief. The idea of belonging before belief appeals to this age, especially if they are considering Confirmation. It is important to let them know that there is no person who is not structured by and tied to community, even though there are times when we might be tempted to seek a certain fulfillment apart from God, apart from the community of faith, and apart from family. To turn away from God is only a futile attempt to escape from ourselves (cf. Saint Augustine,

Confessions VIII, 7). God is with us in the reality of life, not the fantasy! It is embrace, not escape, that we seek!

Consider the ways the Holy Spirit gently but surely steers us back to what is real, what is lasting, what is true. Together name the kind of communities they belong to, and then consider their belief in the Trinity. Remember, only about 48% of children who attend church every Sunday continue to do so as teens or young adults. Faith then is a gift of the Holy Spirit. The work of the teen is to be an agent of mission. It is the Spirit who leads us back into the communion of the Blessed Trinity!

Activities to do with youth:

- Take a look at the symbols for the Trinity, i.e. clover, triangle, fleur de lis, three interconnected circles, and talk about the relationship one to another.
- Consider the prayers in the prayer book that refer to the Trinity—what is it that we are praying for?
- The *Perichoresis*—the Greek term for the mysterious exchange of God (as the Divine) and the love between the Father, the Son, and the Holy Spirit—do they believe in that mystery?
- Encourage them to draw, write, or demonstrate what they believe to be the relationship between God, Son, and Holy Spirit.
- Name a Trinitarian Mission Action they would like to develop.

Symbols and Traditions of Trinity Sunday

- Color—white, the color of joy.
- Equilateral triangle—three in one.
- Three interlocking circles—inseparability and unity.
- Blessing—the cross is signed in the name of the Father, Son, and Holy Spirit.
- We celebrate the Trinity in the *Gloria in excelsis*.
- All collects and many prayers end with ascription to the Holy Trinity.

Great Hymns of Trinity Sunday

FROM *THE HYMNAL 1982*

- Trinity hymns 362–371, including:
- I bind unto myself today (Hymn 370)
- Come, thou almighty King (Hymn 365)

- Holy God we praise thy Name (Hymn 366)
- Thou, whose almighty word (Hymn 371)

FROM *LIFT EVERY VOICE AND SING*

- How like a gentle Spirit (Hymn 113)

FROM *WONDER, LOVE AND PRAISE*

- O threefold God of tender unity (Hymn 743)
- O Trinity of blessed light (Hymn 744)
- I believe in God almighty (Hymn 769)

FROM *VOICES FOUND*

- God of all time (Hymn 86)
- God, creator, source of healing (Hymn 93)
- Bring many names (Hymn 106)
- People of God (Hymn 109)

FROM *MY HEART SINGS OUT*

- In the night, in the day (Hymn 116)
- Glory to God (Hymn 117)

Trinity Sunday in the Book of Common Prayer

PRAYERS AND THANKSGIVINGS

- The three prefaces of the Lord's Day (BCP 377–378) summarize our understanding of the three persons of the Trinity.
- The Collect for Trinity Sunday (BCP 228)
- An additional collect concerning the Holy Trinity (BCP 251)

CANTICLES

- Canticle 7 or 21: Te Deum laudamus (You are God) (BCP 52, 95)
- Canticle 2 or 13: Benedictus es, Domine (A Song of Praise) (BCP 49, 90)

Trinity Themes in the Book of Common Prayer

- Holy Baptism has a trinitarian emphasis throughout. Notice especially the Baptismal Covenant (BCP 304–305), the Thanksgiving over the Water (BCP 306–307), and the baptism itself (BCP 307–308).
- The prayer for renewal of the Baptismal Covenant said by the bishop before confirmation (BCP 309) refers to each of the persons of the Trinity in their relationship to the life of a committed Christian.

- The historic creeds that appear in the prayer book are sources of our understanding of the Trinity:
  - The Apostles' Creed (BCP 96)
  - The Nicene Creed (BCP 326–327)
  - The Creed of St. Athanasius (BCP 864–865)

Living Trinity Sunday at Home and Church

- A banner or altar cloth can be made to express the theme of praise to the Trinity. A line from prayers or even an entire canticle could serve as the basis for these illustrations.
- "The Grace" from 2 Corinthians 13:13 is a text that lends itself to illustration in a number of ways, including poetry, sentence completion (such as "The fellowship of the Holy Spirit makes me think of . . ."), hangings, sculptures, murals, and mobiles.
- Ask questions that will encourage people to talk about their experiences of God in different "persons," such as God as a loving parent, a forgiving savior, a strengthening companion.

THE SEASON AFTER PENTECOST

Definition

The numbered weeks after Pentecost are sometimes referred to as "Ordinary Time" because these weeks of the year are not associated with specific seasons, such as Lent and Easter, with their overriding themes. The Season after Pentecost begins with Trinity Sunday (the first Sunday after Pentecost) and ends on the last Sunday after Pentecost, just before Advent begins, sometimes called the Feast of Christ the King. The numbered Proper to be used on each of the Sundays after Pentecost is determined by the calendar date of that Sunday (see BCP 158). The liturgical color for the Season after Pentecost is green, and these weeks during the summer and fall months in the northern hemisphere have often been connected with growth and fruitfulness in the Christian life. Although in this time of the Church Year it may seem that nothing of note happens, we understand that our "ordinary" lives are how we live out our Christian faith.

82

Holy Days in the Season After Pentecost

Since Pentecost is a movable feast, depending on the date of Easter, check the calendar. The holy dates below are after June 1 through Christ the King (Last Sunday After Pentecost):

- Saint Barnabas the Apostle (June 11)
- The Nativity of John the Baptist (June 24)
- Saint Peter and Saint Paul, Apostles (June 29)
- Independence Day (July 4)
- Saint Mary Magdalene (July 22)
- The Transfiguration of Our Lord Jesus Christ (August 6)
- Saint Mary the Virgin, Mother of Our Lord Jesus Christ (August 15)
- Saint Bartholomew the Apostle (August 24)
- Holy Cross Day (September 14)
- Saint Matthew, Apostle and Evangelist (September 21)
- Saint Michael and All Angels (September 29)
- Saint Luke the Evangelist (October 18)
- Saint James of Jerusalem, Brother of Our Lord Jesus Christ, and Martyr (October 23)
- Saint Simon and Saint Jude, Apostles (October 28)
- All Saints (November 1)
- Thanksgiving Day
- Saint Andrew the Apostle (November 30)

The Season After Pentecost Themes

- Sanctification is the work of the Holy Spirit in the day-to-day life of the Christian.
- Through the gift of faith that comes only from the Holy Spirit, Christians are enabled to trust in Christ and proclaim him in their daily lives by service to their neighbors.
- The church stresses vocation, evangelism, missions, stewardship, almsgiving, and other works of mercy and charity as ways in which Christ empowers us by his grace to share the Gospel with others.

When we gather to celebrate in the presence of Christ in our own generation, we too must allow the unexpected initiative of God to burst through the ordinary, the predictable, and the unlikely.

Great Words in the Season After Pentecost

Vocation	Almsgiving
Stewardship	Child of God
Mission	Relationships
Evangelism	Action
Parable	Presence

The Season After Pentecost Through the Eyes of a Child

Formation in faith is a life-long journey. Life itself is the context of any religious education program:

- The needs of children change over time. Therefore, a variety of teaching methods are required.
- The children's lives influence their expressions of faith. Thus teaching and learning strategies will respond to and respect the diversity of children in terms of maturation, experience, and culture within their families;
- The family is the basic community of the church. Links between the home, parish, and school are discovered and encouraged.

The weeks after Pentecost are the time to attend to spiritual growth. It is important to set an environment as well as provide the opportunities to share with a child what you see. Put your thinking into words about God, your relationships in Christ, and the faith journey. Emphasis is upon the journey; we are on a pilgrimage together, a journey that is marked by physical, emotional, intellectual, and spiritual growth.

"God calls us to be open to the presence and action of the Holy Spirit every day."

The Season After Pentecost Through the Eyes of Youth

Youth are modern-day pilgrims; they can be agents of mission. Offer an environment to the teens that:

- Gives them time with adults to demonstrate and explore their beliefs and faith. Adults can provide a positive relationship as a mentor, joining the teen on the faith journey;
- Demonstrates how leaders practice sacrificial love, and teaches through Scripture how to be a Christian in a post-modern world;
- Accepts failure as a way to learn, as a way to change the heart, as a way to forgive and reconcile.

Offer opportunities to grow spiritually and learn how to practice a variety of spiritual disciplines through multiple experiences:

- Intellectually: by knowing and understanding;
- Experientially: through a mystical experience or event;
- Ideologically: learning about the beliefs of others as well as self;
- Ritualistically: experiencing a variety of worship practices and rituals;
- Consequentially: learning what guides our behavior as Christians.

The Season After Pentecost Through the Eyes of Daily Life

The twenty-nine Collects for the Sundays that follow Pentecost fall broadly under four themes. Each theme is a statement of a basic Christian truth, which applies to us at any age. As organizing principles for learning, these truths enhance the educational life of the church community and make teaching more than mythology, because they are directly related to our lives.

We are God's children:
- Throughout his life on earth, Jesus told others about his Father, and did what he knew to be God's will for his life. Jesus served and honored his Father in all ways in his life and in his death.
- As we grow in faith and in years, to know ourselves as children of God calls for increasingly mature responses, but the underlying truths are there for us at any age.
- Because we are God's children we trust him, we believe in him, we want to worship him, and most of all we want to discover his will for our lives.

We have a personal relationship with Jesus Christ and a ministry of love to other people:
- Through our prayers, the sacraments, and the life in the community of the church we have a relationship of faith with the living Christ and his mission.
- We know that Jesus is God. We know, too, that he is our brother. His incarnation, death, resurrection, and ascension are faith events for us, centered in the celebration of the Eucharist.
- We try faithfully to respond to the commandment of Jesus Christ that we love one another as he has loved us.

God calls us to be open to the reality of the presence and action of the Holy Spirit:
- We learn to understand the nature of the Holy Spirit as shown to us in the teaching of Jesus and elsewhere in the Bible.
- We increase our ability to recognize the action of the Holy Spirit in our lives and in the world through prayer and thoughtful listening.

We believe in the church as the Body of Christ in the world and in the church's mission:

- We believe in and work with the church as it carries on its mission of bringing about the Kingdom of God in the world through prayers, service, and witness.

The Season After Pentecost Through the Eyes of Our Global Community

We pray in our Collects as well as the proper preface during the Great Thanksgiving that we go out into the world spreading the Good News of God in Jesus Christ through the gift of the Holy Spirit. Our call is to be missionaries in our community as well as in the world. By bringing our prayers into action, we are called to think and respond in mission and ministry. Consider the following Collects as ways to direct us to the wider call to serve Christ in the world by being in relationship with others globally:

PROPER 6

Keep, O Lord, your household the Church in your steadfast faith and love, that through your grace we may proclaim your truth with boldness and minister your justice with compassion.

PROPER 9

O God, you have taught us to keep all your commandments by loving you and our neighbor: Grant us the grace of your Holy Spirit, that we may be devoted to you with our whole heart, and united to one another with pure affection.

PROPER 14

Grant to us, Lord, we pray, the spirit to think and do always those things that are right, that we, who cannot exist without you, may by you be enabled to live according to your will.

PROPER 24

Almighty and everlasting God, in Christ you have revealed your glory among the nations: Preserve the works of your mercy that your Church throughout the world may persevere with steadfast faith in the confession of your Name.

Pentecost is a wonderful season to strengthen or join the Companion Diocesan Link through the Anglican Communion. The Lambeth Conference declared in 1998, "The time has come for significant new initiatives in encouraging all dioceses to develop companion relationships across provincial boundaries, as part of the process of developing the cross-cultural nature of the Communion." Our prayers during the season of Pentecost call us to be in active relationship and ministry. This is the time to build upon the ministry you already share or encourage the development of new global mission and ministries: www.anglicancommunion.org/ministry/mission/companion/.

Symbols and Traditions of the Season After Pentecost

- Color—green, the color of life and growth
- Vacation Bible School
- Local traditions

Great Bible Stories for the Season After Pentecost

There are many Bible stories from the Old and New Testaments during this season. Summertime can be a time to develop creative intergenerational programming that builds week upon week. Storytelling, enhanced by simple dramatics, creative writing, painting, and other experiences, can be fully explored. The "Common Lectionary" breaks away from the thematic harmony principle of all the Sunday readings during this long season of the church year.

- *Year A:* Stories of our roots (Genesis) and liberation (Exodus), a semi-continuous reading of the biblical story beginning with the call of Abraham and Sarah to the death of Moses (along with readings from Matthew).
- *Year B:* Stories of God's Word and will revealed through the anointed leader of the nation shares the story of King David from First and Second Samuel followed by selections from Wisdom literature (along with readings from Mark).
- *Year C:* Stories of God's Word revealed as it confronts those who govern and guide the people of the world beginning with the reign of Solomon. The great stories of the prophets Elijah and Elisha from First and Second Kings are told followed by a fifteen-week focus on the writings of the great prophets (read alongside Luke).

Great Hymns for the Season After Pentecost

The following are hymns that tell the Biblical story, praise God's Creation, speak of the mission of the church, or are appropriate for specific feast days during this long season. Each can also be the central theme for creative activities:

FROM *THE HYMNAL 1982*

- All things bright and beautiful (Hymn 405)
- Earth and all stars (Hymn 412)
- For the beauty of the earth (Hymn 416)
- All hail the power of Jesus' Name! (Hymn 450)
- God is working his purpose out (Hymn 534)
- Open your ears (Hymn 536)
- God, who stretched the spangled heavens (Hymn 580)
- Go down, Moses (Hymn 648)
- Amazing grace! (Hymn 671)
- Guide me, O great Jehovah (Hymn 690)

FROM *WONDER, LOVE AND PRAISE*

- Will you come and follow me (Hymn 757)
- We all are one in mission (Hymn 778)
- Peace before us (Hymn 791)
- Holy God, you raise up prophets (Hymn 792)
- I, the Lord of sea and sky (Hymn 812)

FROM *LIFT EVERY VOICE AND SING*

- Lift every voice and sing (Hymn 1)
- I love to tell the story (Hymn 64)
- Jesu, Jesu (Hymn 74)
- Jesus in the morning (Hymn 76)
- God is so good (Hymn 214)
- Joshua fit de Battle of Jericho (Hymn 223)
- Ezek'el saw de wheel (Hymn 224)

FROM *VOICES FOUND*

- Join us, Christian children (Hymn 134)
- Bless now (Hymn 142)

FROM *MY HEART SINGS OUT*

- Halle, halle, hallelujah! (Hymn 18)
- God it was (Hymn 85)

- What does it mean to follow Jesus? (Hymn 89)
- We are on our way (Hymn 96)
- One, two, three, Jesus loves me (Hymn 144)
- Peace before us (Hymn 152)

The Season After Pentecost in the Book of Common Prayer

PRAYERS AND THANKSGIVINGS
- Collect for the Nation (BCP 207/258)
- Collect for Labor Day (BCP 210/261)
- Prayers and Thanksgivings (BCP 810–841)

AN OUTLINE OF THE FAITH
- The Church (BCP 854–855)
- The Ministry (BCP 855–856)

Living the Season After Pentecost at Home and Church

This season covers two different time frames in our day-to-day life—summer and autumn. Because summer is the time for family vacations, summer camp, and visits to friends and relatives who live in distant places, church attendance is less regular and the patterns of congregational Christian education often change in summer. The summer Sundays after Pentecost bring the gift of time to plan ahead for the coming academic year as well as time to introduce special emphases for educational focus, such as mission study, social justice issues, and intergenerational participation and study. When programs are cut off for the season it becomes an invitation for people to drop out or stay away.

Offer a variety of activities that say summer is different, but still a time for learning and discovery. Some ideas include:
- Intergenerational activities and study around a common theme. People of every age can be teachers and learners.
- Interest Centers designed around a central theme in one large room or separated in smaller rooms. The centers could be planned for adults and children of all ages or in specific groupings. Interest Centers might include:
  - Arts activities, such as painting, lettering, clay modeling, stitching, mobiles, photography, film making;
  - Creative writing, interviews, or news stories;
  - Simple creative drama, puppets, shadow plays, or pantomime;

- Choral readings, recording of sound effects;
- Projects that will take several weeks, such as making banners, shields, research on a subject, displays, models or dioramas, field trips, outreach projects, nature or ecology activities;
- Learning hymns or folk songs, exploring Christianity in the arts.

- Take families and individuals to a local camp or conference site and spend the weekend together. Offer intergenerational and/or age-grouped opportunities for worship, art, and a variety of other activities.
- A Vacation Church School for a specified period, perhaps one or two weeks.
- Meet in different locations and at different times (such as outdoors, in each others' homes, at some place of recreation) for meals, overnight camping, or retreats.
- Ideas for summer projects:
  - Reenact the life of the early Christians. Build a house, make costumes.
  - Write scrolls, and have some of the saints of that time "visit."
  - Build a house or town of the Holy Land.
  - Build a puppet stage for use all year.
  - Cook and enjoy some foods mentioned in the Bible.
  - Plant an herb garden using the herbs mentioned in the Bible. Dry the herbs in the fall and use them for cooking or decorations.
  - Relive the entire church year, Advent to Pentecost, devoting one or two days to each season, depending on the time available (a good idea for a summer camp program).

SOCIAL JUSTICE ISSUES

Identify issues in your community, the nation, or the world. Gather the information you need. Plan to invite local resource people who are involved in the issues. Develop sessions for research, field trips, movies, keeping in mind the question: How can we as Christians respond to the situation?

Learn about how to participate in the mission activities of the larger church.

Information about Episcopal Relief & Development: http://www.er-d.org/ or the United Thank Offering: http://www.episcopalchurch.org/uto/ may be obtained from the Episcopal Church Center in New York.

ALL SAINTS' DAY

Definition

On November 1 the church remembers the saints of God—all faithful servants and believers. The day is seen as a communion of saints who have died and of all Christian persons. All Hallows' Eve, October 31 (from which our Hallowe'en traditions come); All Saints' Day; and All Souls' Day, November 2 (the Day of the Faithful Departed), are connected by tradition and are often celebrated together.

All Saints' Day Themes

A day to remember those who came before us:

- We are always surrounded by a cloud of witnesses (Hebrews 12:1)—those faithful Christians who have died.
- When we die, a new and everlasting life begins with God and others who have died before us.
- The sacredness of persons is celebrated, remembering that they are all creations of God.
- Baptism is a sacrament of Christian initiation in which all Christian saints, living and dead, share as members of the Body of Christ.
- The unique personality, gifts, talents, and experiences of every individual are given by God to be valued and used in the building of the Kingdom. Being good stewards of God's gifts means looking at our lives for clues about what we have to offer that will serve others in Christ's name. To become the people God intends us to be is to find our greatest happiness and deepest fulfillment.

Great Words of All Saints' Day

Baptism	Kingdom of God
Cloud of witnesses	Martyr
Communion of saints	Ministry
Eternity	Obedience
Fellowship of the faithful	Saint
Gifts and talents	Service

All Saints' Day Through the Eyes of a Child

- We are all called to be saints, using our talents and lives to serve others, loving them as God loves us.
- Famous saints are examples, showing us how to be followers of Jesus.
- When we die, it is the beginning of a new life in which we join with others who have died and are close to God and Jesus.
- Life in the Kingdom of God is life in a new way, without sorrow or pain, a life of joy.

All Saints' Day Worship Sentence for Young Children

"We give thanks for all the saints who showed us the way to God and rejoice that we, too, are children of God."

Suggested hand motions: Arms in the air, wiggle fingers overhead; swing arms behind body then in front of body; arms end in upraised position.

All Saints' Day Through the Eyes of Youth

Together with those who came before us, we all make up the Body of Christ. This particular day on our church's calendar we remember those who have died, the famous and not-so-famous. Youth can also recognize those saints we are living amongst us today. Discuss, "What are the qualities of a saint?"

If our destiny and purpose in life are to become more and more deeply united with God and one another, then it doesn't make sense that this process would stop at the time of our deaths. Jesus' Resurrection shows us that this life is only the entryway into an even fuller kind of living. Because it's our relationships with one another that give our lives meaning, a fuller experience of life must bring us into even closer relationships with others. This is the concept of the "body of Christ," first described by St. Paul in the New Testament (Romans 12:4-8). The Church has often used the word mystical before the word body, meaning spiritual or invisible. (It doesn't mean magical!) St. Paul wanted us to understand that we are intimately related to one another and to Jesus. He explained that the Church functions as a human body does. Every Christian is a member of this body. We all depend on one another like parts of the body do. (For instance, try leaving your heart at home for a few days.) All the parts of your body (its members) unite toward the purpose of keeping the body alive and healthy. All the parts of our body are connected: All the parts of the body of Christ are connected as well.

Symbols and Traditions of All Saints' Day

- Color—white for joy and festival
- The Cross and Crown—for faithfulness and the Crown of Life (Revelation 2:10)
- Reading the names of those who have died during the year, with the prayer
- Local traditions often involve special services in the church cemetery

Great Bible Stories for All Saints' Day

Any of the stories related to the disciples, Paul, early church leaders found in Acts of the Apostles, or persons found in *Lesser Feasts and Fasts* can be heard on this day. Don't forget modern-day saints!

Great Hymns of All Saints' Day

FROM *THE HYMNAL 1982*
- Hymns for saints 231–293, including:
- For all the saints (Hymn 287)
- I sing a song of the saints of God (Hymn 293)

FROM *WONDER, LOVE AND PRAISE*
- No saint on earth lives life to self alone (Hymn 776)

FROM *LIFT EVERY VOICE AND SING*
- Black saints (Hymns 44–51)

FROM *VOICES FOUND*
- Hymns for saints (Hymns 65–66)

FROM *MY HEART SINGS OUT*
- We sing of the saints (Hymn 118)

All Saints' Day in the Book of Common Prayer

PRAYERS AND THANKSGIVINGS
- Opening sentence of Scripture—Morning Prayer (BCP 40/77)
- Antiphon—Morning Prayer (BCP 44/82)
- Prefaces—Holy Eucharist (BCP 347/380); for the day commemorating a particular saint there are Prefaces on (BCP 348/380–81)

- For the Saints and Faithful Departed (BCP 838)
- "O God, the King of Saints . . . " (BCP 489/504)
- Eucharistic Prayer D (BCP 372) from the Liturgy of St. Basil
- Number 8 of the Concluding Collects (set at the end of the Prayers of the People) speaks of our being supported and surrounded by "your saints in heaven and on earth . . ." (BCP 395)
- Notice what the Anthem of Commendation in the Burial Service has to say about what life in heaven with the saints will be like (BCP 482–83/499)
- Prayer: For those who suffer for the sake of Conscience (BCP 823)

CANTICLES

- Canticle 7 or 21: "We Praise Thee" or "You are God" (Te Deum laudamus) BCP 52/95

A SERVICE WITH ALL SAINTS' DAY THEMES

- A Form of Commitment to Christian Service (BCP 420)

Living All Saints' Day at Home and Church

- Look at the list of saints in the prayer book's calendar (BCP 19–33). Refer also to *Lesser Feasts and Fasts* to begin study of those whom the church especially honors.
- Think about the many ways that people in any period of history (including our own) have expressed their love for God in service to others. Show the qualities of people's lives, whether famous or ordinary, in some visual form: a mural, a display, a mobile, an altar-hanging, a collection of objects that symbolize loving acts, a parade of costumed persons showing how they help or serve, or banners hung or carried in procession.
- Many groups, especially Asian-Americans, use All Saints' Day as an opportunity to remember and respect family members who are elderly or who have lived in other generations. This might be the occasion for telling about where our families have come from and lived, what their lives were like, and what values we honor that they have passed on to us.
- Our names are symbols of who we are, and our Christian names tell who we are in our new life in Christ. A study of names and their meanings, of how our names show we are particular people loved individually and personally by God, can help us see ourselves as particular saints of God whose lives are offered in loving service.
- A design of everyone's name in a congregation or family or other group can make an interesting All Saints' Day bulletin board or Sunday bulletin

cover, or other display. Photos can be made into a mobile or PowerPoint presentation to help convey our common Christian calling to be saints.

- Biblical illustrations of Jesus' calling of the disciples, or invitations to others to follow him, can stimulate discussions and art or drama projects about how we, and others, can be followers today. Think of people in your local community whom are contemporary examples of discipleship today, who provide genuine inspiration when we take time to notice and celebrate their often quiet and unnoticed acts.

- Share with a family or other group the lives of persons (living or dead) whom you have always admired or wished to meet, saying what particularly attracts you to them and giving their names if you wish. Perhaps you might want to cite family and friends who have been influences or have helped you in some way. Writing such people a letter of gratitude, however simple, might be rewarding for everyone.

- Visit a cemetery and read examples of how friends and loved ones have honored the dead on tombstones both now and long ago. Rubbings might be made from the tombstones, with appropriate permission and using the proper tools.

- Making and discussing a "living will" is another way to render service to others.

- Look at the memorials in your church and talk about what they have meant.

Days of Special Importance

LESSER FEASTS AND FASTS

The Episcopal Church publishes *Lesser Feasts and Fasts,* which contains feast days for the various men and women the church wishes to honor. It gives the Collects, Psalms, and lessons as well as a short historical description of the individuals and events.

This book is updated every three years following General Convention, and notable persons are added to the liturgical calendar. The Episcopal Church does not canonize individuals, holding instead that all baptized Christians are saints of God and have the potential to be examples of faith to others. Episcopalians pray for each other and for all Christians as members of the Communion of Saints, including both the living and the dead, since all are in the hands of God. With this understanding, a wide variety of Christians from various denominations and traditions are thought of as "saints" in the Episcopal Church, such as Martin Luther and Augustine of Canterbury. Others recognized as "saints," while not of major ecclesiastical significance, are rather examples of holding moral positions that may have compromised their acceptance by society at the time they lived. Such "saints" include William Wilberforce and Elizabeth Cady Stanton, for example.

Develop a spiritual discipline based upon these days of remembrance. Using the brief statement regarding the person's significance and faith in *Lesser Feasts and Fasts,* reflect on his or her life to see if it provides any insight into your own. The Collect of the Day's purpose is to focus our minds on some particular characteristic of the person. Refer to pp. 237–250 in the Book of Common Prayer to discover other ways to celebrate and remember the Feast Day of any particular "saint."

EMBER DAYS

In each of the four seasons of the year, the Calendar of the Church designates a Wednesday, Friday, and Saturday as Ember Days. The origin of the custom of setting aside these days, and the meaning of "Ember," are hidden in long-ago church history, but the days have continuing importance as traditional times for prayer for the ministry of the church.

- Spring: after the first Sunday in Lent
- Summer: after Pentecost
- Autumn: after September 14 (Holy Cross Day)
- Winter: after December 13

ROGATION DAYS

Rogation Days (BCP 258–59) are observed on the Monday, Tuesday, and Wednesday before Ascension Day. "Rogation" comes from the Latin *rogare*, to ask. These days were originally set aside as times of prayer for bountiful harvests on land and sea. They have been expanded and are now times of prayer for commerce and industry and for the stewardship of creation. The Propers note that they are for use on the traditional days or at other times.

- Proper I—for fruitful seasons
- Proper II—for commerce and industry
- Proper III—for stewardship of creation

INDEPENDENCE DAY

Definition

The church recognizes the anniversary of the birth of our nation and our ongoing quest for liberty and justice.

Independence Day Themes

- Freedom and liberation are human rights, allowing God-given gifts and potential to grow and develop.
- Importance of the rights of people.
- The Fourth of July is a time to reaffirm our Christian call to justice and to pray for God's grace to assist and inspire and strengthen us.

- As citizens of this "nation under God," we are called to speak out against oppression of any person, including our fellow citizens, and to speak out for human rights in government, in institutions, in systems, and in social and personal life.
- The Declaration of Independence offers us a way to examine and evaluate how faithfully we as a nation have brought about its promises for all our citizens.

Great Words of Independence Day

Freedom	Justice
Human family	Liberation
Human rights	One nation under God
In God we trust	Righteousness

Independence Day Through the Eyes of a Child

- We celebrate the birth of our nation.
- We continue to work for what is right for all people with God's help.
- It is our responsibility to be good stewards of our nation's freedom, heritage, and resources.

Symbols and Traditions of Independence Day

- United States flag
- Local traditions

Great Hymns of Independence Day

FROM *THE HYMNAL 1982*

- National Songs (Hymns 716–720)
- God of our fathers, whose almighty hand (Hymn 718)

Independence Day in the Book of Common Prayer

PRAYERS AND THANKSGIVINGS

- Collect for a Nation (BCP 207/258)
- Collect for Social Justice (BCP 209/260)
- Collect for Social Service (BCP 209/260)

- Collect for Peace (BCP 57/69/99)
- Prayers for the National Life (BCP 820–823)
- Prayers for the Social Order (BCP 823–827)
- Thanksgiving for National Life (BCP 838–839)
- Prayer Attributed to St. Francis (BCP 833)
- Additional Prayers for Peace (BCP 207/258, 815–816)

HISTORICAL DOCUMENTS

- The Preface to the Book of Common Prayer was written at Philadelphia in October 1789. The government of The Episcopal Church was organized by many of the same persons who established our nation's government (BCP 9–11).

Living Independence Day at Home and Church

- Enjoy a family or church picnic with prayers, a reading of the Declaration of Independence, sharing stories of our forebears, and thinking of those places in the world where independence and freedom are being sought.
- "Whose service is perfect freedom" from the Collect for Peace might serve as a theme for a visual display, perhaps a PowerPoint presentation, mobile, or collage showing examples of freedom in our lives and of freedom denied, using photographs and news stories. A litany and other prayers based on these topics can be used in worship, including asking God's help to stir and strengthen and renew us in bringing "liberty and justice for all."
- Read the words of famous Americans and talk about how their lives have enriched our nation. Many such persons can be found in *Lesser Feasts and Fasts*, such as Martin Luther King, Jr., William Wilberforce, Jonathan Myrick Daniels, and Florence Nightingale.

THANKSGIVING DAY

Definition

The church recognizes the traditional Thanksgiving holiday as a holy day for our land, life, and heritage.

Thanksgiving Day Themes

- All our many blessings come from God's good Creation.
- Christians are to live their lives in a spirit of thankfulness.
- We are to be faithful stewards of the earth as God's Creation, given to us as a sacred trust.

Great Words of Thanksgiving Day

Blessings
Creation
Daily bread

Stewardship
Thankful hearts

Thanksgiving Day Through the Eyes of a Child

- We thank God for everything we have.
- We live our lives in a spirit of thankfulness for God's goodness.

Symbols and Traditions of Thanksgiving Day

- The meaning of Eucharist is Thanksgiving.
- Feasting to share with others our celebration of thankfulness.
- Cornucopia—fruits and grains and the earth's bounty.
- We remember our heritage of struggle for freedom.
- Simple living, with respect for each other and the earth's resources, is a way to be thankful stewards of our blessings so that all may share them.

Great Bible Stories for Thanksgiving Day

- Injunction for life in the Promised Land (Deuteronomy, Chapter 8)

Great Hymns of Thanksgiving Day

FROM *THE HYMNAL 1982*

- Come, ye thankful people, come (Hymn 290)
- We plow the fields, and scatter (Hymn 291)

Thanksgiving Day in the Book of Common Prayer

- The General Thanksgiving (BCP 58/71/101)
- Litany of Thanksgiving (BCP 836)
- The Thanksgiving Day Collect (BCP 194/246)
- Rogation Day Collects (BCP 207/258)

PART II:
THE REVISED COMMON LECTIONARY
FOR CHRISTIAN EDUCATION

Reading Scripture in Worship

The Scriptures emerged from the experience of a community who believed that God had been and was mysteriously, but clearly, present and active in their midst. Beginning as an oral tradition, the Hebrew people and the Church gradually gathered and developed its sacred texts and established a final, unchanging canon to be a measuring rod or standard for the Christian life of faith. These Scriptures, however, were intended to be interpreted and reinterpreted over and over again in the light of contemporary knowledge and experience within a believing and worshiping community open to the leading of God's Spirit into new truth.

The Scriptures taken as a whole are foundational in God's revelation. Each part is to be heard in relation to every other part. Christianity is a religion of a person, Jesus Christ, and not a book. Because this is so, special authority is given to the Gospels, which contain the narrative of Jesus' life, death, resurrection, and of his teachings. While Christ is the head (mind and heart) of the "Church, which is his body" (Ephesians 1:23), even he did not claim to know the mind of God fully (Mark 13:32). He did promise, however, that "the Holy Spirit whom the Father will send in my name, will teach you everything and remind you of all that I have said to you" (John 14:25–26).

The beginning of each service of Holy Eucharist is called The Word of God. A technical term for this part of the Eucharist that precedes the Offertory is *synaxis*. This comes from the same Greek word as 'synagogue," reminding us of the source of the ministry of the Word. Each Sunday is provided with three lessons, or readings. One is from the Old Testament or Apocrypha. One is from the Epistles (letters), Acts of the Apostles, or The Revelation to John. One is from the Gospels. A Psalm or Canticle usually follows the Old Testament reading. The sequence hymn follows the 2nd reading, or Epistle.

An Explanation of The Lectionary

A *Lectionary* is a table of readings from Scripture, appointed to be read at public worship. The association of particular texts with specific days began in the 4th century. The Lectionary [1969, revised 1981] was developed by the Roman Catholic Church after Vatican II provided for a three-year cycle of Sunday readings. This Roman lectionary provided the basis for lectionary in The Book of Common Prayer 1979 as well as those developed by many other denominations.

The Common Lectionary, published in 1983, was an ecumenical project of several American and Canadian denominations, developed out of a concern for the unity of the Church and a desire for a common experience of Scripture. It was intended as a harmonization of the many different denominational approaches to the three-year lectionary. It has been in trial use in the Episcopal Church and among the member denominations since 1983.

The Revised Common Lectionary, published in 1992, takes into account constructive criticism of the Common Lectionary based on the evaluation of its trial use and, like the current prayer book lectionary, is a three-year cycle of Sunday Eucharistic readings. (Year A: Matthew. Year B: Mark. Year C: Luke. John is read during the Easter Season.)

The 75th General Convention in June 2006 directed that the Revised Common Lectionary replace the Book of Common Prayer lectionary "effective the First Sunday of Advent 2007; with the provision for continued use of the previous Lectionary for purposes of orderly transition, with the permission of the ecclesiastical authority, until the First Sunday of Advent 2010" (2006 Resolution A077). The Revised Common Lectionary preserves about 90% of the Gospel readings in the Lectionary of The Book of Common Prayer but also provides these new features:

- The option of semi-continuous reading of the great Old Testament narratives on the Sundays after Pentecost, to provide exciting new preach-

ing opportunities, vacation Bible School ideas, or informal summer story-telling for adults as well as children.
  - Year A: Genesis through Judges;
  - Year B: The Davidic Covenant and Wisdom literature;
  - Year C: The prophets—Elijah, Elisha, Amos, Hosea, Isaiah, Jeremiah, Joel and Habbakuk.

- The option of lections in thematic harmony with the Gospel of the day for the Sundays after Pentecost. This follows the pattern of the present lectionary in which the readings from the Old Testament and the New Testament are chosen in relation to the Gospel.

- The inclusion of women and their role in salvation history, offering texts about women never heard on Sunday before. The most notable example is the account of the woman anointing Jesus at Bethany [Mark 14:3-9]. Jesus responded by saying "wherever the good news is proclaimed in the whole world, what she has done will be told in remembrance of her." This text, omitted in the present lectionary, is included in the Revised Common Lectionary as part of the Passion narrative read on Palm Sunday in Year B.

The Revised Common Lectionary is a truly ecumenical lectionary shared by most Protestant denominations and widely used throughout the Anglican Communion. It provides new opportunities for ecumenical Bible study and shared resources for teaching and preaching.

A Summary of the Lectionary Text

Year A

The First Sunday of Advent, Year A

THEME OF THE LECTIONS

The day will come when God's wisdom and presence will be fully revealed. It will be a time of both tremendous hope and promise, but it will also be a time of judgment. God's people must live in readiness for that great day to come.

- *The Collect* (BCP 159/211): God's grace to help us; light and darkness; Christ the giver of our immortal life.
- *Isaiah 2:1–5:* The Prophet Isaiah looked ahead to a time when the people of the earth would learn God's ways, when God would judge his people, and they would give up war forever and live in peace "in the light of the Lord."
- *Psalm 122:* The song echoes the theme of Isaiah, ". . . the tribes go up . . . to praise the Name of the Lord. For there are the thrones of judgment, . . ."
- *Romans 13:11–14:* Paul teaches that all the commandments are fulfilled when people love one another. He calls people to live in the full light of day; the time for leading new lives and being Christ's people is at hand.
- *Matthew 24:36–44:* Jesus tells his disciples of the judgment that will come without warning when the Lord returns.

KEY WORDS, IDEAS, AND CONCEPTS TO EXPLORE

- Mountain of the Lord (Jerusalem or Mount Zion)
- Light and darkness
- Seeking world peace
- Salvation
- Readiness for judgment

- The Day of the Lord (the "Second Coming" — see Acts 1:11; 1 Corinthians 15:23; Hebrews 9:28; Revelation 1:7)

CHRISTIAN PRACTICE AND LITURGICAL TRADITION

- The "memorial acclamation" at the Eucharist expresses the Advent theme in one sentence, "Christ will come again."
- "Swords into plowshares" is a theme often cited by groups working for peaceful solutions to the world's problems, including the Episcopal Peace Fellowship: http://www.epfnational.org/.

FORMATION IN BAPTISMAL DISCIPLESHIP

Christians are called to live expectantly. The good news of Christ's coming again is balanced with the understanding that God comes in judgment. Part of living expectantly is to know that all that is hidden will be revealed.

The season of Advent is a time when the church is called to prepare itself and individuals for baptism on the First Sunday after the Epiphany, the Baptism of our Lord. In Advent, those preparing for their baptism (and their parents and sponsors) are offered a glimpse of God's ultimate vision for creation and humanity. They are challenged to set life goals around that vision. Advent invites the church to dream of what God's will being done fully "on earth as in heaven" might mean in light of Jesus' words and acts.

LESSER FEASTS AND FASTS

- Nicholas Ferrar, Deacon, 1637 (December 1)
- Channing Moore Williams, Missionary Bishop in China and Japan, 1910 (December 2)
- John of Damascus, Priest, c. 760 (December 4)
- Clement of Alexandria, Priest, c. 210 (December 5)
- Nicholas, Bishop of Myra, c. 342 (December 6)

The Second Sunday of Advent, Year A

THEME OF THE LECTIONS

John the Baptist proclaims the coming of Jesus and calls people into repentance through baptism.

- *The Collect* (BCP 159/211): The prophets, sent as messengers to preach repentance and to bid God's people prepare for salvation.
- *Isaiah 11:1–10:* The prophet promises that God will send a wise and understanding Judge who will be righteous and faithful in his decisions.

Even animals that are traditional enemies shall be at peace with one another. "They will not hurt or destroy on all my holy mountain; for the earth will be full of the knowledge of the Lord as the waters cover the sea."

- *Psalm 72:1–7, 18–19:* The expected Messiah will rule with righteousness and justice, and there will be peace to the end of time.
- *Romans 15:4–13:* Paul brings a message of hope to all people, and prays that the God of hope will fill the church in Rome with "all joy and peace in believing, so that you may abound in hope by the power of the Holy Spirit."
- *Matthew 3:1–12:* John the Baptist issues a strong warning to his hearers that they must repent and prepare for the coming of the Messiah.

KEY WORDS, IDEAS, AND CONCEPTS TO EXPLORE

- Baptism
- Jesse (the Jesse tree)
- Spirit of the Lord
- The Day of the Lord ushering in a time of peace
- Circumcision as a mark of the covenant
- John the Baptist: Preparing the way and pointing the way
- Repentance; preparing hearts to accept the gift of Christ
- The church is called to prepare the way of the Lord
- Baptism with the Holy Spirit
- Harvest practices of biblical times

STORIES TO TELL

- The story of John the Baptist, including the narrative details from the gospel of Luke (Luke 1:5–80).

CHRISTIAN PRACTICE AND LITURGICAL TRADITION

- The beautiful imagery of all creation being at peace (Isaiah 11) has inspired poets and artists for generations.
- Today's gospel text helps to define the sacrament of baptism. John baptized with water for repentance; Jesus came to baptize with the Holy Spirit and fire. At baptism, the priest anoints the new Christian and says, "N., you are sealed by the Holy Spirit in Baptism and marked as Christ's own forever" (BCP 308).

FORMATION IN BAPTISMAL DISCIPLESHIP

The call to defend the weakest of society and to stand for social justice is inherent in scripture, and therefore must be an integral part of preparing persons for baptism, confirmation, reaffirmation, or reception.

The Third Sunday of Advent, Year A

THEME OF THE LECTIONS

The promised day of God is dawning. John is the herald of that day. Jesus proclaimed the kingdom of God by everything he said and did.

- *The Collect* (BCP 160/212): God's great power, grace, and mercy are among us now to help us.
- *Isaiah 35:1–10:* Isaiah describes a time of glorious growth and healing for the people of Israel, when God will bring judgment and salvation, and his redeemed people will walk on the Holy Way.
- *Psalm 146:4–9:* A song of praise for God's healing and hope, because God who feeds the hungry is faithful forever. (Canticle 3 or 15: The Song of Mary—Magnificat)
- *James 5:7–10:* We are reminded that the coming of the Lord is at hand; to wait patiently without complaining about the people among whom we live; to remember the patience of the prophets who spoke in the Lord's name.
- *Matthew 11:2–11:* When John the Baptist, who was in prison, sent his followers to Jesus to ask if he was the person whose coming had been promised, Jesus sent them back to John with words of healing and good news, very much like the healing described in the lesson from Isaiah, leaving the implication that people must decide for themselves if Jesus is the promised one. Jesus spoke in strong words about John's ministry of preparation for Jesus' coming.

KEY WORDS, IDEAS, AND CONCEPTS TO EXPLORE

- John the Baptist
- The Day of the Lord inaugurates a time of peace
- The coming of the Lord (or "Second Coming")
- Messenger; proclaiming the "Good News of God in Christ"
- Preparing the way

STORIES TO TELL

- The story of John the Baptist continues this Sunday.
- The stories of Jesus that lie behind his statement to John's disciples, such as healing a paralyzed man (Mark 2:1–12) and restoring a girl to life (Luke 8:40–42, 49–56).

CHRISTIAN PRACTICE AND LITURGICAL TRADITION

- We pray for God's Kingdom to come every time we pray the Lord's Prayer.

FORMATION IN BAPTISMAL DISCIPLESHIP

The Baptismal Covenant provides the vision for the baptized:

> *Will you continue in the apostles' teaching . . . persevere in resisting evil . . . proclaim by word and example the Good News of God in Christ . . . seek and serve Christ in all persons . . . strive for justice and peace among all people?*
> (BCP 304–305)

It is in living out this covenant call that the church responds to the question raised by John, "Are you the one who is to come, or are we to wait for another?" (Matthew 11:3). The first reading and the gospel lection lie behind the church's call to be deeply involved in the ministry of service and justice. The church continues in the role of Jesus, pointing out God's coming reign in such actions.

The Fourth Sunday of Advent, Year A

THEME OF THE LECTIONS

Jesus' imminent birth is proclaimed in the scriptures; his continued presence in the world is proclaimed by the church today.

- *The Collect* (BCP 160/212): Asking God, among us now, to purify our consciences and help to make us prepared when Christ comes.
- *Isaiah 7:10–17*: A sign in the time of Isaiah was an extraordinary event. The Lord, through Isaiah, offered to give a sign to Ahaz, King of Judah, and Ahaz refused, saying he would not expect God to perform some special feat on demand. Isaiah responded that the Lord himself would give Ahaz a sign: a young woman would bear a son to be called Immanuel (God with us), and before the child was old enough to make decisions, the threat of the two kings would be ended.
- *Psalm 80:1–7, 16–18*: A communal lament in which the people confirm that God is their Sovereign.

- *Romans 1:1–7:* Paul introduces the gospel concerning the Son of God, and the blessings that come to those who are called to belong to Jesus Christ.
- *Matthew 1:18–25:* Matthew's story of the birth of Jesus includes a quotation from Isaiah, "Behold, a virgin shall conceive and bear a son, and his name shall be called Emmanuel."

KEY WORDS, IDEAS, AND CONCEPTS TO EXPLORE

- Sheol
- Gospel
- Prophets
- Significance of King David
- Mary and Joseph
- Significance of the name "Jesus"

STORIES TO TELL

- The stories from Matthew and Luke leading up to Jesus' birth.

CHRISTIAN PRACTICE AND LITURGICAL TRADITION

- We prepare to celebrate the birth of the one born to save us from the power of sin and death.
- We see signs of God's love in birth, in love, in creation, and in gifts that we receive in this season.

FORMATION IN BAPTISMAL DISCIPLESHIP

The role of the Christian congregation, and the individual Christian, is to reflect the presence of God in the world today. From the Fourth Sunday of Advent through the Feast of the Epiphany, the church celebrates the Incarnation; God is present "in the flesh" of human life. God meets us in the midst of our human struggle. The collect for the First Sunday after Christmas Day expresses this idea well:

> *Almighty God, you have poured upon us the new light of your incarnate Word: Grant that this light, enkindled in our hearts, may shine forth in our lives. . . .* (BCP 213)

The Days of Christmas

Christmas Day, All Years

THEME OF THE LECTIONS

God came in Jesus of Nazareth to reveal the power of God's love and healing. In the birth of Jesus we realize that God shares life with us intimately. We meet God "in the flesh" of human struggle and most especially in the midst of human love. Christmas celebrates the incarnation of God; God "in the flesh of" human life. (*Carne* comes from the Latin for meat or flesh.)

- *The Collects* (BCP 160/161 and 212/213): God makes us joyful with the yearly celebration of the birth of his only Son Jesus Christ; OR God made this holy night bright with the true light of Jesus Christ; OR We ask that we who are God's children by adoption and by his grace may be made new every day through his Holy Spirit.
- Christmas Day I:
  - *Isaiah 9:2–7:* For Christians the words of the prophet are fulfilled by the coming of Jesus Christ. "Peace," as used in this reading, means more than the absence of war. It points to the presence of justice and righteousness.
  - *Psalm 96:* A song of joyful praise to God—King, Creator, and Judge.
  - *Titus 2:11–14:* The grace of God has dawned upon the world with healing for all persons; and Christians lead sober, honest, and godly lives while waiting for Jesus Christ to come in glory.
  - *Luke 2:1–14 (15–20):* The story of the birth of Jesus.
- Christmas Day II:
  - *Isaiah 62:6–12:* The watchmen on the walls of Jerusalem are to pray constantly and give God no rest until his promises are fulfilled and salvation comes for Jerusalem. His people shall be called a holy people, redeemed by the Lord, long sought for, and not forsaken.
  - *Psalm 97:* The Lord is king, and he will rule over all peoples.
  - *Titus 3:4–7:* God has saved us through baptism, sending the Spirit to us through Jesus Christ our Savior, so that we may become heirs in hope of eternal life.
  - *Luke 2:(1–7) 8–20:* After the angels who brought the good news of the Savior's birth had left them, the shepherds decided to go at once to Bethlehem to see for themselves what the Lord had made known to them. They found their way to Mary, Joseph, and the child, and told what they had heard about the child. The shepherds went back to their sheep, praising God.

- Christmas Day III:
  - *Isaiah 52:7–10:* A song celebrating the joyous return of the Lord and his people to the holy city.
  - *Psalm 98:* A song of praise for the final victory of God, who will judge the earth and establish justice.
  - *Hebrews 1:1–4, (5–12):* God once spoke directly to his people, and after that he spoke to them through his prophets. Now he speaks to us through his Son, who has suffered for us and reigns at the right hand of God, supreme over the angels.
  - *John 1:1–14:* A hymn to the coming of Christ, who is described as the Word who was with God from the beginning, and through whom all things come to be.

KEY WORDS, IDEAS, AND CONCEPTS TO EXPLORE
- Christian hope
- Expectation
- Highway-building as a metaphor of hope
- The role of sentinels in biblical times
- Salvation
- Incarnation
- Grace
- Royal courtroom imagery as descriptive of Jesus' relationship with God the Father

STORIES TO TELL
- The story of the birth of Jesus in Luke's gospel. (Note that the story of the visit of the magi in Matthew's gospel is a story associated with the Feast of the Epiphany, rather than Christmas Day.)

CHRISTIAN PRACTICE AND LITURGICAL TRADITION
- Christmas pageants are a way of participating in the wonderful story of Jesus' birth.
- The candlelight service at midnight on Christmas Eve reflects the awe and wonder of the angels' visit to the shepherds at night.

FORMATION IN BAPTISMAL DISCIPLESHIP
Luke's account of Jesus being placed in a manger at his birth because there was no room in the inn serves as a constant reminder to the Christian that God identifies with the weak, the poor, and the outcast.

The First Sunday after Christmas, All Years

THEME OF THE LECTIONS

God came in Jesus fully to reveal God's love and forgiveness to all.

- *The Collect* (BCP 161/213): God has poured the new light of the incarnate Word upon us.
- *Isaiah 61:10–62:3:* The promise of a new name for Jerusalem given by God speaks of a Jerusalem redeemed and delivered according to God's promise.
- *Psalm 147:* A hymn of praise featuring God's power over nature and in history, redeeming those who are faithful.
- *Galatians 3:23–25, 4:4–7:* Now that faith has come we are all children of God, baptized into union with Jesus Christ.
- *John 1:1–18:* Christ is described as the Word who was with God from the beginning and through whom all things come to be. No one has ever seen God. The only Son, who is with the Father, has made him known.

KEY WORDS, IDEAS, AND CONCEPTS TO EXPLORE

- Incarnation
- Logos (Word)
- Clothing as metaphor of joy

CHRISTIAN PRACTICE AND LITURGICAL TRADITION

- The wearing of vestments reflects the reading from Isaiah: "he has clothed me with the garments of salvation." In the early church, those who were baptized were given new white garments to wear as a sign of their redeemed relationship with God and the church. Later, the vesting of the priest became associated with being clothed with "the robe of righteousness."
- Though technically Christmas is not a season, since the Sundays are numbered after Christmas, the tradition of the "twelve days of Christmas" is familiar partly from the well-known carol. Twelfth Night, the night before the Feast of the Epiphany, traditionally ends the Christmas "season."

LESSER FEASTS AND FASTS

- Thomas Becket, 1170 (December 29)
- Frances Joseph Gaudet, Educator and Prison Reformer, 1934 (December 30)

The Feast of the Holy Name (January 1), All Years

THEME OF THE LECTIONS

God's identity is revealed as "merciful and gracious" (Exodus 34:6). Jesus' name has significance: it is the Greek form of the Hebrew name Joshua, meaning "God saves."

- *The Collect* (BCP 162/213): We pray that God will make the love of Jesus Christ grow in every heart.
- *Numbers 6:22–27:* The priestly blessing offering protection, favor and graciousness.
- *Psalm 8:* A psalm of David praising the majesty of God.
- *Galatians 4:4–17:* Jesus' humanity redeems all of God's children; OR
- *Philippians 2:5–11:* A hymn on Jesus' unselfish disposition that calls us to submit to Christ and give up privileges for the sake of others to the glory of God.
- *Luke 2:15–21:* Mary's son is given the name "Jesus," which in Hebrew means "The Lord saves."

KEY WORDS, IDEAS, AND CONCEPTS TO EXPLORE

- Significance of Mt. Sinai
- God's steadfast love and mercy
- Gospel
- The importance of names
- Covenant and circumcision
- Blessings
- Adoption

STORIES TO TELL

- The story of the naming of Jesus.

CHRISTIAN PRACTICE AND LITURGICAL TRADITION

- The naming of the person being baptized is an important element in the baptismal rite, as in scripture: "You shall be called by a new name that the mouth of the Lord will give" (Isaiah 62:2). In some traditions a child was literally named at baptism and given the name of a Christian saint. Whether or not the name is given at baptism, one's given name takes on new significance as one is adopted into the family of Christ.
- *A Thanksgiving for the Birth or Adoption of a Child* (BCP 439–445) comes from the ancient traditions of naming and dedicating expressed in the gospel text.

The Second Sunday after Christmas, All Years

THEME OF THE LECTIONS

- *The Collect* (BCP 162/214): The restoration of human nature through the divine life of Jesus.
- *Jeremiah 31:7–14:* Israel will be united and the covenant will be restored.
- *Psalm 84:* A hymn praising the Temple of the Lord, and proclaiming the happiness of the pilgrims as they come to worship.
- *Ephesians 1:3–6; 15–19a:* Praising God who has given us all spiritual blessings in Christ and adopted us as children through Jesus Christ.
- *Matthew 2:13–15, 19–23:* The Holy Family flees to Egypt; OR
- *Luke 2:41–52:* The boy Jesus in the temple; OR
- *Matthew 2:1–12:* The visit of the magi.

KEY WORDS, IDEAS, AND CONCEPTS TO EXPLORE

- Adoption as a metaphor of our relationship with God
- "Glorious inheritance"
- Egypt
- The temple in Jerusalem

STORIES TO TELL

- The story in Matthew of the Holy Family fleeing to Egypt.
- The story in Luke of Jesus as a boy visiting the temple.
- The story in Matthew of the visit of the magi.

CHRISTIAN PRACTICE AND LITURGICAL TRADITION

The adoption language associated with baptism comes from the reading from Ephesians heard this week. See also:

> All praise and thanks to you, most merciful Father, for adopting us as your own children, for incorporating us into your holy Church. (BCP 311)

THE SUNDAYS OF EPIPHANY

The Epiphany, All Years

THEME OF THE LECTIONS

The significance of Jesus' birth is revealed to the world beyond Judea.

- *The Collect* (BCP 162/214): By the leading of a star, God showed his only-begotten Son to the people of the earth.
- *Isaiah 60:1–6, 9:* The promise of the New Jerusalem. Though darkness covers the earth, Jerusalem will shine with the glory of the Lord. The wealth of the nations, gold and frankincense, will be brought to honor the Lord.
- *Psalm 72:1–2, 10–14:* All kings shall bow down before him and all the nations do him service.
- *Ephesians 3:1–12:* ". . . the Gentiles have become fellow-heirs, members of the same body, and sharers in the promise in Christ Jesus through the gospel." We all find unity in Christ.
- *Matthew 2:1–12:* The story of the wise men from the east who came to Jerusalem to find the child born to be King of the Jews, having been sent by Herod. Following the star that they had seen in the east, these representatives from distant nations worship the child and offer gifts of gold, frankincense, and myrrh.

KEY WORDS, IDEAS, AND CONCEPTS TO EXPLORE

- Mysteries hidden that are now revealed
- "Eternal purpose"
- Hope for the restoration of Judea
- The significance of gold, frankincense, and myrrh

STORIES TO TELL

- The story of the visit of the magi.
- The story of the Week of Prayer for Christian Unity.

CHRISTIAN PRACTICE AND LITURGICAL TRADITION

- The magi join the nativity scene at the crèche on the Feast of the Epiphany.
- Twelfth Night celebrations of pageantry, drama, singing, festivity, and a banquet of lamb is given in honor of the coming of the magi.

FORMATION IN BAPTISMAL DISCIPLESHIP

Christians are to continue "revealing the mystery" to the world. As God appeared in Jesus, so God appears through the Holy Spirit in the people of God who are the church.

LESSER FEASTS AND FASTS

- Harriet Bedell, Deaconess and Missionary, 1969 (January 8)
- Julia Chester Emery, 1922 (January 9)
- William Laud, Archbishop of Canterbury, 1645 (January 10)

The First Sunday after the Epiphany:
The Baptism of our Lord, All Years

THEME OF THE LECTIONS

The baptism of Jesus.

- *The Collect* (BCP 162/214): We ask that all who are baptized into Jesus' name may be strengthened to keep the covenant they have made and acknowledge Jesus as Lord and Savior.
- *Isaiah 42:1–9:* Thus says the Lord, "Here is my servant, whom I uphold, my chosen, in whom my soul delights; I have put my spirit upon him; he will bring forth justice to the nations."
- *Psalm 29:* An enthronement psalm where the king provides for his people in a land of *shalom* ("peace").
- *Acts 10:34–43:* Peter tells the household of the centurion Cornelius about Jesus, his baptism, and how God anointed Jesus with the Holy Spirit and with power. Peter has come to recognize that God-fearing people from every nation are acceptable to him.
- *Matthew 3:13–17* (Year A): The story of Jesus' baptism, John the Baptist's question, and Jesus' answer. A voice from heaven says, "This is my Son, the Beloved, with whom I am well pleased."
- *Mark 1:7–11* (Year B): John the Baptist preached that a person greater than he would come who would baptize people with the Holy Spirit. Jesus came to John and was baptized by him in the River Jordan. After Jesus' baptism, a voice from heaven declared that Jesus is God's Son.
- *Luke 3:15–16, 21–22* (Year C): People wondered whether John the Baptist might be the Christ; but he told them plainly that someone was to come who would baptize with divine power and judgment. After Jesus' baptism, and while he was praying, a voice came from heaven, saying "You are my Son, the Beloved; with you I am well pleased."

KEY WORDS, IDEAS, AND CONCEPTS TO SHARE

- Justice
- Servant
- Jesus as "Lord of all"
- Baptism with water and the Holy Spirit
- Water
- Role of John the Baptist

STORIES TO TELL

- Jesus' baptism

CHRISTIAN PRACTICE AND LITURGICAL TRADITION

This Sunday is one of the five most appropriate times for baptism in the church (see BCP 312).

FORMATION IN BAPTISMAL DISCIPLESHIP

The words of calling and anointing for ministry heard in connection with Jesus' baptism are the words that frame the church's understanding of the ministry of all the baptized today: "You are my . . . Beloved; with you I am well pleased." The radical nature of our calling is to bring justice and to serve the cause of right, to be part of God's own mission of liberating the suffering, the oppressed, and the hungry.

LESSER FEASTS AND FASTS

- Aelred, Abbot of Rievaulx, 1167 (January 12)
- Hilary, Bishop of Poitiers, 367 (January 13)
- Antony, Abbot in Egypt, 356 (January 17)

The Second Sunday after the Epiphany, Year A

THEME OF THE LECTIONS

Responding to God's call to be a "light to the nations."

- *The Collect* (BCP 163/215): Through the light of God's Word and Sacraments, we ask that God's people may shine with Christ's glory and that Christ may be known, worshipped, and obeyed throughout the world.
- *Isaiah 49:1–7:* The servant of the Lord speaks of his call and his mission to restore Israel; and of God's promise to become his strength. God will make his servant a light to the nations.
- *Psalm 40:1–12:* A song of gratitude for deliverance; the righteous one values God's will above ritual sacrifice: "I delight to do your will, O my God."
- *1 Corinthians 1:1–9:* Paul writes from Ephesus to the Christian congregation in Corinth, thanking God for the spiritual growth that has come to them in Christ. (This Sunday begins a serialized reading of 1 Corinthians 1–4; therefore, the epistle reading will not usually be in thematic harmony with the Old Testament, psalm, and gospel lections.)
- *John 1:29–42:* John the Baptist tells of Jesus' coming to him as he was baptizing; and John bears witness that Jesus is God's Chosen One. The

next day Andrew and another follower of John the Baptist go home with Jesus, and Andrew tells his brother Simon Peter, "We have found the Messiah!"

KEY WORDS, IDEAS, AND CONCEPTS TO EXPLORE

- "Light to the nations"
- Servant
- Salvation
- Redeemer
- Overview of 1 Corinthians
- Lamb of God
- Rabbi—How did Jesus teach?
- The apostles Andrew and Simon Peter

STORIES TO TELL

During the early Sundays after the Epiphany, we hear the stories of Jesus calling his disciples. Explore these stories from all three years of the lectionary.

CHRISTIAN PRACTICE AND LITURGICAL TRADITION

- The baptismal rite includes elements of being called that reflect Jesus' call to the first disciples: "I present N. to receive the sacrament of baptism . . . Do you renounce Satan . . . Do you turn to Jesus?"
- "The Lamb of God" figures strongly in our Eucharistic language (Prayer of Consecration and the Agnes Dei).

FORMATION IN BAPTISMAL DISCIPLESHIP

Christians see their baptism as a calling into discipleship. Christ calls people into servanthood today as the first disciples were called on the lakeshore and in the counting house.

LESSER FEASTS AND FASTS

- Wulfstan, Bishop of Worcester, 1095 (January 19)
- Fabian, Bishop and Martyr of Rome, 250 (January 20)
- Agnes, Martyr at Rome, 304 (January 21)
- Vincent, Deacon of Saragossa, and Martyr, 204 (January 22)
- Phillips Brooks, Bishop of Massachusetts, 1893 (January 23)
- Ordination of Florence Li Tim-Oi, 1944 (January 24)

This is also the *Week of Prayer for Christian Unity* (annually the third week in January). Resources can be found through the World Council of Churches at http://www.oikoumene.org/en/home.html.

The Third Sunday after the Epiphany, Year A

THEME OF THE LECTIONS

The calling of the disciples, yesterday and today.

- *The Collect* (BCP 163/215): Our Savior Jesus Christ calls us, and we ask for grace to answer eagerly without holding back.
- *Isaiah 9:1–4*: A light in the darkness of Assyrian destruction will come, ushering in a new era of peace and hope.
- *Psalm 27:1, 5–13*: Imagery of entrusting one's self to God.
- *1 Corinthians 1:10–18*: Paul appeals to the members of the new congregation to be joined with one another in unity of mind and thought, and not to form cliques centered upon the person who introduced them to the faith.
- *Matthew 4:12–23*: Jesus' ministry, preaching, and teaching; Simon Peter, Andrew, James, and John called to be disciples, "fishers of men."

KEY WORDS, IDEAS, AND CONCEPTS TO EXPLORE

- The role of prophets
- Divisions in the church
- Repentance
- The calling of the disciples

STORIES TO TELL

The stories of Jesus calling his disciples continue from Epiphany 2.

CHRISTIAN PRACTICE AND LITURGICAL TRADITION

See Epiphany 2, Year A.

FORMATION IN BAPTISMAL DISCIPLESHIP

We begin to focus on mission, ministry, and discipleship in our readings. Just as Jesus called his disciples (followers) who became his apostles (ambassadors) after the resurrection, he calls men and women to be his followers. In our baptism we too are called by the Lord to point beyond ourselves to God's eternal presence in creation.

LESSER FEASTS AND FASTS

- John Chrysostom, Bishop of Constantinople, 407 (January 27)
- Thomas Aquinas, Priest and Friar, 1274 (January 28)

The Fourth Sunday after the Epiphany, Year A

THEME OF THE LECTIONS

The Sermon on the Mount: God's word is revealed. God's way is proclaimed.

- *The Collect* (BCP 164/215): God governs all things in heaven and earth. We pray earnestly that God will grant us his peace in our time.
- *Micah 6:1–8:* God accuses his wayward people Israel, reminding them of all he has done for them and what he requires of them: "To do justice, to love kindness, and to walk humbly with your God."
- *Psalm 15:* An entrance liturgy used as worshippers entered the Temple, portraying the lifestyle of those who are "righteous."
- *1 Corinthians 1:18–31:* Paul reminds the Corinthians that God uses the powerless, the people of lowly origin, and even the simple and despised, to bring about his purposes. "Let the one who boasts, boast in the Lord."
- *Matthew 5:1–12:* In the opening words of the Sermon on the Mount (The Beatitudes), Jesus commends attitudes that are different from the values of the world, and promises that those who suffer for the cause of the right will experience the Kingdom of Heaven.

KEY WORDS, IDEAS, AND CONCEPTS TO EXPLORE

- Doing justice
- Courtroom proceedings to express God's anger at the nation
- God's wisdom
- The Sermon on the Mount

CHRISTIAN PRACTICE AND LITURGICAL TRADITION

The powerful words of Micah are reflected in the call for justice in the Baptismal Covenant:

> "Will you strive for justice and peace among all people, and respect the dignity of every human being?" (BCP 305)

FORMATION IN BAPTISMAL DISCIPLESHIP

Worship is an act in which the Christian assembly envisions the reign of God in word and sacrament. That is, the values of God's reign are enacted in the ancient pattern of the worship service. ("He has told you, O mortal, what is good . . . to do justice, and to love kindness, and to walk humbly with your God") (Micah 6:8).

- We gather in God's name.
- We hear God's radical Word.
- We respond in prayer and thanksgiving.
- We offer ourselves to God (the offertory).

- We share a foretaste of the heavenly banquet (communion).
- We go forth to love and serve.

LESSER FEASTS AND FASTS
- Brigid (Bride), 523 (February 1)
- Anskar, Archbishop of Hamburg, Missionary to Denmark and Sweden, 865 (February 3)
- Cornelius the Centurion (February 4)
- The Martyrs of Japan, 1597 (February 5)

The Fifth Sunday after the Epiphany, Year A

THEME OF THE LECTIONS
The Sermon on the Mount: God's people are to give witness to God's grace and power by leading righteous lives.

- *The Collect* (BCP 164/216): We ask God to release us from the bonds that are our sins and to give us the freedom of the abundant life shown to us in Jesus Christ.
- *Isaiah 58:1–9a (9b–12):* Public displays of piety, if deeds are unaccompanied by compassion and concern for the less fortunate, are meaningless to God.
- *Psalm 112:1–9 (10):* Those who are generous in their lives model God's will.
- *1 Corinthians 2:1–12 (13–16):* The secret and hidden wisdom of God is not the wisdom of human beings. God reveals himself through the Spirit.
- *Matthew 5:13–20:* Jesus tells his disciples that they are the salt of the earth and the light of the world and that he has come to fulfill the purpose of the law and the prophecies. Only those who give their lives to God's will can enter the Kingdom of Heaven.

KEY WORDS, IDEAS, AND CONCEPTS TO EXPLORE
- God's wisdom
- The Holy Spirit as the revealer of God's wisdom
- Salt of the earth and light of the world
- God's law (Torah)
- Role of the scribes and Pharisees
- The Sermon on the Mount

CHRISTIAN PRACTICE AND LITURGICAL TRADITION

The tradition of giving candles as a gift at the time of baptism symbolizes the role of the baptized to be lights to the world.

FORMATION IN BAPTISMAL DISCIPLESHIP

Light and darkness are frequent themes in the Bible and prayer book. Ministry is bringing Christ's light into the world in the daily life of each Christian and in the corporate witness of the church.

LESSER FEASTS AND FASTS

- Absalom Jones, Priest, 1818 (February 13)
- Cyril, Monk, and Methodius, Bishop, Missionaries to the Slavs, 869, 885 (February 14)
- Thomas Bray, Priest and Missionary, 1730 (February 15)

The Sixth Sunday after the Epiphany, Year A

THEME OF THE LECTIONS

The Sermon on the Mount: Jesus' commandments call for a profound commitment, leading the Christian to witness to a distinctive way of life.

- *The Collect* (BCP 164/216): We ask God to accept our prayers because we are weak human beings who can do nothing without God.
- *Deuteronomy 30:15–20:* Israel's choice is simple—obey and live, or disobey by worshipping other gods and perish; OR
- *Sirach 15:15–20:* Wisdom is portrayed as an attribute of the Lord.
- *1 Corinthians 3:1–9:* Paul compares himself and other missionaries to workers in a field who plant and water, but the growth is from God.
- *Matthew 5:21–37:* Jesus speaks of the inner dimensions of our actions and calls his followers to change their lives.

KEY WORDS, IDEAS, AND CONCEPTS TO EXPLORE

- Freedom to choose
- Conflicts within the church
- The Sermon on the Mount
- The higher law of Jesus

CHRISTIAN PRACTICE AND LITURGICAL TRADITION

- The offertory at the Eucharist continues the ancient temple practice of offering gifts at the altar as an act of commitment to and reconciliation with God.
- The passing of the peace at the Eucharist expresses the command of Jesus to leave one's gift at the altar and be reconciled with one's brother and sister and then offer the gift. Since it follows the confession and absolution, the peace is an acting-out of the need to forgive as we have been forgiven.

FORMATION IN BAPTISMAL DISCIPLESHIP

The church must take seriously the call for unity and peace within the Body of Christ. Harsh judgments and enmity have no place in the congregation.

LESSER FEASTS AND FASTS

- Janani Luwum, Archbishop of Uganda and Martyr, 1977 (February 17)
- Martin Luther, 1546 (February 18)

The Seventh Sunday after the Epiphany, Year A

THEME OF THE LECTIONS

The Sermon on the Mount: our covenant with God calls us to live a life of justice and compassion that surpasses expected behavior.

- *The Collect* (BCP 164/216): We pray that God will send the Holy Spirit to fill our hearts with love, which is his greatest gift.
- *Leviticus 19:1–2, 9–18:* Through Moses, God calls the people of Israel to live upright and charitable lives, to be righteous because God is righteous, loving their neighbors as themselves.
- *Psalm 119:33–40:* A petition requesting of God that the psalmist be completely oriented toward God.
- *1 Corinthians 3:10–11, 16–23:* Paul, still troubled by disruptions in the church at Corinth, says: "Do you not know that you are God's temple and that God's Spirit dwells in you? . . . you are Christ's, and Christ is God's."
- *Matthew 5:38–48:* Jesus teaches that it is not enough for us to love our neighbors who love us. We must love our enemies so that we may be children of our Father in heaven.

KEY WORDS, IDEAS, AND CONCEPTS TO EXPLORE

- Temple of God
- Covenant

- Justice
- Compassion
- The Sermon on the Mount

CHRISTIAN PRACTICE AND LITURGICAL TRADITION

There are many hymns connected with how we are called to be neighbors to one another, such as "Jesu, Jesu" found in *The Hymnal 1982* (602) and *Lift Every Voice and Sing* (74).

FORMATION IN BAPTISMAL DISCIPLESHIP

The Baptismal Covenant stresses the need to "seek and serve Christ in all persons" and to "strive for justice and peace among all people" (BCP 305) A congregation living out the biblical and Baptismal Covenant imperative will be constantly exploring issues of justice and compassion. Throughout history the church has stood for justice and compassion in society, out of response to the biblical imperative to be holy as God is holy (Leviticus 19:2).

LESSER FEASTS AND FASTS

- Polycarp, Bishop and Martyr of Smyrna, 156 (February 23)
- George Herbert, Priest, 1633 (February 27)

The Eighth Sunday after the Epiphany, Year A

THEME OF THE LECTIONS

The Sermon on the Mount: the vision of the kingdom of God.

- *The Collect* (BCP 165/216): We ask that we be kept safe from fears and anxieties that come from lack of trust in God and that no difficulties in our lives may hide from us the light of God's immortal love, shown to us in Jesus Christ our Lord.
- *Isaiah 49:8–16a:* The prophet, speaking to the people of Israel in exile in Babylon, promises that God will comfort and redeem Israel: God will never forsake his people.
- *Psalm 131:* An expression of humble trust. As a child relies on its mother, so we rely on God.
- *1 Corinthians 4:1–5:* Paul describes in caustic terms his understanding of what it means to be a disciple.
- *Matthew 6:24–34:* Jesus urges his followers to trust in God to know their needs and to provide for them. Concern about material needs will draw them away from the fullness of life that God has promised.

KEY WORDS, IDEAS, AND CONCEPTS TO EXPLORE

- God's motherly love
- Steward
- Trust in God
- "Mysteries of God"
- Righteousness
- Mammon
- Compassion
- The Sermon on the Mount

CHRISTIAN PRACTICE AND LITURGICAL TRADITION

- The Daily Office from the prayer book expresses the call to live each moment in thanksgiving and praise. The service of Morning Prayer opens with words calling the congregation to praise: "Lord, open our lips. And our mouth shall proclaim your praise" (BCP 80).
- The Lenten customs of living more simply and exercising self-control reflect Jesus' words about setting priorities in life.
- The readings for today are also appointed for Thanksgiving Day. It is not what we Christians have that leads us to thanksgiving. It is what we feel and experience together with Christ that rings wholeness and the response of thanksgiving.

FORMATION IN BAPTISMAL DISCIPLESHIP

Today's gospel is a vivid statement about the values and lifestyle of the Christian congregation and each baptized member of the Body of Christ. As we devote our hopes and energies to what we can accumulate for ourselves in reputation and possessions, we lose touch with the source of our life and creativity.

The Last Sunday after the Epiphany, Year A

THEME OF THE LECTIONS

The Transfiguration of our Lord.

- *The Collect* (BCP 165/271): We pray that we who see the light of the presence of our Lord through faith may be given strength to bear our crosses and be changed into his likeness from glory to glory.
- *Exodus 24:12–18:* Moses receives the Ten Commandments on God's mountain, which was covered by a cloud. Moses enters the cloud, which is a sign of God's presence.
- *Psalm 2:* Today is the day of enthronement—the Lord and the anointed proclaim God's universal reign; OR

- *Psalm 99:* A hymn in praise of God that speaks of experiences of Moses, Aaron, and Samuel. God is to be worshipped upon his holy hill, because he is the Holy One.
- *2 Peter 1:16–21:* Peter's eyewitness account of Jesus' transfiguration, a prophecy of Jesus' return in glory. There is nothing more important than knowing Christ.
- *Matthew 17:1–9:* In this account of the Transfiguration, Peter, James, and John see Jesus, shining with brilliant light, talking with Moses and Elijah. They hear the affirmation of the voice from the cloud, and are cautioned after the experience to tell no one what they have seen until the Son of Man is raised from the dead.

KEY WORDS, IDEAS, AND CONCEPTS TO EXPLORE

- Transfiguration
- Resurrection
- The role of Moses and Elijah in the Hebrew Scriptures
- Mount Sinai

STORIES TO TELL

- The story of Moses on the mountain.
- The story of Jesus' transfiguration.

CHRISTIAN PRACTICE AND LITURGICAL TRADITION

The Sundays after the Epiphany are framed both by the Feast of Epiphany, with its star in the heavens, and Jesus' face shining like sun at the Transfiguration. The light of God's revelation in Jesus becomes clearer in the ensuing weeks as disciples are called and his word is proclaimed.

FORMATION IN BAPTISMAL DISCIPLESHIP

Like Moses, Elijah, and Jesus, it is in those mountaintop, seeing-the-light experiences that we begin to understand what the Lord is calling us to do in our covenant relationship.

LESSER FEASTS AND FASTS

- Anna Julia Hayward Cooper, Educator, 1964 (February 28)
- David, Bishop of Menevia, Wales, c. 544 (March 1)
- Chad, Bishop of Lichfield, 672 (March 2)
- John and Charles Wesley, Priests, 1791, 1788 (March 3)

THE SUNDAYS IN LENT

An Overview of the Readings

During Lent, the readings of the five weeks of the season provide us with a short course in the meaning of baptism. This is no accident, of course. When the early church prepared candidates for baptism, it let the liturgy do the teaching. Some of the Lenten texts found in the lectionary of our prayer book were teaching texts for candidates for baptism in the early centuries of Christianity.

With that thought in mind, the outline below for the Sundays in Lent differs from the treatment of Sunday lections for the rest of the year. The focus of the lections each week has a direct reference to parts of the baptismal rite in the Book of Common Prayer. Following the theme of the lectionary texts week by week, the congregation will have an opportunity to explore the baptismal rite in Year A and Year B. In Year C, five great themes of baptism are explored during Lent.

If Lent provides a natural way of discovering the meaning of baptism, there is no need to wonder what we should be doing for a Lenten program! The lectionary provides the "program," one that developed out of the early church's preparation of candidates for their baptism at the Easter Vigil. The church's renewed interest in adult formation and the catechumenal process makes baptismal teaching even more relevant to the congregations of the church.

Notice the close connection among all three readings in the five weeks of Lent. Unlike the epistle lections in the Sundays after the Epiphany and after Pentecost, when entire epistles are read independently of the gospel, the epistle lections during Lent are linked directly with the baptismal theme expressed in the other two readings.

Since baptism and Lent are all about conversion, the themes for these five weeks also provide us with a process for "conversion therapy" (a term used by Aidan Kavanagh to describe the purpose behind the catechumenate) as we move through the season and Holy Week. First we turn away from evil and toward Jesus Christ (Lent 1 and 2). Then we look at what we thirst for in life and ask for the empowerment of the Holy Spirit (Lent 3 and 4). Then we put our whole life and trust in Christ, who leads us even through death into life (Lent 5).

LESSER FEASTS AND FASTS

Since the days of Lent are not fixed, the following persons are remembered during these weeks, or in the latter weeks of Epiphany and first weeks of Easter. They are listed here for ease of reference in the months to come.

- Perpetua and Her Companions, Martyrs at Carthage, 202 (March 7)
- Gregory, Bishop of Nyssa, c. 394 (March 9)

- Gregory the Great, Bishop of Rome, 604 (March 12)
- James Theodore Holly, Bishop of Haiti and Dominican Republic (March 13)
- Patrick, Bishop and Missionary to Ireland, 461 (March 17)
- Cyril, Bishop of Jerusalem, 386 (March 18)
- Cuthbert, Bishop of Lindisfarne, 687 (March 20)
- Thomas Ken, Bishop of Bath and Wells, 1711 (March 21)
- James DeKoven, Priest, 1780 (March 22)
- Gregory the Illuminator, Bishop and Missionary of Armenia, c. 332 (March 23)
- Oscar Romero, Archbishop of San Salvador, 1980 (March 24)
- Charles Henry Brent, Bishop of the Philippines and of Western New York, 1929 (March 27)
- John Keble, Priest, 1866 (March 29)
- John Donne, Priest, 1631 (March 31)

The First Day of Lent: Ash Wednesday (Years A, B, and C)

THEMES OF THE LECTIONS

- *The Collect* (BCP 166/217): God hates nothing he has made and forgives us when we are truly repentant. We ask God to give us new and contrite hearts, asking for God's perfect forgiveness through Jesus Christ our Lord.
- *Joel 2:1–2, 12–17:* The day of the Lord is described as a time of darkness; "and yet," the Lord says, "Yet even now, says the Lord, return to me with all your heart." The Lord will be gracious and compassionate if his people return to him; OR
- *Isaiah 58:1–12:* God requires more than fasts made for private devotion. He requires that we share what we have with the hungry, take the homeless and poor into our homes, clothe those in need, and be responsible for our families if we are to offer a fast acceptable to the Lord.
- *Psalm 103:* A song of gratitude for God's fatherly care. He remembers that we are but dust.
- *2 Corinthians 5:20b–6:10:* "See, now is the acceptable time; see, now is the day of salvation!" Paul calls the congregation at Corinth to be reconciled to God, and describes the incredible hardships he and other servants have endured for the sake of the Gospel.
- *Matthew 6:1–6, 16–21:* Fasting, prayer, and support for the needy are not to be public demonstrations of piety. They are part of our private relationship with God.

The First Sunday in Lent, Year A

THE BAPTISMAL RITE

The renunciations:

- Do you renounce Satan and all the spiritual forces of wickedness that rebel against God?
- Do you renounce the evil powers of this world which corrupt and destroy the creatures of God?
- Do you renounce all sinful desires that draw you from the love of God? (BCP 302)

BAPTISMAL THEME EXPRESSED IN THE LECTIONARY READINGS

- Saying "no" to evil so that the Christian can say "yes" to Christ.

THEME OF THE LECTIONS

During Lent in Year A, the readings provide a primer in Christianity as outlined in Paul's letters to the Romans and Ephesians. These epistle readings pick up the theme from the Hebrew Scripture readings and the gospel.

- *The Collect* (BCP 166/218): Just as God's Son was led by the Spirit to be tempted by Satan, we are assaulted by temptations from every direction. We pray that each of us may find God's mighty salvation through Jesus Christ our Lord.
- *Genesis 2:15–17, 3:1–7:* The second story of the Creation and Fall of man and woman in the garden of Eden. God has given us the choice of disobedience and awareness of good and evil so that we may come to recognition of our need for God's saving grace.
- *Psalm 32:* A penitential psalm contrasting righteousness and disobedience.
- *Romans 5:12–19:* Paul contrasts human sin from the time of Adam with God's gift of salvation through Jesus Christ.
- *Matthew 4:1–11:* After his baptism, Jesus was led by the Spirit into the wilderness. Hungry after a long fast, Jesus was tempted to prove that he was indeed the Son of God, possessed with supernatural powers. Jesus' response to the devil is "no."

The Second Sunday in Lent, Year A

THE BAPTISMAL RITE

Turning and accepting Jesus as Savior and Lord:

- Do you turn to Jesus Christ and accept him as your Savior?
- Do you put your whole trust in his grace and love? Do you promise to follow and obey him as your Lord? (BCP 302–303)

BAPTISMAL THEME EXPRESSED IN THE LECTIONARY READINGS

- Saying "yes" to Jesus.

THEME OF THE LECTIONS

- *The Collect* (BCP 167/218): We ask God, who is always merciful, to bring back those people who have strayed from his ways, to give them penitent hearts and firm faith in Jesus Christ.
- *Genesis 12:1–4a:* God calls Abram (Abraham) and Sarai (Sarah) to leave their country and people and go to the land of Canaan.
- *Psalm 121:* A psalm of trust in which God offers protection for one's journey.
- *Romans 4:1–5, 13–17:* It is not through law that Abraham and his descendents were promised that theirs should be a great inheritance, but through faith.
- *John 3:1–17:* Nicodemus, a member of the Jewish Council, believing Jesus to be a teacher sent by God, came in the night to talk with him, wondering how it could be possible to be born again. Jesus tells him that this gift comes through water and the Spirit (baptism).

The Third Sunday in Lent, Year A

THE BAPTISMAL RITE

The waters of baptism:

> Now sanctify this water, we pray you, by the power of your Holy Spirit, that those who here are cleansed from sin and born again may continue for ever in the risen life of Jesus Christ our Savior. (BCP 307)

BAPTISMAL THEME EXPRESSED IN THE LECTIONARY READINGS

The baptismal waters become for the Christian "a spring of water gushing up to eternal life" (John 4:14).

THEME OF THE LECTIONS

- *The Collect* (BCP 167/218): God knows that we have no power to help ourselves. We ask God to keep us from anything that might hurt our bodies or our souls.
- *Exodus 17:1–7:* The trust of the people of Israel disappeared in the face of difficulties of they journey, and they were in open defiance of Moses' authority because they were thirsty. Despite this, God leads the thirsty Israelites to water from the rock at Meribah.
- *Psalm 95:* The psalmist warns people not to harden their hearts against God, as he speaks of the event of God's anger with the people of Israel (as in today's Old Testament reading).
- *Romans 5:1–11:* God accepts us on the basis of our faith, which leads to salvation.
- *John 4:5–42:* The Samaritan woman who comes to the well for water finds her thirst assuaged by Jesus, who promises her living water.

The Fourth Sunday in Lent, Year A

THE BAPTISMAL RITE

The anointing of baptism:

> *N., you are sealed by the Holy Spirit in Baptism and marked*
> *as Christ's own forever.* (BCP 308)

BAPTISMAL THEME EXPRESSED IN THE LECTIONARY READINGS

The Christian is given the gift of enlightenment through the Holy Spirit.

THEME OF THE LECTIONS

- *The Collect* (BCP 167/219): Jesus Christ came to be the true bread that gives life to the world.
- *1 Samuel 16:1–13:* As David was being anointed by Samuel, he was empowered to speak for God as Israel's king.
- *Psalm 23:* Guided by the Lord, whom we often call the Good Shepherd, goodness and love follow the psalmist through life.
- *Ephesians 5: 8–14:* Paul calls Christians to live in the light of Christ, which illumines everything, and to have no part in the deeds of darkness.
- *John 9:1–41:* The story of the healing of the man born blind. Jesus spat on the ground and make a paste with his spittle with which he anointed the man's eyes. Through the anointing of Jesus the blind man could see to follow Jesus: "'Lord, I believe.' And he worshiped him" (John 9:38).

Through the anointing of the Holy Spirit at baptism the Christian can see to follow Jesus. The early church saw the healing of the man born blind as a metaphor of enlightenment: the Christian is called to see things differently.

The Fifth Sunday in Lent, Year A

THE BAPTISMAL RITE

The forgiveness of sins and new life through baptism:

> *Heavenly Father, we thank you that by water and the Holy Spirit you have bestowed upon these your servants the forgiveness of sin, and raised them to the new life of grace.* (BCP 308)

BAPTISMAL THEME EXPRESSED IN THE LECTIONARY READINGS

In baptism the Christian is freed from the tomb of sinfulness. Dry bones take on flesh and those who were dead are filled with the breath of God. The raising of Lazarus points ahead to the Resurrection.

THEME OF THE LECTIONS

- *The Collect* (BCP 167/219): We ask that God give us grace to love what he commands and to want what he promises, so that our hearts will center on the true joys of God's Kingdom.
- *Ezekiel 37:1–14:* In an intense vision, Ezekiel sees the dry bones of the house of Israel lying in a valley. As Ezekiel speaks God's words over the bones, they take on sinew and flesh and come alive in the breath of God.
- *Psalm 130:* The psalmist speaks out of hopelessness, and recognizes that his hope is in the Lord.
- *Romans 8:6–11:* God's life-giving Spirit is unleashed in Christ, replacing the Mosaic law that sin uses to produce death.
- *John 11:1–45:* The raising of Lazarus, the ultimate sign of Jesus as the Son of God who was to come to the world.

THE DAYS OF HOLY WEEK

An Overview of Holy Week

Holy Week is an entering into Jesus' death through baptism so that "just as Christ was raised from the dead by the glory of the Father, so we too might walk in newness of life" (Romans 6:4b).

The origins of Holy Week are found in the practices of Cyril, Bishop of Jerusalem, who died in 386; fortunately, these practices were witnessed and recorded by a pilgrim nun named Egeria.[5] As pilgrims poured into the holy city for their baptism on Easter Sunday morning, Cyril would lead them out to sites that were significant to the events leading up to Golgotha.

With prayer, a dramatic reading of the story associated with the place, the singing of hymns and symbolic actions, these events were re-experienced again by the pilgrims. By the time of their baptism, Paul's powerful words of dying in order to have new life could be appreciated. They were truly raised with Christ, they felt, because they had walked through his death in their baptism.

Bishop Cyril should be honored as the patron saint of church educators! He knew the importance of the Christian story in forming a people, and he moved it right into their lives by involving them in experiences of drama, worship, and prayer during Holy Week. Later, during the Great Fifty Days of Easter, he helped the newly baptized reflect on the meaning of those stories for their new life in Jesus Christ.

Holy Week becomes an "in-house" retreat for candidates and their sponsors for baptism or the reaffirmation of their baptismal vows. They take part in prayer vigils, prepare the Maundy Thursday meal, participate in foot washing, read the biblical texts at the Easter Vigil, and so forth.

The Sunday of the Passion (Palm Sunday), All Years

LECTIONS

THE LITURGY OF THE PALMS

- **Year A:** *Matthew 21:1–11:* In fulfillment of an ancient prophecy, Jesus enters Jerusalem riding on a donkey. Crowds of people spread their cloaks in the road and cut branches from trees to spread in his path. The people shouted "Hosanna to the Son of David," and other cries of praise and blessing.

---

5 Excerpts from Egeria's writings can be found in *Readings for the Daily Office from the Early Church*, ed. J. Robert Wright (New York: Church Hymnal Corporation, 1991).

- **Year B:** *Mark 11:1–11:* Jesus and his disciples were close to Jerusalem when he sent two of his followers to bring him a colt that had not ever been ridden. Jesus mounted the colt, and the people carpeted the road with their cloaks, and cut branches to spread in his path. The people shouted, "Hosanna! Blessed is he who comes in the name of the Lord!" Jesus went into Jerusalem and entered the temple, but it was late in the day, and he went with his friends to stay at Bethany. [Or John 12:12–16.]
- **Year C:** *Luke 19:28–40:* As Jesus reached the hill called Olivet, he sent two of his disciples to find a colt that no one had ever ridden. His followers threw their cloaks on the colt or cast them into the road as he passed by. In joy, the whole company of Jesus' disciples loudly sang praises to God in words that recall the angels' song at the time of Jesus' birth. Some Pharisees in the crowd were not pleased.
- *Psalm 118:1–2, 19–29:* The Hosanna psalm, "Bind the festal procession with branches."

THE LITURGY OF THE WORD

- *The Collect* (BCP 168/229): We ask God to help us to understand the spirit in which Christ suffered and to share in his resurrection.
- *Isaiah 50:4–9a:* The third of the Servant Songs of Isaiah showing the servant undergoing humiliation and rejection in the course of fulfilling his mission.
- *Psalm 31:9–16:* Petition showing trust in God and turning one's life over to God.
- *Philippians 2:5–11:* Paul describes Jesus, who was born as a human being and who took the form of a servant, obedient in all things, even to his death. God has greatly exalted Jesus, and all people who know him acknowledge that Jesus Christ is Lord to the glory of the Father.
- **Year A:** *The Passion from Matthew 26:14–27:66 or 27:11–54:* Jesus in Gethsemane; his trials; his sufferings and death.
- **Year B:** *Mark 14:1–15:47 or 15:1–39, (40–47):* Jesus in Gethsemane; his trials; his sufferings and death.
- **Year C:** *Luke 22:14–23:56 or 23:1–49:* Jesus' prayers; his trials; his sufferings and death.

Monday in Holy Week, All Years

LECTIONS

- *The Collect* (BCP 168/220): We pray that we may find the way of the Cross to be the way of life and peace.
- *Isaiah 42:1–9:* A poem that speaks of the relation between God and his servant (Israel).
- *Psalm 36:5–11:* The psalm speaks of the priceless love of God, of his faithfulness, righteousness, and justice. The well of life is with God.
- *Hebrews 9:11–15:* Christ's death is the perfect atonement, once for all.
- *John 12:1–11:* (See Fifth Sunday of Lent, Year C); OR
- *Mark 14:3–9:* The anointing of Jesus. In John, Mary anoints Jesus "for his burial"; in Mark, the woman is unnamed. In both texts a woman anoints Jesus with expensive perfume. Jesus understood this as symbolizing the anointing of his body for burial, which he knew would be soon.

Tuesday in Holy Week, All Years

LECTIONS

- *The Collect* (BCP 168/220): Through God, Jesus' shameful death on the Cross has become the means of life for us.
- *Isaiah 49:1–7:* God's servant tells of the mission to which the Lord has called him, for which the Lord made him the restoration of Israel. But God intends his servant to do even more—"that my salvation may reach to the end of the earth."
- *Psalm 71:1–14:* The lament of one who is in deep trouble, who cries out for the Lord's help, and reminds God of his faithfulness in years past.
- *1 Corinthians 1:18–31:* Paul's description of the paradox of the Cross. What is folly to those on their way to ruin is the power of God to those on their way to salvation.
- *John 12:20–36:* Abundant life-giving through death interprets both Jesus' death and the service of the disciples to a new mission.

Wednesday in Holy Week, All Years

LECTIONS

- *The Collect* (BCP 169/220): We ask God for the grace to accept our present sufferings joyfully, secure in the glory that will be revealed.

- *Isaiah 50:4-9a:* The servant of the Lord speaks of his mission to listen like one who is taught. The servant offered his back to those who beat him, he did not hide his face from spitting, because the Lord God was with him.
- *Psalm 70:* A prayer for help, affirming that God stands with the poor and needy.
- *Hebrews 12:1-3:* In addition to the cloud of witnesses, Jesus offers the ideal example of faithfulness in God.
- *John 13:21-32:* Jesus predicts his betrayal by Judas Isacariot. Jesus gives his friends a new commandment: that you love one another as I have loved you.

Maundy Thursday, All Years

LECTIONS

- *The Collect* (BCP 169/221): We pray that Jesus will give us grace to receive the Sacrament of his Body and Blood thankfully, remembering that in these holy mysteries we have been given a promise of eternal life.
- *Exodus 12:1-4, (5-10), 11-14:* While the people of Israel were still in Egypt, the Lord gave Moses and Aaron directions for preparing and eating the Passover meal, and explained to them how he would judge Egypt and lead the people of Israel from their slavery.
- *Psalm 116:1, 10-17:* In a song of thanksgiving, the psalmist recalls former distress and recalls deliverance from death to living while affirming with faith in God.
- *1 Corinthians 11:23-26:* Paul tells the people of Corinth how he received the tradition he has transmitted to them, and how Jesus instituted the new covenant of bread and wine.
- *John 13:1-17, 31b-35* or *Luke 22:14-30:* Jesus, in love and humility, washes his disciples' feet during his last Passover meal with them.

Good Friday, All Years

LECTIONS

- *The Collect* (BCP 169/221): We ask God to look with kindness at us his family, for whom our Lord Jesus Christ died on the Cross and lives and reigns forever with God and the Holy Spirit.
- *Isaiah 52:13-53:12:* The song of the suffering servant of the Lord, sometimes thought of as Israel, humiliated and in pain like an individual. The

servant bears his suffering without complaint because he is suffering for others.

- *Psalm 22:1–21:* A cry for help from one who feels forsaken by God.
- *Hebrews 10:16–25:* Christ has given us a new covenant by making for all time a single sacrifice for sin; OR
- *Hebrews 4:14–16; 5:7–9:* Christ, the perfect high priest.
- *John 18:1–19:40:* Jesus' trials before the high priest and Pilate, his sufferings, and his death.

Holy Saturday, All Years

LECTIONS

- *The Collect* (BCP 170/221): We ask God that we may wait with Christ for the coming of the third day and rise with him to newness of life.
- *Job 14:1–14:* The life of an individual is limited and its end is death. Job thought God was angry with him and Job wanted to hide from God in Sheol (the place of departed spirits in early Hebrew thought, where God was not present) for a period of time, rather than in death, from which he could not be waked; OR
- *Lamentations 3:1–9, 19–24:* An individual's lament, blaming God for his troubles.
- *Psalm 31:1–4, 15–16:* A cry of deliverance and redemption.
- *1 Peter 4:1–8:* An appeal to Christians to accept the sufferings they endure for their faith, to pray and to love one another because "love covers a multitude of sins."
- *Matthew 27:57–66* or *John 19:38–42:* After the crucifixion, Jesus was buried in the unused tomb of Joseph of Armathea. On the morning after that Friday, due to the fear of the Pharisees that Jesus' body would be moved, Pilate posts a guard at the tomb and seals it with a stone.

THE EASTER VIGIL

An Overview of the Easter Vigil

The Easter Vigil is the most important service of the Christian year. In the early church the catechumens, their sponsors, and catechists gathered for an all-night storytelling session that culminated in baptism, the proclamation of the resurrection, and the Eucharist. The baptisms were by total immersion. As candidates were lowered into the water, they would remember the words about dying with Christ in baptism so that they could be raised with Christ in his resurrection. They were given white robes to wear after their immersion and anointing and then were led out to the congregation for the Holy Eucharist.

Such an event would have had a powerful effect. Today the drama and significance of baptism can be emphasized in a number of ways. Many congregations have all-night "lock-ins" with youth, and Easter sunrise services are already a standard practice in churches around the world. Consider holding an all-night storytelling time with candidates for baptism or reaffirmation. Gather the rest of the congregation together at thirty minutes before sunrise for the full Vigil service.

The Easter Vigil is an event in which the church tells the salvation story again with the candidates for baptism, summarizing the whole story as people prepare to turn their lives around. The message of the nine readings appointed from the Bible (though as few as two can be read as long as one lesson is from Exodus) can be lost if they are read one after another interspersed only with psalms and prayers, but can be offered dramatically in a variety of ways to encourage the joyful participation and reflection of the people gathered.

The nine readings from the Vigil are outlined below, listed as "chapters" in salvation history. Along with the biblical citations are suggestions for sharing the texts at the Vigil. These suggestions are offered only to stimulate your own imagination. Consider the gifts of your congregation: music, dance, dramatic reading, storytelling, visual arts, and poetry are but a few of the talents that can be exercised in the Great Vigil of Easter.

At the end of the fourth "chapter" in the salvation story, the texts move from remembering God's past deeds done on behalf of God's people and turn to the future promises of God. There is a dramatic shift here from "remember what God has done" to "hear what God is going to do." Without the memory, the future vision has no meaning. Only as the people of Israel recall the past actions of God can they have confidence in God's promises for the future.

A movement from one space to another might heighten the sense of this dramatic shift. For example, offer the first four readings around the baptismal font to emphasize the memories associated with God's past actions. Three of the four memories include water imagery, making the font as a focal point particularly appropriate. Move to the altar for the five promises, since it represents the promise of the kingdom of God that is coming: "For I tell you that from now on I will not drink of the fruit of the vine until the kingdom of God comes" (Luke 22:18). The places where the Vigil readings are offered do not have to be in the nave or sanctuary. Use the parish hall, an area out of doors, the columbarium, or other places that make sense in light of the texts.

Chapters in the Salvation Story of the Easter Vigil

CHAPTER 1: GENESIS 1:1–2:4A (THE STORY OF CREATION)

Read the text as a poem, with one person taking the part of the narrator and the other the part of God. At the end of each "day" in the text, invite the congregation to repeat the refrain, "Good. Good. Very, very good!"

CHAPTER 2: GENESIS 7:1–5, 11–18, 8:6–18, 9:8–13 (THE FLOOD)

Read this text as a choral reading, assigning parts to two or more persons.

CHAPTER 3: GENESIS 22:1–18 (ABRAHAM'S SACRIFICE OF ISAAC)

Encourage an informal telling of the story rather than a reading from the Bible, thus capturing the way this text was shared in ancient times. A second alternative is to offer the story as a dramatic reading with persons taking the parts of the narrator, Abraham, and Isaac.

This is a reading that many of us would rather leave out of the Easter Vigil! How could the God we know in Jesus possibly have "tested" Abraham in such a way? Jews and Christians over many generations have been bothered by that very question, but they have also seen in this story the faith of the patriarch Abraham who trusted God to do what had to be done for the salvation of a people. Abraham's response is not unlike Mary's recorded in Luke: "Here am I, the servant of the Lord; let it be with me according to your word" (Luke 1:38a). Christians see in this story a direct connection to the death of God's beloved Son on the cross. The cross on Jesus' back was foreshadowed in the wood for the fire that Isaac carried up the hill.

CHAPTER 4: EXODUS 14:10–31; 15:20–21 (ISRAEL'S DELIVERANCE AT THE RED SEA)

Here is a second opportunity for storytelling. Do not worry about including every word of the text in the telling of the story; shape the story in a way that makes it easier to tell. Again, a dramatic reading of the text is an excellent option. Movement as well as oral interpretation can be included: let Moses' arm be raised over the waters of the sea, and have several people move across the space with a sense of awe and wonder.

CHAPTER 5: ISAIAH 55:1–11 (SALVATION OFFERED FREELY TO ALL)

If there are two readers, have the first reader offer Isaiah 55:1–5, with the second reader taking verses 6 through 11. (The second segment of this text is printed on page 86 of the Book of Common Prayer as Canticle 10, "The Second Song of Isaiah.")

CHAPTER 6: BARUCH 3:9–15, 32– 4:4 (IN PRAISE OF WISDOM)

This reading is a portion of a hymn in praise of Wisdom, exalting the law of Moses as the unique gift of God to Israel, the observance of which is the way to life and peace. Baruch was the well-known secretary of the prophet Jeremiah. A dramatic reading of someone dressed in period costume as one transcribing the thoughts of the prophet during the period after the fall of Jerusalem can set the scene for the readings to come.

OR

PROVERBS 8:1–8, 19–21; 9:4B–6 (THE GIFTS OF WISDOM)

One of the most striking features of Proverbs is its way of presenting the abstract concept of Wisdom as a woman. In this reading, a woman can give this speech as if she were in a town square, inviting passersby to listen to the promises of the future for those who would be her disciples.

CHAPTER 7: EZEKIEL 36:24–28 (A NEW HEART AND A NEW SPIRIT)

The imagery of this prophetic promise invites dramatic movement. Consider asking someone who signs for those who are hearing impaired to express the text in sign language while someone else reads aloud.

CHAPTER 8: EZEKIEL 37:1–14 (THE VALLEY OF THE DRY BONES)

Here is a text that cries out for a dramatic rendering. The whole group could be drawn into the acting out of the reading. Have some participants lie on the floor as "dried bones." Put people in the four corners of the space to "breathe upon these slain, that they may live" (Ezekiel 37:9b). They rise up as the breath of the Spirit is proclaimed from the four corners of the earth. If lying down on the floor is not practical, have people sit with eyes closed so that they hear the words of the spirit coming from all around them.

CHAPTER 9: ZEPHANIAH 3:14–20 (THE GATHERING OF GOD'S PEOPLE)

Have a single voice read the first two verses. Ask everyone to read the remainder of the text together in unison. If you have done the Vigil readings outside the nave, the text is an invitation for the people to move in procession into the nave for baptism and the proclamation of the gospel: "At that time I will bring you home, at the time when I gather you" (Zephaniah 3:20a).

THE SUNDAY OF THE RESURRECTION (EASTER DAY)

Lections

- *The Collect* (BCP 170/222): Celebrating Christ's glorious resurrection, we pray that we may be renewed in body and mind, being raised from the death of sin by God's life-giving Spirit.

Early Service (Great Vigil of Easter)

- *Romans 6:3–11:* All of us who have been baptized into Christ Jesus were baptized into his death, but if we have died with Christ, we believe that we shall also live with him.
- **Year A:** *Matthew 28:1–10:* Mary Magdalene and the "other Mary" go to the grave at daybreak on Sunday and discover the stone rolled from the tomb by an angel who tells them not to fear. In running to tell the disciples, they encounter the Risen Christ.
- **Year B:** *Mark 16:1–8:* Three women friends of Jesus came to the tomb early Sunday morning to find the huge stone that had been placed in front of the door rolled away. They went into the tomb and saw a young man, who told them that Jesus had risen. They were to tell his disciples that Jesus would go ahead of them to Galilee. The women were petrified with terror and said nothing to anyone.
- **Year C:** *Luke 24:1–24:* The women approach the tomb with spices to find the stone rolled away and the tomb empty. They share the good news with the other disciples. Later that day, two of the disciples encounter the Risen Christ on the road to Emmaus.

Easter Day (Principle Service)

The reading from Acts of the Apostles is read in place of either the Old Testament or New Testament lesson each year.

YEAR A LECTIONS

- *Acts of the Apostles 10:34–43:* The centurion Cornelius (commander of a hundred soldiers) had been told in a vision that he should ask Peter to come to him and his relatives and friends to hear what the Lord had commanded Peter to say. Peter's answer to Cornelius is the beginning of the mission to the Gentiles. Peter speaks of Christ crucified and resurrected, the good news for all people.

- *Jeremiah 31:1–6:* All of Israel will be united and the covenant with God will be restored.
- *Psalm 118:1–2, 14–24:* A song of thanksgiving, rejoicing in the wonderful acts of God; and praising God that the stone the builders rejected has become the chief cornerstone.
- *Colossians 3:1–4:* Paul stresses our present sharing in the risen life of Christ.
- *John 20:1–18:* Mary Magdalene finds the empty tomb and runs to tell Simon Peter and another disciple that the body of the Lord has been taken from the tomb. They see the linen cloths that had been used at the burial, and the other disciple sees and believes that Jesus has risen from the dead. Mary Magdalene sees the risen Christ.

YEAR B LECTIONS

- *Isaiah 25:6–9:* Justice comes when God overcomes the power of death itself.
- *Psalm 118:1–2, 14–24:* See Year A.
- *1 Corinthians 15:1–11:* Paul describes one of the earliest teachings of the resurrection, including the key moments in the Passion story as if he had been present himself as a witness to the events.
- *Mark 16:1–8:* Three women friends of Jesus came to the tomb early Sunday morning to find the huge stone that had been placed in front of the door rolled away. They went into the tomb and saw a young man, who told them that Jesus had risen. They were to tell his disciples that Jesus would go ahead of them to Galilee. The women were petrified with terror and said nothing to anyone.

YEAR C LECTIONS

- *Isaiah 65:17–25:* God is still in control of human history and is about to create new heavens and a new earth.
- *Psalm 118:1–2, 14–24:* See Year A.
- *1 Corinthians 15:19–26:* Like Adam, Christ stands at the beginning of a new order of humanity, the first fruits of resurrection for all.
- *Luke 24:1–10:* Women followers of Jesus learned of his resurrection as very early Sunday morning came, bringing spices. They found the tomb open and empty, when "two men in dazzling garments" suddenly appeared and asked them why they were looking among the dead for the living. Jesus had told them what would happen, how he would be crucified and must rise on the third day. The women went back and told the eleven disciples all they had seen.

Easter Evening (All Years)

- *Isaiah 25:6–9:* See Easter Day, Year B.
- *Psalm 114:* A psalm of praise telling how God saved Israel at the Exodus. The earth itself enters into the awe and joy of salvation.
- *1 Corinthians 5:6b–8:* Leaven (yeast), used in making bread, deteriorates and spoils, and to this day there is a Jewish household custom of throwing away all the yeast and all the bread baked with yeast before making the unleavened bread that is used at Passover. Paul speaks of Christ as the lamb offered as the Passover sacrifice, so we who observe the festival must be new like the unleavened bread of sincerity and truth.
- *Luke 24:13–49:* Two of the disciples met Jesus on the road to Emmaus. Something kept them from knowing who he was. In response to his question they told him all that had happened in Jerusalem, and Jesus responded with scriptural passages referring to the Messiah. Night was coming, and the disciples invited Jesus to stay with them. He sat at the table and took bread and said the blessing, broke the bread and offered it to them, and in that act the disciples recognized Jesus. They knew him as we know him, in the words of scripture and the breaking of bread.

THE GREAT FIFTY DAYS OF EASTER

An Overview of the Great Fifty Days

The Great Fifty Days of Easter, beginning with Easter Week, are the time when those who have reaffirmed their baptismal vows or have been baptized at the Easter Vigil reflect on the meaning of their baptism. Through the lectionary texts they explore the "mysteries" of their faith. The early church called this period of the process *mystagogia*. Today the whole church enters into this period of uncovering anew the mysteries of faith expressed in sacrament, word, and life lived for others. Each time we celebrate the Holy Eucharist using Eucharistic Prayer A, we say these words:

> We proclaim the mystery of faith: Christ has died. Christ is
> risen. Christ will come again. (BCP 363)

Some overall themes need to be kept in mind as the Great Fifty Days unfold:

- The role of the church is to continue the proclamation of the resurrection expressed with such joy at that first Easter. We hear the proclamation of the resurrection in order to pass on the Good News.

- In a sense, Christ rose again *within* the church. Through the Holy Spirit, the risen Christ is revealed in every new generation. The apostles found themselves filled with the power to continue the acts of Jesus that revealed God's presence: Peter healed the man at the Beautiful Gate (Acts 3:1–10); "Many signs and wonders were done among the people through the apostles" (Acts 5:12a); Philip unfolded the meaning of God's word to the Ethiopian eunuch on the road to Gaza (Acts 8:26–39).
- The Great Fifty Days traditionally were a time when the mysteries of the faith were revealed to the recently baptized. The meaning of all that the candidates experienced in Holy Week and the Easter Vigil unfolds in this time of intense theological reflection on just what it means to live as a covenant people.
- For congregations involved in the catechumenal process, the Great Fifty Days are a time of reflection on baptism. "What difference does my baptism make?" ask the recently baptized as they gather with priest, catechist, sponsor, and those who have reaffirmed their Baptismal Covenant.
- A question to ask each week: How will we know the risen Christ in our lives today?

The Weeks of Easter, Year A

Sequential readings from the Acts of the Apostles are read during the Great Fifty Days because we need to hear the story of the first-century church in order to understand our mission in the church of today. In the Acts of the Apostles, the followers of Jesus suddenly realize that through the Holy Spirit they have the power to heal, to preach, to turn lives around, to witness to the presence of God and the coming reign of God in the world.

A course of readings from 1 Peter is heard each Sunday of the weeks of Easter in Year A. Some scholars believe that this letter is actually an early baptismal rite that included exhortations, sermons, and so forth. Thus we are formed during Easter with the same understanding of baptism that was given to the earliest converts.

Alternative selections from the Hebrew Scripture that are in thematic harmony with the gospel lections or with the Easter themes are provided in all three years. When the Hebrew Scripture selection is used, it replaces either the reading from Acts or the reading from 1 Peter.

Easter Day (Principle Service)

THEME OF THE LECTIONS

The Resurrection of Jesus the Christ is proclaimed.

- *Acts of the Apostles 10:34–43:* The centurion Cornelius (commander of a hundred soldiers) had been told in a vision that he should ask Peter to come to him and his relatives and friends to hear what the Lord had commanded Peter to say. Peter's answer to Cornelius is the beginning of the mission to the Gentiles. Peter speaks of Christ crucified and resurrected, the Good News for all people.
- *Jeremiah 31:1–6:* All of Israel will be united and the covenant with God will be restored.
- *Psalm 118:1–2, 14–24:* A song of thanksgiving, rejoicing in the wonderful acts of God; and praising God that the stone the builders rejected has become the chief cornerstone.
- *Colossians 3:1–4:* Paul stresses our present sharing in the risen life of Christ.
- *John 20:1–18:* Mary Magdalene finds the empty tomb and runs to tell Simon Peter and another disciple that the body of the Lord has been taken from the tomb. They see the linen cloths that had been used at the burial, and the other disciple sees and believes that Jesus has risen from the dead. Mary Magdalene sees the risen Christ.

The Second Sunday of Easter, Year A

THEME OF THE LECTIONS

Knowing the risen Christ through faith.

- *The Collect* (BCP 172/224): We pray that all the people who have been reborn into Christ's Body the Church may live their faith.
- *Acts of the Apostles 2:14a, 22–32:* Peter preaches a bold sermon on the street in Jerusalem on Pentecost, fifty days after Jesus' resurrection. Testifying to Jesus' resurrection, Peter says that all the apostles can bear witness to the risen Christ.
- *Psalm 16:* A prayer and profession of faith, trust, and loyalty to God.
- *1 Peter 1:3–9:* God has given us new birth into a living hope by the resurrection of Jesus Christ. Nothing can destroy our inheritance, which is God's continuing love.
- *John 20:19–31:* The risen Lord appeared twice to his friends. During his first appearance Jesus gave the power to forgive sins to the church. Jesus

affirmed the power of belief that does not depend upon physical evidence when Thomas' doubts vanish after touching the Lord.

HOW WILL THE RISEN CHRIST BE KNOWN IN THE GENERATIONS TO COME?

We may not see the risen Christ but we will know the risen Christ as we gather in faith-filled community on the "eighth day." Blessed are those who have not seen and yet have come to believe (John 20:29b).

LESSER FEASTS AND FASTS

Feast appointed on fixed days in the calendar are not observed on the days of Holy Week or of Easter Week. Major feasts falling in these weeks are transferred to the week following the Second Sunday of Easter, in the order of their occurrence. Those in the month of April and May are noted here.

- Frederick Denison Maurice, Priest, 1872 (April 1)
- James Lloyd Breck, Priest, 1876 (April 2)
- Richard, Bishop of Chichester, 1253 (April 3)
- Martin Luther King, Jr., Civil Rights Leader, 1968 (April 4)
- Tikhon, Patriarch of Russia and Confessor, 1925 (April 7)
- William Augustus Muhlenberg, Priest, 1877 (April 8)
- Dietrich Bonhoeffer, 1945 (April 9)
- William Law, Priest, 1761 (April 10)
- George Augustus Selwyn, Bishop of New Zealand and Lichfield, 1878 (April 11)
- Alphege, Archbishop of Canterbury and Martyr, 1012 (April 19)
- Anselm, Archbishop of Canterbury, 1109 (April 21)
- Catherine of Siena, Monastic, 1380 (April 29)
- Athanasius, Bishop of Alexandria, 373 (May 2)
- Monnica, Mother of Augustine of Hippo, 387 (May 4)
- Dame Julian of Norwich, c. 1417 (May 8)
- Gregory of Nazianzus, Bishop of Constantinople, 389 (May 9)
- Martyrs of Sudan, 1983 (May 16)
- Dunstan, Archbishop of Canterbury, 988 (May 19)
- Alcuin, Deacon and Abbot of Tours, 804 (May 20)
- Jackson Kemper, First Missionary Bishop in the United States, 1870 (May 24)
- Bede, the Venerable, Priest and Monk of Jarrow, 735 (May 25)
- Augustine, First Archbishop of Canterbury, 605 (May 26)

The Third Sunday of Easter, Year A

THEME OF THE LECTIONS

Sacramental life.

- *The Collect* (BCP 173/224): We pray that God will open the eyes of our faith so that we may recognize Christ in all his redemptive work.
- *Acts of the Apostles 2:14a, 36–41:* The conclusion of Peter's sermon on Pentecost speaks of Jesus, whom they had crucified, the Lord and Messiah. Peter told them to repent and be baptized; three thousand were baptized that day.
- *Psalm 116:1–3, 10–17:* In a song of thanksgiving, verbal gratitude and sacrifice are to be given to the Lord.
- *1 Peter 1:17–23:* A letter about the calling of a Christian, written to Christians who once were pagans, reminds them that the price of their freedom from their old lives was the blood of Christ. They have been born as a new people through the living and enduring Word of God.
- *Luke 24:13–35:* The disciples on the road to Emmaus (see Easter Day, Evening Service).

HOW WILL THE RISEN CHRIST BE KNOWN IN THE GENERATIONS TO COME?

The risen Christ is known in the sharing of the word and in the breaking of bread. This text reflects the form of the Eucharist celebrated each week in the congregation: the Liturgy of the Word and the Liturgy at the Table.

> Lord Jesus, stay with us, for evening is at hand and the day is past; be our companion in the way, kindle our hearts, and awaken hope, that we may know you as you are revealed in Scripture and the breaking of bread. Grant this for the sake of your love. (BCP 124)

The Fourth Sunday of Easter, Year A

THEME OF THE LECTIONS

Ministry as a way of revealing the risen Christ through word, action, and prayer.

- *The Collect* (BCP 173/225): We ask God to help us recognize the Good Shepherd's voice and follow where he leads.
- *Acts of the Apostles 2:42–47:* A view of the early church—the apostles' teaching and fellowship, the breaking of the bread and the prayers—sharing all thing in common with one another.

- *Psalm 23:* The shepherd psalm of our pilgrimage of earthly life. The Lord will be our guide and host, and his unfailing love will be with us always.
- *1 Peter 2:19–25:* Christ suffered for us, and left us an example to follow. He bore our sins when he was crucified, so that we might die to sin and live to righteousness. By his wounds we have been healed. Although we have strayed, we have now come back to the Shepherd of our souls.
- *John 10:1–10:* Jesus, teaching through a parable, describes himself as a shepherd who cares for his sheep, whose sheep follow him because they know his voice. He describes himself as the door of the sheepfold; those who enter through him shall be safe. He has come that people may have life in all its fullness.

HOW WILL THE RISEN CHRIST BE KNOWN IN THE GENERATIONS TO COME?

The risen Christ is known through the ministry of the church modeled by Jesus, the Good Shepherd.

The Fifth Sunday of Easter, Year A

THEME OF THE LECTIONS

One cannot be Christian alone; apart from the Body, we can do nothing.

- *The Collect (BCP 173/225):* We ask that we may follow Jesus' example in the way that leads to eternal life.
- *Acts of the Apostles 7:55–60:* The story of the stoning of Stephen, the first follower of Jesus to die following the pattern of Jesus' death.
- *Psalm 31:1–5, 15–16:* A prayer for help, with expressions of trust that accompany each petition.
- *1 Peter 2:2–10:* Christians are described as chosen by God to be a royal priesthood, the people of God.
- *John 14:1–14:* Part of Jesus' last conversation with his friends, he tells them to trust God and to trust him and to be easy in their troubled minds; He is going to make it possible for the Father, the Son, and the disciples to be truly part of one another. "I am the way, and the truth, and the life."

HOW WILL THE RISEN CHRIST BE KNOWN IN THE GENERATIONS TO COME?

The church will reveal the risen Christ to the world and to each other through the community of faithful gathered and scattered as the Body of Christ. We are "made one body with him, that he may dwell in us, and we in him" (BCP 336).

The Sixth Sunday of Easter, Year A

THEME OF THE LECTIONS

(Continued from Easter 5) One cannot be Christian alone; apart from the Body we can do nothing.

- *The Collect* (BCP 174/225): We ask God to fill our hearts with such great love for him that we may receive his promises, which are infinitely more than we can desire.
- *Acts of the Apostles 17:22–31:* Paul's message to the people of Athens proclaiming God and our relation to him and his Son, Christ Jesus.
- *Psalm 66:7–18:* A communal song of thanksgiving and deliverance for the individual as well as the community.
- *1 Peter 3:13–22:* Just as Christ suffered and was made alive in the Spirit, we too are given spiritual washing through our baptism into new birth.
- *John 14:15–21:* The Holy Spirit is promised to all believers, as well as God's continuing love for those who keep Jesus' commandments.

HOW WILL THE RISEN CHRIST BE KNOWN IN THE GENERATIONS TO COME?

(Continued from Easter 5) The church will reveal the risen Christ to the world and to each other through the community of faithful: "I am the vine, you are the branches. Those who abide in me and I in them bear much fruit, because apart from me you can do nothing" (John 15:5).

The Seventh Sunday of Easter, Year A

THEME OF THE LECTIONS

The church consecrated as the Body of Christ.

- *The Collect* (BCP 175/226): We pray that God will send us his Holy Spirit to comfort and strengthen us and raise us to the place where our Savior has gone before us.
- *Acts of the Apostles 1:6–14:* The ascension of Jesus, followed by the disciples' return to Jerusalem to the upper room, where with Mary the mother of Jesus and his brothers they spent their time in prayer.
- *Psalm 68:1–10, 33–36:* A hymn praising God as King.
- *1 Peter 4:12–14, 5:6–11:* The significance of suffering as a Christian. A joyful acceptance of undeserved suffering shows trust in God, as Peter's exhortations to the church echo Jesus' words.

150

- *John 17:1–11:* Jesus prays for his disciples, asking God to reveal his glory and protection.

HOW WILL THE RISEN CHRIST BE
KNOWN IN THE GENERATIONS TO COME?

The Holy Spirit empowers the church. The text for this Sunday might be called a "Prayer of Consecration" for the church. The Body of Christ becomes a living sacrament to the world, an "outward and visible sign" of Christ's redeeming presence in history.

> *The words that you gave to me I have given to them, and they have received them and know in truth that I came from you; and they have believed that you sent me . . . And now I am no longer in the world, but they are in the world, and I am coming to you. Holy Father, protect them in your name that you have given me, so that they may be one, as we are one.* (John 17:8, 11)

ASCENSION DAY

Ascension Day, All Years

THEME OF THE LECTIONS

The risen Jesus is lifted up into heaven and no longer seen by the disciples.

- *The Collect* (BCP 174/226): Jesus Christ ascended far above the heavens so that he might fulfill all things and continue to be with us to the end of the ages.
- *Acts 1:1–11:* The close of Jesus' ministry on earth and how he appeared to his disciples, taught them, and promised them they would receive power through the Holy Spirit so they would be witnesses throughout the world.
- *Psalm 47:* A hymn celebrating God, King of all the earth; OR
- *Psalm 93:* A proclamation that God is king.
- *Ephesians 1:15–23:* The writer gives thanksgiving and prays for the people of the church at Ephesus. He speaks of the infinite power of God in raising Christ from the dead to enthronement at God's right hand.
- *Luke 24:44–53:* Jesus promised his disciples to send them his Father's promised gift. He led them to Bethany and blessed them with his hands raised. As he blessed them he parted from them, and was carried to heaven.

KEY WORDS, IDEAS, AND CONCEPTS TO EXPLORE

- Authority
- Christ as high priest
- "Seated at God's right hand"
- Head of the church
- Kingdom or reign of God

STORIES TO TELL

The story of Christ's ascension from Luke and Acts.

CHRISTIAN PRACTICE AND LITURGICAL TRADITION

- Belief in Christ's ascension is an important element in the major creeds of the church.
- We pray to God "through Christ" as a recognition that Christ intercedes for us "at the right hand of the Father." The familiar refrain that closes many of our prayers and collects captures this image:

    . . . through Jesus Christ our Lord, who lives and reigns with
    you and the Holy Spirit, one God for ever and ever.

FORMATION IN BAPTISMAL DISCIPLESHIP

The Baptismal Covenant affirms our belief that after his death and resurrection Jesus Christ "ascended into heaven, and is seated at the right hand of the Father" (BCP 304).

PENTECOST

The Day of Pentecost, Year A

THEME OF THE LECTIONS

The gift of the Holy Spirit empowers Christians for ministry in the world.

- *The Collect* (BCP 175/227): God has opened the hearts of his faithful people by sending them the light of his Holy Spirit. We pray that God will give us right judgment in all things and joy in the strengthening of the Holy Spirit.
- *Acts of the Apostles 2:1–21:* The experience of the apostles on the Day of Pentecost, when the Holy Spirit filled them and they were able to tell the people of "every nation under heaven" in their own languages the great things God has done for us.

- *Ezekiel 37:1–14:* Ezekiel's vision of dry bones symbolizes the restoration of the people of Israel.
- *Psalm 104:25–35, 37:* A creation hymn through which praise is given for God's wonderful and benign order, the source of new life on earth.
- *Romans 8:22–27:* Believers share both suffering and glory with Christ, and the Spirit is our intercessor with God.
- *John 15:26–27; 16:4b–15:* Jesus' departure is the means by which he is able to send the Holy Spirit, our Advocate and Guide.

LESSER FEASTS AND FASTS
- The anniversary of the introduction of the first Book of Common Prayer in 1549 is appropriately observed on a weekday following the Day of Pentecost.

TRINITY SUNDAY

Trinity Sunday, Year A

THEME OF THE LECTIONS
The God who creates, redeems, and sanctifies is revealed to us in three persons.
- *The Collect* (BCP 176/228): Through his divine power, God has given us grace to confess a true faith and to acknowledge the glory of the eternal Trinity and to worship the Unity.
- *Genesis 1:1–2:4a:* The story of the Creation.
- *Psalm 8* or *Canticle 2* OR *Canticle 13:* Praising God.
- *2 Corinthians 13:11–13:* Paul closes with a benediction that has become a familiar part of our worship: "The grace of the Lord Jesus Christ, the love of God, and the communion of the Holy Spirit be with all of you."
- *Matthew 28:16–20:* Jesus' last appearance to the eleven disciples, directing them to go and make all nations his disciples, to baptize everywhere in the name of the Father, the Son, and the Holy Spirit.

KEY WORDS, IDEAS, AND CONCEPTS TO EXPLORE
- Trinity
- Names of God
- God's power revealed in Creation and history
- Creeds of the church

CHRISTIAN PRACTICE AND LITURGICAL TRADITION

- "The Grace" from 2 Corinthians appears at the conclusion of both versions of Morning Prayer and Evening Prayer.
- Following Jesus' directive to his disciples in Matthew 28, Christians are baptized in the name of the Trinity.

  N., I baptize you in the Name of the Father, and of the Son, and of the Holy Spirit. (BCP 307)

FORMATION IN BAPTISMAL DISCIPLESHIP

The relationship of love among the three persons of the Trinity serves as a model for communities of baptized Christians living together in unity.

THE SUNDAYS AFTER PENTECOST

An Overview of the Readings

During the Sundays after Pentecost, both the Old Testament, epistle, and gospel lections are heard in semi-continuous readings. Using the Revised Common Lectionary, the inclusion of women and their role in salvation history is now heard on Sundays as they never have been before. The first reading and the psalm are in thematic relationship to one another and not necessarily with the epistle or gospel. The theme listed here for each set of Propers is often the theme set by the gospel text. These sequential readings give a delightful opportunity to "walk through" one of the stories from the Hebrew scriptures, an epistle or gospel in sermons and educational offerings, as well as Vacation Bible School ideas or informal summer story-telling for adults as well as children.

- *Hebrew scriptures:* During Year A, the great stories from Genesis through the settling of the Hebrews in the Promised Land are heard. In Year B, stories of the great kings are heard, along with readings from the Wisdom literature, following the Davidic covenant. Year C offers semi-continuous readings from the great literature of the prophets, highlighting Jeremiah as well as Elijah, Elisha, Amos, Hosea, Joel, and Habbakuk.
- *Epistles:* The sequential reading of several of the epistles also offers the opportunity for more in-depth study of their context and overall message in the educational setting or in a serialized sermon during the liturgy. Year A provides a sixteen-week, semi-continuous reading of Romans (Proper 4 through Proper 19). Year B offers a six-week reading of 2 Corinthians (Proper 4 through Proper 9) and an eight-week semi-continuous reading of Ephesians (Proper 10 through Proper 16), followed by four weeks of

James (Proper 17 through 21) and seven weeks of Hebrews. Year C begins with a six-week reading of Galatians (Proper 4 through Proper 9), then four weeks reading Colossians (Proper 10 through 13), four weeks from Hebrews (Proper 14 through 17), and a seven-week reading of 1 and 2 Timothy (Proper 19 through 26).

- *Gospel Readings:* In Year C, reading the Gospel according to Luke, Jesus is "on the road to Jerusalem" from Luke 9:51 through 13:21. In the lectionary, the "journey" portion of the gospel is read from Proper 8 (the Sunday closest to June 29) through Proper 26 (the Sunday closest to November 2). All summer we hear the gospel texts in the context of the shadow of the cross. As Jesus and the disciples draw closer to Jerusalem, the immediacy of Jesus' suffering and death is heightened. Scholars remind us that the gospel writers did not always know the context of the narratives they included in their gospels, but from Luke's perspective his "on the road" stories are to be read with the crisis of the cross increasingly in mind. Posters, banners, and bulletin covers can carry the common theme of "on the road with Jesus," week after week. Similar ideas can be tried in Year A with Matthew and Year B with Mark.

As always, during these months let the lectionary establish the focus for education and liturgy. These sequential readings offer wonderful opportunities for summertime storytelling and education in the congregation. We can share the Bible in serialized fashion: "Come back to find out what happens next week!"

For those congregations following the alternative sets of readings from the Hebrew scripture that are in thematic harmony with the gospel lections, these are listed separately.

Except for Trinity Sunday, the numbered proper to be used on each of the Sundays after Pentecost is determined by the calendar date of that Sunday. Propers 1, 2, and 3 are the same as the Propers for Epiphany 6, 7, and 8. When Easter falls early in the calendar, we hear these Propers after Pentecost; with a late Easter, we hear them after the Feast of the Epiphany. Since Propers 1, 2, and 3 are covered in this book during the Epiphany season, we begin herewith Proper 4. See page 158 of the Book of Common Prayer for instructions concerning the Propers of the church year.

Proper 4, Year A (The Sunday Closest to June 1)

THEME OF THE LECTIONS

The Sermon on the Mount: living by God's word must be at the center of every Christian's life.

- *The Collect* (BCP 177/229): God's unfailing providence sets all things in order in heaven and on earth.
- *Genesis 6:9–22; 7:24; 8:14–19:* Noah and the flood: To be righteous means to be in a trusting and loyal relationship with God. To walk with God means to be in a trusting and loyal relationship with God.
- *Psalm 46:* A Song of Zion proclaiming God's cosmic sovereignty.
- *Romans 1:16–17, 3:22b–28, (29–31):* It is one's faith that brings salvation.
- *Matthew 7:21–29:* False prophets follow Jesus and call him Lord, but only those who do the will of the Father will enter the kingdom of heaven. The people who do God's will as well as talk about it are like those who build their houses on solid rock.

ALTERNATIVE READINGS

- Deuteronomy 11:18–21, 26–28
- Psalm 31:1–5, 19–24

KEY WORDS, IDEAS, AND CONCEPTS TO EXPLORE

- The Sermon on the Mount
- Covenant
- Justification by faith
- Kingdom of heaven
- This Sunday begins a sixteen-week reading of Romans. Offer an overview of Paul's important letter.

CHRISTIAN PRACTICE AND LITURGICAL TRADITION

- A covenant is a formal agreement or promise made between two parties. In today's reading in Genesis, God makes a covenant with Noah and his family, which is further explained (9:8–17). God makes several important covenants throughout the Old Testament. Our Baptismal Covenant is our promise to God and one another.
- Justification by faith (Romans 3:28) played a central role in the Protestant Reformation.

FORMATION IN BAPTISMAL DISCIPLESHIP

The words from the Baptismal Covenant call us to persevere in resisting evil, and, whenever we fall into sin, repent and return to the Lord (BCP 304).

LESSER FEASTS AND FASTS
- Justin, Martyr at Rome, c. 167 (June 1)
- Blandia and Her Companions, 177 (formerly Martyrs of Lyons) (June 2)
- The Martyrs of Uganda, 1886 (June 3)
- Boniface, Archbishop of Mainz, Missionary to Germany and Martyr, 754 (June 5)

Proper 5, Year A (The Sunday Closest to June 8)

THEME OF THE LECTIONS

Calling of outcasts into a faithful relationship with God.
- *The Collect* (BCP 178/229): All good comes from God. We pray that our thoughts may be right, and through God's guidance we may act on them.
- *Genesis 12:1–9:* God calls Abram and promises his descendents will be a great nation that will be extended to all the families of the earth. Abram obeys God's command and enters into the land of Canaan where he builds an altar in thanksgiving to God.
- *Psalm 33:1–12:* A song praising God's steadfast love that fills the earth.
- *Romans 4:13–18:* It is faith, not law, that makes one righteous before God.
- *Matthew 9:9–13, 18–26:* Jesus calls Matthew, a tax collector, to follow him. Jesus' disciples were asked why their master ate with tax collectors and sinners. (Tax collectors were scorned as servants of the Roman occupation.) Jesus heard their question and replied that healthy people do not need doctors. He said he had not come to call righteous people, but sinners, to repentance. He suggested that they think about the words in scripture: "I desire mercy, not sacrifice."

ALTERNATIVE READINGS
- Hosea 5:15–6:6
- Psalm 50:7–15

KEY WORDS, IDEAS, AND CONCEPTS TO EXPLORE
- Sacrifice and burnt offerings
- Righteousness
- Faith

- Promise
- Grace
- Sinners
- Role of the Pharisees
- Tax collectors in Jesus' time

STORIES TO TELL
- The calling of Abram.
- The calling of Matthew.

CHRISTIAN PRACTICE AND LITURGICAL TRADITION

Each week as we reflect on the readings, we need to confront our own reasons for participating in the liturgy. If we are not careful, the sacraments can become mere good-luck omens or empty payments for our sins. What the Lord wants from us is mercy and justice and a true self-offering. The Great Thanksgiving (Eucharistic Prayer or Prayer of Consecration) reflects the feelings in today's readings. "And we earnestly desire thy fatherly goodness mercifully to accept this our sacrifice of praise and thanksgiving . . . And here we offer and present unto thee, O Lord, our selves, our souls and bodies . . ." (Rite I, BCP 335–336) and "Sanctify us also that we may faithfully receive this holy Sacrament, and serve you in unity, constancy, and peace . . ." (Rite II, BCP 363).

FORMATION IN BAPTISMAL DISCIPLESHIP

The church is called to follow Jesus' example of reaching out to those who are considered outcasts by society.

LESSER FEASTS AND FASTS
- Columba, Abbot of Iona, 597 (June 9)
- Ephrem of Edessa, Syria, Deacon, 373 (June 10)
- Enmegahbowh, Priest and Missionary, 1902 (June 12)
- Basil the Great, Bishop of Caesarea, 379 (June 14)

Proper 6, Year A (The Sunday Closest to June 15)

THEME OF THE LECTIONS

God calls a people into intimate covenant relationship.
- *The Collect* (BCP 178/230): We ask that God will keep his household the church firm in faith and love for him so that we may serve with justice and compassion.

- *Genesis 18:1–15, (21:1–7):* Abraham and Sarah are promised the birth of a son by three strangers who visit them at the oaks of Mamre. Sarah's laughter at the impossible promise of a child leads to the birth of their son, Issac, later in the reading. God's promise is fulfilled.
- *Psalm 116:1, 10–17:* A song of thanksgiving in which the psalmist recalls former distress and affirms faith in God.
- *Romans 5:1–8:* Christ died so that the world may know the power of God's saving love. We rejoice in God through our Lord Jesus; through him we have been granted reconciliation.
- *Matthew 9:35–10:8, (9–23):* As Jesus went through the towns and villages, he was moved to pity by the needs of the people he saw. He said to the disciples that the harvest was plentiful, but that there were few workers to gather it; they should pray to the Lord to send laborers to gather the crop. The names of the twelve disciples are given and Jesus gives them authority over unclean spirits and the ability to cure every disease and sickness.

ALTERNATIVE READINGS
- Exodus 19:2–8a
- Psalm 100

KEY WORDS, IDEAS, AND CONCEPTS TO EXPLORE
- Kingdom of priests
- Apostolic authority
- Disciples
- Christ's sacrificial death for sinners
- Names of the disciples (gospel accounts show some variations)

STORIES TO TELL
- The story of Abraham and Sarah and the events leading up to Issac's birth.

CHRISTIAN PRACTICE AND LITURGICAL TRADITION
Bishops receive and pass on the apostolic authority of the disciples.

FORMATION IN BAPTISMAL DISCIPLESHIP
The Baptismal Covenant (BCP 304–305) becomes the focus for life in the church. The church can measure its faithfulness to the gospel by setting the life of the congregation alongside the provisions of the covenant.

LESSER FEASTS AND FASTS
- Evelyn Underhill, 1941 (June 15)

- Joseph Butler, Bishop of Durham, 1752 (June 16)
- Bernard Mizeki, Catechist and Martyr in Rhodesia, 1896 (June 18)

Proper 7, Year A (The Sunday Closest to June 22)

THEME OF THE LECTIONS:

The cost of discipleship.

- *The Collect* (BCP 178/230): God never fails to help and direct the people he has placed upon the secure foundation of his loving-kindness.
- *Genesis 21:8–21*: Abraham and Sarah send Hagar and Ishmael away. God remains with each individual as they journey different ways.
- *Psalm 86:1–10, 16–17*: A prayer for help, trusting in God's steadfast love to lift up the poor and needy.
- *Romans 6:1b–11*: When we were baptized into union with Christ, we were baptized into his death, and we believe that we shall also come to life with him. We must regard ourselves as dead to sin and alive to God in Christ Jesus.
- *Matthew 10:24–39*: Matthew supports an egalitarian community in terms of leadership (although the language is male-centered). Members are to proclaim their faith through their actions and attitudes in which believers must choose between church and family.

ALTERNATIVE READINGS

- Jeremiah 20:7–13
- Psalm 69:8–11, (12–17), 18–20

KEY WORDS, IDEAS, AND CONCEPTS TO EXPLORE

- Righteousness
- Grace
- Witness
- Radical nature of discipleship

CHRISTIAN PRACTICE AND LITURGICAL TRADITION

- The sentences the bishop says at the time of confirmation speak of the cost of taking up the role of disciple in the world today:
  Strengthen, O Lord, your servant N. with your Holy Spirit;
  empower him for your service; and sustain him all the days
  of his life . . . Defend, O Lord, your servant N. with your
  heavenly grace, that he may continue yours for ever . . .
  (BCP 309)

- There have been Christian saints and martyrs who have suffered as a result of witnessing to their faith. These can be found in *Lesser Feasts and Fasts*.

FORMATION IN BAPTISMAL DISCIPLESHIP

The church must witness to the radical call of the gospel, which often means a conflict with family members and even secular authority.

LESSER FEASTS AND FASTS

- Alban, First Martyr of Britain, c. 304 (June 22)
- Irenaeus, Bishop of Lyons, c. 202 (June 28)

Proper 8, Year A (The Sunday Closest to June 29)

THEME OF THE LECTIONS

The cost of discipleship.

- *The Collect* (BCP 178/230): God has built the church on the foundation of the apostles and prophets with Jesus Christ as the cornerstone.
- *Genesis 22:1–14:* God puts Abraham through a remarkable test of his obedience and trust by asking him to sacrifice his only remaining son, Issac. God reaffirms the earlier promises of many descendents because of Abraham's extraordinary obedience and trust in God.
- *Psalm 13:* A prayer for help in which the psalmist looks back in gratitude for deliverance through God's steadfast love.
- *Romans 6:12–23:* Sin can cause physical death and separation from God. With changed loyalties come a purer life, sanctification, and ultimately eternal life. Our obedience must be to God alone.
- *Matthew 10:40–42:* Exhortation in community leadership that will lead to reward in heaven.

ALTERNATIVE READINGS

- Jeremiah 28:5–9
- Psalm 89:1–4, 15–18

KEY WORDS, IDEAS, AND CONCEPTS TO EXPLORE

- Discipleship
- Baptism
- Newness of life
- Enslaved to sin
- Resurrection

CHRISTIAN PRACTICE AND LITURGICAL TRADITION

- The traditions associated with Holy Week come from the early church. With Paul's words in mind, candidates for baptism were led through an experience of participating in the death of Jesus so that they could participate in his resurrection.
- Liberation theology focuses on God's liberating action among the oppressed. From this theological perspective, God is always on the side of the oppressed. He led the Israelites out of the oppression of Egypt into the Promised Land. He is acting through the oppressed in Latin America, Africa, and in our own land. The Magnificat or Song of Mary (BCP 91) says, ". . . he has cast down the mighty from their thrones, and has lifted up the lowly" (Luke 1:52).

FORMATION IN BAPTISMAL DISCIPLESHIP

The congregation must enter into the struggle for justice that comes from proclaiming the gospel to an often hostile world. What is our role as disciples and prophets called to speak out in Jesus' name? What problems in our local community call for our direct participation as Christians?

Proper 9, Year A (The Sunday Closest to July 6)

THEME OF THE LECTIONS

God's wisdom, which brings rest and peace, is personified in Jesus.

- *The Collect* (BCP 179/230): God has taught us that all the commandments are kept if we love God and our neighbor.
- *Genesis 24:34–38, 42–49, 58–67:* Isaac receives a wife (Rebekah) via Abraham's servant.
- *Psalm 45:11–18:* A love song, probably written in honor of and for use at a wedding of a king; OR
- *Canticle: Song of Solomon 2:8–13:* The Song of My Beloved.
- *Romans 7:15–25a:* Paul discusses his struggles to do good despite the sins "that dwells within me."
- *Matthew 11:16–19, 25–30:* Jesus speaks as the representative of Sophia (wisdom). He thanks God for his revelations and trust. He calls all those whose work is at hand and whose load is heavy to come to him and learn from his teachings; in them burdened souls will find relief.

ALTERNATIVE READINGS
- Zechariah 9:9–12
- Psalm 145:8–15

KEY WORDS, IDEAS, AND CONCEPTS TO EXPLORE
- God's wisdom (revealed through Jesus)
- The reign (or kingdom) of God
- God's gift of rest
- Evil
- Law of God
- Deliverance through Jesus Christ

CHRISTIAN PRACTICE AND LITURGICAL TRADITION
The gospel text can be found in the words of comfort said during the Holy Eucharist, Rite I (BCP 332).

FORMATION IN BAPTISMAL DISCIPLESHIP
The church is called to witness to the wisdom of God, which often contradicts the "wisdom" of the culture. The church is to proclaim the way of God's wisdom and peace in its every action and word.

LESSER FEASTS AND FASTS
- Benedict of Nursia, Abbot of Monte Casino, c. 540 (June 11)

Proper 10, Year A (The Sunday Closest to July 13)

THEME OF THE LECTIONS
God's word is power (The Parable of the Sower).
- *The Collect* (BCP 179/231): We ask God to receive our prayers when we call upon him, knowing that God understands us and gives us grace and power to act faithfully.
- *Genesis 25:19–34:* The birth and rivalry of Isaac and Rebekah's twin sons, Jacob and Esau.
- *Psalm 119:105–112:* Like God's own self, God's word is a light.
- *Romans 8:1–11:* Those in Christ no longer feel doomed. God's life-giving Spirit is unleashed in Christ. Through him we are children and heirs of God.
- *Matthew 13:1–9, 18–23:* Jesus taught the crowds that gathered around him on the beach the parable of the sower and the seed, and its inner meaning.

ALTERNATIVE READINGS
- Isaiah 55:10–13
- Psalm 65:(1–8), 9–14

KEY WORDS, IDEAS, AND CONCEPTS TO EXPLORE
- Parable
- Planting and reaping
- God's word
- Living in the Spirit

STORIES TO TELL
- The story of Jacob and Esau.
- The parable of the sower.

CHRISTIAN PRACTICE AND LITURGICAL TRADITION
Paul's description of living in the Spirit is conveyed in the anointing at baptism: "You are sealed by the Holy Spirit in Baptism and marked as Christ's own for ever" (BCP 308).

FORMATION IN BAPTISMAL DISCIPLESHIP
The church must challenge the assumptions of society. The power of story and drama is seen as a tool of prophetic witness.

LESSER FEASTS AND FASTS
- William White, Bishop of Pennsylvania, 1836 (July 17)
- Macrina, 379 (July 19)

Proper 11, Year A (The Sunday Closest to July 20)

THEME OF THE LECTIONS
God's patience and mercy.
- *The Collect* (BCP 179/231): God is the source of all wisdom.
- *Genesis 28:10–19a:* The story of Jacob's encounter with God and God's blessing; a reaffirmation of the promises made to Abraham and Isaac also belong to Jacob.
- *Psalm 139:1–11, 22–23* OR
- *Wisdom 12:13, 16–19:* A song of God's strength in mercy.
- *Romans 8:12–25:* God's glory surpasses the suffering of the present moment. With the whole universe, we want to be set free from bondage to mortality and to receive the glorious freedom that is our heritage as children of God.

- *Matthew 13:24–30, 36–43:* Jesus tells another parable of the kingdom of heaven: the story of the weeds in the wheat field.

ALTERNATIVE READINGS
- Isaiah 44:6–8
- Psalm 86:11–17

KEY WORDS, IDEAS, AND CONCEPTS TO EXPLORE
- Blessing
- Parable
- Judgment
- Mercy
- Glory to be revealed
- Hope

STORIES TO TELL
- The story of Jacob's dream: a ladder to heaven.
- The parable of weeds among the wheat.

CHRISTIAN PRACTICE AND LITURGICAL TRADITION
This section of Romans is often read at a burial service because it expresses with power the Christian hope.

FORMATION IN BAPTISMAL DISCIPLESHIP
The church must reflect God's patience and avoid passing judgment on others.

LESSER FEASTS AND FASTS
- Elizabeth Cady Stanton, Amelia Bloomer, Sojourner Truth, and Harriet Ross Tubman (July 20)
- Thomas à Kempis, Priest, 1471 (July 24)
- The Parents of the Blessed Virgin Mary (July 26)

Proper 12, Year A (The Sunday Closest to July 27)

THEME OF THE LECTIONS
The hidden power of the kingdom of God.
- *The Collect* (BCP 180/231): God protects everyone who trusts in God. Without God nothing is strong, nothing is holy.
- *Genesis 29:15–28:* Jacob marries Leah and Rachel following years of work for their father, Laban.

- *Psalm 105:1–11, 45b:* A historical psalm, its recital of God's saving acts is offered in the form of a song of praise; OR
- *Psalm 128:* To be happy involves orienting one's life fully to God, in work as well as family life.
- *Romans 8:26–39:* Through the Spirit's intercession, God's love and care support us in our weakness. God's purpose is for us to be like his Son. It is Christ who is at God's right hand, who intercedes for us.
- *Matthew 13:31–33, 44–52:* Jesus tells more parables about the Kingdom of heaven: the mustard seed, the yeast, the hidden treasure, the fine pearl, a net.

ALTERNATIVE READINGS

- 1 Kings 3:5–12
- Psalm 119: 129–136

KEY WORDS, IDEAS, AND CONCEPTS TO EXPLORE

- Trust
- Intercession
- Predestined
- Justification
- Parables
- Mustard seeds
- Kingdom of heaven

STORIES TO TELL

- The story of Jacob, Laban, Leah and Rachel.
- The short parables of Jesus as told in today's gospel.

FORMATION IN BAPTISMAL DISCIPLESHIP

The epistle reading points to the dynamic role of the Holy Spirit in the life of the individual and the church.

LESSER FEASTS AND FASTS

- William Reed Huntington, Priest, 1909 (July 27)
- Mary and Martha of Bethany (July 29)
- William Wilberforce, 1833 (July 30)
- Ignatius of Loyola, 1556 (July 31)
- Joseph of Arimathaea (August 1)

Proper 13, Year A (The Sunday Closest to August 3)

THEME OF THE LECTIONS

God continues to show steadfast love and compassion. Jesus' compassion for the people leads him to respond with food for mind and body. The feeding of the five thousand expresses the significance of the Holy Eucharist.

- *The Collect:* (BCP 180/232): We pray that God's continual mercy will cleanse and defend the church, asking for protection and safety.
- *Genesis 32:22–31:* Jacob's name is changed to Israel after he wrestles with God, limping away from the fight with a blessing.
- *Psalm 17:1–7, 16:* A prayer for help from one who claims innocence, seeking refuge in God.
- *Romans 9:1–5:* Paul expresses his great grief at Israel's unbelief in Jesus Christ. The people of Israel were made God's sons; they had covenants, the law, the worship in the temple, and God's promises. The patriarchs were part of their history, and the Messiah himself came from their roots.
- *Matthew 14:13–21:* Feeding of the Five Thousand—Jesus blessed and broke the loaves and the disciples gave them to the people. All ate and were satisfied; and there were twelve baskets of food left over.

ALTERNATIVE READINGS

- Isaiah 55:1–5
- Psalm 145:8–9, 15–22

KEY WORDS, IDEAS, AND CONCEPTS TO EXPLORE

- Israel
- God's chosen people
- Covenant
- Eucharistic actions (took bread, blessed, broke, gave)
- Blessing
- Reconciliation
- Steadfast love

STORIES TO TELL

- Jacob's wrestling with God.
- The feeding of the five thousand.

CHRISTIAN PRACTICE AND LITURGICAL TRADITION

There are Eucharistic overtones to this day's gospel story. Jesus "took bread, blessed the bread, broke it, and distributed it among the people." Notice that Jesus "feeds" the people first with teaching and then with bread. At the Eucharist we first hear the word and then receive the Eucharistic bread: word and sacrament lie at the heart of Christian life.

FORMATION IN BAPTISMAL DISCIPLESHIP

Christ has compassion for the people of the church and the world that hunger for God's word. When we offer the risen Christ our time, talent, and commitment, he can bring about the Kingdom.

LESSER FEASTS AND FASTS

- John Mason Neale, Priest, 1866 (August 7)
- Dominic, Priest and Friar, 1221 (August 8)

Proper 14, Year A (The Sunday Closest to August 10)

THEME OF THE LECTIONS

God's infinite mercy far surpasses our understanding. God's power is revealed as Jesus controls the waters.

- *The Collect* (BCP 180/232): We ask that God will give us the spirit to think and do the things that are right. We cannot exist without God.
- *Genesis 37:1–4, 12–28:* The story of the family of Jacob, including the jealousy and scheming of his sons that led them to sell favored son, Joseph, to a caravan of Ishmaelites traveling to Egypt.
- *Psalm 105:1–6, 16–22, 45:* A historical psalm that tells of God's wonderful works and recounts God's saving acts for the wandering matriarchs and patriarchs who have been left in Egypt.
- *Romans 10:5–15:* Paul speaks of righteousness through faith. There is no distinction between Jew or Greek; we are to proclaim Jesus is Lord.
- *Matthew 14:22–33:* Following the feeding of the five thousand, Jesus sends the disciples to the other side of the lake in a boat while he goes off to pray. A storm arises on the water, and Jesus appears to the frightened men, walking on the water toward them. Peter leaves the boat and begins to walk toward Jesus. Matthew portrays the disciples as comprehending Jesus as the Son of God.

ALTERNATIVE READINGS

- 1 Kings 19:9–18
- Psalm 85:8–13

KEY WORDS, IDEAS, AND CONCEPTS TO EXPLORE

- Descendents of Abraham continue to interact with God's chosen people, Israel.
- God's power of protection.
- God's power over the waters (first expressed in Genesis 1).

STORIES TO TELL

- The story of Joseph and his brothers.
- The story of Jesus walking on the water.

CHRISTIAN PRACTICE AND LITURGICAL TRADITION

The Thanksgiving over the water in the baptismal rite (BCP 306) emphasizes the times in salvation history when God's power and calling were revealed through the waters.

FORMATION IN BAPTISMAL DISCIPLESHIP

We come to the new life of God in Christ through the waters of baptism.

LESSER FEASTS AND FASTS

- Lawrence, Deacon and Martyr at Rome, 258 (August 10)
- Clare, Abbess at Assisi, 1253 (August 11)
- Florence Nightingale, Nurse and Social Reformer, 1910 (August 12)
- Jeremy Taylor, Bishop of Down, Connor and Dromore, 1667 (August 13)
- Jonathan Myrick Daniels, 1965 (August 14)

Proper 15, Year A (The Sunday Closest to August 17)

THEME OF THE LECTIONS

Faith brings salvation to Jews and Gentiles alike.

- *The Collect* (BCP 180/232): God has given his only Son to be a sacrifice for our sin and an example of godly life.
- *Genesis 45:1–15:* Joseph reveals his true identity to his brothers and recognizes that his coming to Egypt was part of a larger divine plan to preserve life for both his own family and "all the families of the earth."
- *Psalm 133:* Family imagery is shown when kindred live together in unity.
- *Romans 11:1–2a, 29–32:* Paul speaks as a missionary to the Gentiles, still seeking to save some of his own fellow Jews. If their rejection of Jesus Christ meant the reconciliation of the world, their acceptance of him would be like life from the dead.

- *Matthew 15:(10–20), 21–28:* Jesus heals a Canaanite woman's daughter, reluctantly after a conversation with her, and in the light of her faith.

ALTERNATIVE READINGS
- Isaiah 56:1, 6–8
- Psalm 67

KEY WORDS, IDEAS, AND CONCEPTS TO EXPLORE
- Forgiveness
- Canaanites
- Providence
- Gentiles
- Evangelizing society's outcasts

CHRISTIAN PRACTICE AND LITURGICAL TRADITION
The Reconciliation of a Penitent (BCP 447) is available to all who desire it. The ministry of reconciliation, which has been committed by Christ to his Church, is exercised through the care each Christian has for others, through the common prayer of Christians assembled for public worship, and through the priesthood of the Church and its ministers declaring absolution.

FORMATION IN BAPTISMAL DISCIPLESHIP
The congregation is called to live for others so that all may know the power of God's salvation revealed through Christ. Evangelism is the means by which the church proclaims the good news of salvation to all peoples.

LESSER FEASTS AND FASTS
- William Porcher DuBose, Priest, 1918 (August 18)
- Bernard, Abbot of Clairvaus, 1153 (August 20)

Proper 16, Year A (The Sunday Closest to August 24)

THEME OF THE LECTIONS
The foundation of faith.

- *The Collect* (BCP 181/232): God's Church is gathered together in unity by his Holy Spirit. We pray that the Church may show forth his power among all peoples.
- *Exodus 1:8–2:10:* A new king arises in Egypt who did not know Joseph or his descendens and forces the Israelites to become slaves. Moses is

saved from Pharaoh's killing of all Israelite newborn males, being found by Pharaoh's daughter in a basket floating on the Nile.

- *Psalm 124:* A communal song of thanksgiving from enslavement.
- *Romans 12:1–8:* Paul appeals to the members of the Christian congregation in Rome to offer themselves to God as living sacrifices, in worship offered by mind and heart. They are no longer to follow the patterns of the world, but to let their whole beings be transformed. The gifts they have been given come from God's grace, and they must be used accordingly.
- *Matthew 16:13–20:* Peter is called "the rock" on which the church will be built. He gives the disciples strict orders to tell no one that he was the Messiah.

ALTERNATIVE READINGS
- Isaiah 51:1–6
- Psalm 138

KEY WORDS, IDEAS, AND CONCEPTS TO EXPLORE
- Salvation
- Deliverance
- Peter as "the rock" ("Peter" means "rock" in Greek)
- "Who do you say that I am?"

STORIES TO TELL
- The birth of Moses.
- Stories about Peter.

CHRISTIAN PRACTICE AND LITURGICAL TRADITION
- The services of Holy Week provide a symbolic way of walking in the way of the cross.
- The offertory at the Holy Eucharist is to express the offering of our lives to God. A phrase from Eucharistic Prayer I (Rite I) reflects Paul's words heard in the second reading: *And here we offer and present unto thee, O Lord, our selves, our souls and bodies, to be a reasonable, holy, and living sacrifice unto thee.* (BCP 336)
- The gospel text establishes a sense of authority for the role of the bishop in the church. As Jesus had authority to act for God in the world, so the church has authority to "bind and loose," and its bishops are seen as symbols of that apostolic authority in the church today. In the Roman Catholic tradition, the gospel text is cited as the authority for the primacy of the Bishop of Rome (the Pope).

FORMATION IN BAPTISMAL DISCIPLESHIP

Peter is a symbol of leadership for the Church. We are called to build our faith on a solid foundation so we can follow in Christ's footsteps, as well as all those who have come before us in recognizing the true nature of Jesus.

LESSER FEASTS AND FASTS

- Louis, King of France, 1270 (August 25)
- Thomas Gallaudet, 1902 and Henry Winter Syle, 1890 (August 27)
- Augustine, Bishop of Hippo, 430 (August 28)

Proper 17, Year A (The Sunday Closest to August 31)

THEME OF THE LECTIONS

The cost of discipleship.

- *The Collect* (BCP 181/233): God is the Lord of all power and might, the source and giver of all good things.
- *Exodus 3:1–15:* Moses encounters God in a burning bush at Mount Horeb, otherwise known as Mount Sinai. God calls Moses to leave Midian and return to Egypt in order to lead Israel out of slavery into freedom.
- *Psalm 105:1–6, 23–26, 45c:* A recital of God's saving acts, featuring how the Israelites came to Egypt, were enslaved and then led to freedom by Moses.
- *Romans 12:9–21:* A letter from Paul on the power of love. He counsels that so far as possible people should live at peace with one another, and not seek revenge.
- *Matthew 16:21–28:* Jesus speaks of his coming suffering and death to his disciples. To become a follower of Jesus, one must deny themselves and take up their cross and follow Jesus.

ALTERNATIVE READINGS

- Jeremiah 15:15–21
- Psalm 26:1–8

KEY WORDS, IDEAS, AND CONCEPTS TO EXPLORE

- Answering God's call
- Discipleship
- Sacrifice
- Taking up the cross

172

STORIES TO TELL

- Moses and the burning bush.

CHRISTIAN PRACTICE AND LITURGICAL TRADITION

The prayer appointed for Fridays in the liturgy for Morning Prayer expresses the concept of the cost of discipleship (BCP 56).

FORMATION IN BAPTISMAL DISCIPLESHIP

- The church remembers and honors saints and martyrs who have borne the cost of discipleship.
- People are truly formed as Christians when they are part of a congregation that lives out Paul's words, "Rejoice with those who rejoice, weep with those who weep."

LESSER FEASTS AND FASTS

- Aidan, Bishop of Lindisfarne, 651 (August 31)
- David Pendleton Oakerhater, Deacon and Missionary, 1931 (September 1)
- The Martyrs of New Guinea, 1942 (September 2)
- Paul Jones, 1941 (September 4)

Proper 18, Year A (The Sunday Closest to September 7)

THEME OF THE LECTIONS

The church is vested with Jesus' authority. Guidelines for discipline and other aspects of church life.

- *The Collect* (BCP 181/233): We ask God to grant us complete trust in him. He never forsakes those who trust in his mercy.
- *Exodus 12:1–14:* The flow of the exodus story (the plagues in Egypt) are interrupted by instructions to Israel for the annual festivals of Passover and Unleavened Bread as the Israelites are about to be delivered from the wrath of Pharaoh.
- *Psalm 149:* A song of praise and glory for all God's faithful.
- *Romans 13:8–14:* Preparation for the end requires moral living, alertness, and an expression of love.
- *Matthew 18:15–20:* Jesus describes the ways in which the disciples are to respond if a member of the community commits a sin; he assures them that where two or three have come together in his Name he will be in the midst of them.

ALTERNATIVE READINGS

- Ezekiel 33:7–11
- Psalm 119:33–40

KEY WORDS, IDEAS, AND CONCEPTS TO EXPLORE

- Preparation
- Discipline
- Excommunication
- Forgiveness
- Judgment
- Repentance

STORIES TO TELL

- The Passover of the Lord.

CHRISTIAN PRACTICE AND LITURGICAL TRADITION

- Deliverance from slavery and sin are themes shared between the Old Testament stories and the gospel. Our salvation story is retold each year at the Great Vigil of Easter (BCP 285–292).
- The Disciplinary Rubrics set forth guidelines for church discipline based on the gospel lection (BCP 409).

FORMATION IN BAPTISMAL DISCIPLESHIP

We have a responsibility to confront the evil that we see in ourselves, in one another, and in our society. On the other side of confrontation is forgiveness. We do not confront to destroy a person. We confront to lead a person into a deeper relationship with God and with neighbor.

LESSER FEASTS AND FASTS

- Constance, Nun, and her Companions, 1878 (September 9)
- Alexander Crummel, 1898 (September 10)
- John Henry Hobart, Bishop of New York (September 12)
- Cyprian, Bishop and Martyr of Carthage, 258 (September 13)

Proper 19, Year A (The Sunday Closest to September 14)

THEME OF THE LECTIONS

Living in community under God's dominion over evil and sin.

- *The Collect* (BCP 182/233): We ask that God's Holy Spirit may direct our lives and rule our hearts in all things.

- *Exodus 14:19-31:* The Lord saves Israel from the Egyptians as Moses divides the waters and the people cross onto dry land. This creation theme helps interpret Israel's exodus out of Egypt as God's defeat of the primal forces of evil and chaos in the world.
- *Psalm 114:* A poetic accounting of the Exodus, wilderness, the crossing of the Jordan into the Promised Land and God's sanctuary; OR
- *(Canticle) Exodus 15:1b–11, 20–21:* The Songs of Moses and Miriam.
- *Romans 14:1–12:* Paul offers instructions about what is required when people from different backgrounds with strongly held opinions try to live together as a community of faith.
- *Matthew 18:21-35:* A lesson on human forgiveness, following Peter's question to Jesus regarding how often he must forgive his brother if his brother continues to wrong him. Jesus shares a story showing that forgiveness has no limit.

ALTERNATIVE READINGS
- Genesis 50:15–21
- Psalm 103:(1–7), 8–13

KEY WORDS, IDEAS, AND CONCEPTS TO EXPLORE
- Deliverance
- Forgiveness
- Sins
- Judgment

STORIES TO TELL
- The deliverance of Israel from slavery in Egypt.
- The parable of the unforgiving servant.

CHRISTIAN PRACTICE AND LITURGICAL TRADITION
- The Lord's Prayer reflects the parable and Jesus' admonition. Each time we gather for worship we pray that we will be forgiven to the extent that we are ready to forgive others. "Forgive us our sins as we forgive those who have sinned against us."
- The passing of the peace is an acting-out of this forgiveness principle. God's forgiveness must be passed on to others if it is to be realized in our own lives. So when you are offering your gift at the altar, if you remember that your brother or sister has something against you, leave your gift there before the altar and go; first be reconciled to your brother or sister, and then come and offer your gift (Matthew 5:23–24).

FORMATION IN BAPTISMAL DISCIPLESHIP

Congregational life must express the forgiveness found in today's texts, including the healing of divisions within the congregation.

LESSER FEASTS AND FASTS

- Ninian, Bishop in Galloway, c. 430 (September 16)
- Hildegard of Bingen, 1170 (September 17)
- Edward Bouverie Pusey, Priest, 1882 (September 18)
- Theodore of Tarsus, Archbishop of Canterbury, 690 (September 19)
- John Coleridge Patteson, Bishop of Melanesia and his Companions, Martyrs, 1871 (September 20)

Proper 20, Year A (The Sunday Closest to September 21)

THEME OF THE LECTIONS

God's gracious compassion for all people extends beyond human understanding.

- *The Collect* (BCP 182/234): We ask God to grant us freedom from anxiety about earthly things and the ability to love heavenly things.
- *Exodus 16:2–15:* The Israelites complain to Moses and Aaron in the wilderness. God rains manna from heaven each morning and meat (quails) each evening in response, showing that he is the "Lord your God."
- *Psalm 105:1–6, 37–45:* A recital of God's saving acts from the time of Abraham through returning Israel to the Promised Land.
- *Philippians 1:21–30:* Paul's desire to be with Christ must be put aside in order that he may be with the church as he still has much to do. He wants to be sure that the Christians at Philippi are firm in the faith.
- *Matthew 20:1–16:* The parable of the laborers in the vineyard. God's way of rewarding people does not conform to human standards. God said, "So the last will be first, and the first will be last."

ALTERNATIVE READINGS

- Jonah 3:10–4:11
- Psalm 145:1–8

KEY WORDS, IDEAS, AND CONCEPTS TO EXPLORE

- God's boundless grace and compassion
- The nature of parables
- "To live in Christ"
- This Sunday begins a four-week, semi-continuous reading of Philippians. Take time to introduce this epistle.

STORIES TO TELL

- Manna and quail from heaven.
- The parable of the laborers in the vineyard.

CHRISTIAN PRACTICE AND LITURGICAL TRADITION

Jesus loves the person who has just been baptized at age ninety just as much as he loves the one who was baptized as an infant. There can be no measuring the total love of God that is offered to all creation. This theme is expressed in the words of comfort read by the presbyter before the Peace (Rite I, BCP 332).

FORMATION IN BAPTISMAL DISCIPLESHIP

The church is called to reach out to the very people who are neglected and despised by society. God calls us to compassion.

LESSER FEASTS AND FASTS

- Philander Chase, Bishop of Ohio and of Illinois, 1852 (September 22)
- Sergius, Abbot of Holy Trinity, Moscow, 1392 (September 25)
- Lancelot Andrews, Bishop of Winchester, 1626 (September 26)

Proper 21, Year A (The Sunday Closest to September 28)

THEME OF THE LECTIONS

Society's outcasts are often more righteous before God than those who consider themselves righteous.

- *The Collect* (BCP 182/234): God declares his almighty power chiefly in showing mercy and pity.
- *Exodus 17:1–7:* The Israelites continue to complain as they wander in the wilderness, this time quarreling with Moses for water to drink. Moses strikes the rock at Horeb and water comes out of it.
- *Psalm 78:1–4, 12–16:* God's gracious activity—the Exodus and guidance in the wilderness.
- *Philippians 2:1–13:* Paul encourages humility and obedience in the members of the congregation at Philippi. He describes the humility of Jesus Christ in the words of an ancient hymn that extols the saving work of Christ. Paul counsels reverence, as they work out their salvation, for it is God who works in them for his purposes.
- *Matthew 21:23–32:* The parable of two sons emphasizes the importance of deeds and denigrates empty promises. Jesus rebukes the Sadducees and Pharisees for rejecting the teachings of John the Baptist while the outcasts were believers.

ALTERNATIVE READINGS

- Ezekiel 18:1–4, 25–32
- Psalm 25:1–8

KEY WORDS, IDEAS, AND CONCEPTS TO EXPLORE

- Christ as God, yet servant
- True righteousness
- Repentance
- Wickedness

STORIES TO TELL

- Moses and the rock at Horeb, giving the people water to drink.
- The parable of the two sons.

CHRISTIAN PRACTICE AND LITURGICAL TRADITION

- The season of Lent points to the need to turn back to God's way.
- Philippians 2:6–11 may have been one of the church's earliest hymns.

FORMATION IN BAPTISMAL DISCIPLESHIP

Christians are called to take on the mind of Christ, full of humility and love for others, and to follow paths of faithfulness.

LESSER FEASTS AND FASTS

- Jerome, Priest and Monk of Bethlehem, 420 (September 30)
- Remigius, Bishop of Rheims, c. 530 (October 1)
- Francis of Assisi, Friar, 1226 (October 4)

Proper 22, Year A (The Sunday Closest to October 5)

THEME OF THE LECTIONS

In the parable of the vineyard, Isaiah and Jesus both warn God's people that they will be held accountable for the fruits of the covenant.

- *The Collect* (BCP 182/234): God is always more ready to hear than we are to pray and to give us more than we desire or deserve.
- *Exodus 20:1–4, 7–9, 12–20:* The Ten Commandments, the ten rules that form the core of Israel's obligation in its relationship with God.
- *Psalm 19:* A proclamation of the all-encompassing importance of God's *torah* (law).
- *Philippians 3:4b–14:* Paul confesses his need to give up arrogance while understanding that all have not reached perfection in Christ as of yet.

- *Matthew 21:33–46:* Jesus tells the story of the wicked tenants to the chief priests and elders. The story is an allegory: The landowner is God, the vineyard is Israel, and the tenants are the people of Israel. The servants are the prophets, and the son is Jesus.

ALTERNATIVE READINGS
- Isaiah 5:1–7
- Psalm 80:7–14

KEY WORDS, IDEAS, AND CONCEPTS TO EXPLORE
- The Ten Commandments
- Stewardship
- Fruits of the kingdom
- Judgment

STORIES TO TELL
- The giving of the Ten Commandments to the Israelites by Moses.
- The parable of the wicked tenants.

CHRISTIAN PRACTICE AND LITURGICAL TRADITION
The Baptismal Covenant provides a way of assessing the church's stewardship of God's vineyard.

FORMATION IN BAPTISMAL DISCIPLESHIP
- Stewardship is more than a financial pledge to the church. It is a way of life in which we all recognize our responsibility to be faithful stewards.
- The Ten Commandments are a central element of the faith of Christianity as well as Judaism.

LESSER FEASTS AND FASTS
- William Tyndale, Priest, 1536 (October 6)
- Robert Grosseteste, Bishop of Lincoln, 1253 (October 9)
- Vida Dutton Scudder, Educator and Witness for Peace, 1954 (October 10)
- Philip, Deacon and Evangelist (October 11)

Proper 23, Year A (The Sunday Closest to October 12)

THEME OF THE LECTIONS
God's coming reign will be like a great banquet (often referred to as the "messianic banquet"), but we must be ready to accept the invitation.

- *The Collect* (BCP 183/234): We pray that God's grace will always go before us and follow us, and that we may be constantly alert to see need and to do good for others.
- *Exodus 32:1–14:* While Moses is on the mountain receiving the Ten Commandments from God, Israel makes an idol in the form of a golden calf and worships it, violating the important prohibition against making idols and worshipping other gods.
- *Psalm 106:1–6, 19–23:* An historical psalm that tells the story of the people's misdeeds.
- *Philippians 4:1–9:* Paul writes of joyful faith and dedication to describe his inner peace and his relationship to others. Paul acknowledges the gift of the Philippians in sharing the burden of his troubles.
- *Matthew 22:1–14:* Two parables are in this reading: the invitation to the wedding feast and the wedding garment. The first parable suggests that the Kingdom of God will become known whether people are ready for it or not. It is God's gift, and all sorts of people will be included, though many may not be worthy by the standards of the world. The second parable reminds us that we must be ready for the King at all times. His invitation comes unexpectedly.

ALTERNATIVE READINGS
- Isaiah 25:1–9
- Psalm 23

KEY WORDS, IDEAS, AND CONCEPTS TO EXPLORE
- Violation of God's commandments
- Peace of God
- Messianic banquet
- Hospitality in the early church
- Kingdom of heaven (or reign of God)

STORIES TO TELL
- The story of the golden calf.
- The parable of the wedding banquet. (The simpler version of this parable is found in Luke 14:16–24; the story of the guest without a proper garment is a separate parable that was added by the writer of Matthew.)

CHRISTIAN PRACTICE AND LITURGICAL TRADITION
- It is often said that the Holy Eucharist is a foretaste of the "messianic banquet." Jesus may have been referring to this coming banquet when he

said, "For I tell you that from now on I will not drink of the fruit of the vine until the kingdom of God comes" (Luke 22:18).

- A portion of the New Testament reading is found in the final blessing given at Holy Eucharist, Rite I (BCP 339).

FORMATION IN BAPTISMAL DISCIPLESHIP

Christians extend the invitation to the banquet in their regular participation in worship and in their involvement in congregational ministry and life.

LESSER FEASTS AND FASTS

- Samuel Isaac Joseph Schereschewsky, Bishop of Shanghi, 1906 (October 14)
- Teresa of Avila, Nun, 1582 (October 15)
- Hugh Latimer and Nichols Ridley, Bishops, 1555 and Thomas Cranmer, Archbishop of Canterbury, 1556 (October 16)
- Ignatius, Bishop of Antioch and Martyr, c. 115 (October 17)

Proper 24, Year A (The Sunday Closest to October 19)

THEME OF THE LECTIONS

God's power and will can be revealed even among those considered enemies or aliens. Since God's power extends to everyone, ultimate authority belongs to God.

- *The Collect* (BCP 183/235): God has shown his glory among the nations in Christ.
- *Exodus 33:12–23:* Moses seeks assurance of God's presence with Israel as they continue in the wilderness and as they enter Canaan.
- *Psalm 99:* An enthronement psalm that proclaims God's holiness.
- *I Thessalonians 1:1–10:* Paul, Sylvanus, and Timothy write to the congregation in Thessalonica, giving thanks for a new and fruitful ministry. Everywhere the faith of this congregation is being praised: how they turned from idol worship to be servants of the living God and wait expectantly for the coming of his son Jesus.
- *Matthew 22:15–22:* The Pharisees attempt to trap Jesus with his own words in a question regarding the payment of taxes to the Emperor of Rome. Jesus' response: "Give therefore to the emperor the things that are the emperor's, and to God the things that are God's."

ALTERNATIVE READINGS

- Isaiah 45:1–7
- Psalm 96:1–9, (10–13)

KEY WORDS, IDEAS, AND CONCEPTS TO EXPLORE
- God's presence with Israel while they wandered in the wilderness
- The construction, use, and location of the tent of meeting during the Exodus period
- The authority of Caesar over Judea in Jesus' time
- This Sunday begins a five-week, semi-continuous reading of 1 Thessalonians, in which Paul deals with the "end times." Take time to introduce the letter and the theology behind it.

CHRISTIAN PRACTICE AND LITURGICAL TRADITION
The rubrics for the Prayers of the People specify that the gathered church must pray for "the Nation and all in authority," and "the welfare of the world" at every celebration of the Eucharist (BCP 383).

FORMATION IN BAPTISMAL DISCIPLESHIP
The church must acknowledge the ultimate allegiance to God. It is important for the congregation to know the stories of those who have witnessed to that ultimate authority with their lives. Dietrich Bonhoeffer, a German theologian killed by the Nazi regime, is an example of the witnesses we have in Christian history.

LESSER FEASTS AND FASTS
- Henry Martyn, Priest and Missionary to India and Persia, 1812 (October 19)
- Alfred the Great, King of the West Saxons, 899 (October 26)
- James Hannington, Bishop of Eastern Equatorial Africa, and his Companions, 1885 (October 29)

Proper 25, Year A (The Sunday Closest to October 26)

THEME OF THE LECTIONS
To be righteous before God means doing right to the neighbor, the sojourner, and the person in need. To love God is to love the neighbor.
- *The Collect* (BCP 183/235): We pray that God will increase in us the gifts of faith, hope, and love and that he will make us love what he commands, so that we may receive what he promises.
- *Deuteronomy 34:1–12*: Moses, not allowed to enter the Promised Land, is shown the expanse of the land from a distance before he dies. Moses was a prophet speaking to the people for God.
- *Psalm 90:1–6, 13–17*: A psalm attributed to Moses, it is a communal prayer

offering a realistic but hopeful response to the despairing questions of being in exile.

- *1 Thessalonians 2:1–8:* Paul reminds the church in Thessalonica of the relationship he established with them when he was in their midst. He, with Sylvanus and Timothy, speak of their frank and fearless preaching of the Gospel.
- *Matthew 22:34–46:* Jesus tells the Pharisees that the greatest commandment in the law is to "love the Lord your God with all your heart, and with all your soul, and with all your mind . . . and the second is . . . You shall love your neighbor as yourself."

ALTERNATIVE READINGS

- Leviticus 19:1–2, 15–18
- Psalm 1

KEY WORDS, IDEAS, AND CONCEPTS TO EXPLORE

- Commandments
- The law of the Lord
- The Shema
- God's compassion for the poor
- Loving our neighbors as ourselves

STORIES TO TELL

- The death of Moses.
- Jesus' teaching of the Great Commandment.

CHRISTIAN PRACTICE AND LITURGICAL TRADITION

The Baptismal Covenant repeats the commandments to love God and neighbor.

FORMATION IN BAPTISMAL DISCIPLESHIP

To embody the covenant means responding to God in praise, seeking and serving Christ in others, and striving for justice and peace (BCP 305).

LESSER FEASTS AND FASTS

- Alfred the Great, King of the West Saxons, 899 (October 26)
- James Hannington, Bishop of Eastern Equatorial Africa, and his Companions, 1885 (October 29)

Proper 26, Year A (The Sunday Closest to November 2)

THEME OF THE LECTIONS

Those in authority must not mislead the people. They must practice what they preach.

- *The Collect* (BCP 184/235): It is only through the gift of God's grace that his faithful people offer him true and worthy service.
- *Joshua 3:7–17:* Joshua leads the Israelites in a religious procession led by the ark across the Jordan River into the Promised Land in a similar fashion to how Moses led them out of Egypt through the Red Sea.
- *Psalm 107:1–7, 33–37:* God delivers from distress through his steadfast love.
- *1 Thessalonians 2:9–13:* Paul rejoices that the congregation at Thessalonica received God's message as what it truly is, the Word of God at work in those who hold the faith.
- *Matthew 23:1–12:* Jesus tells his disciples not to behave as the Scribes and Pharisees and to use no titles of honor. They have one teacher and they are all brothers. The greatest among the disciples must be the servant of all, and the person who exalts himself will be humbled.

ALTERNATIVE READINGS

- Micah 3:5–12
- Psalm 43

KEY WORDS, IDEAS, AND CONCEPTS TO EXPLORE

- Ark of the Covenant
- Leadership
- Servanthood
- Scribes and Pharisees
- Humility
- False prophets
- Injustice
- Ordination

CHRISTIAN PRACTICE AND LITURGICAL TRADITION

Ordination and baptismal rites reflect the call to humility and servanthood, hallmarks of the Christian life.

FORMATION IN BAPTISMAL DISCIPLESHIP

All the ministries of the church are to model the humble servant ministry of Jesus: "The greatest among you will be your servant. All who exalt themselves will be humbled, and all who humble themselves will be exalted" (Matthew 23:11–12).

LESSER FEASTS AND FASTS

- Commemoration of All Faithful Departed (November 2)
- Richard Hooker, Priest, 1600 (November 3)
- William Temple, Archbishop of Canterbury, 1944 (November 6)
- Willibrord, Archbishop of Utrecht, Missionary to Frisia, 739 (November 7)

Proper 27, Year A (The Sunday Closest to November 9)

THEME OF THE LECTIONS

Being ready for judgment means striving for justice and righteousness. (Note: The themes of the season of Advent begin to be expressed this week, offering an opportunity to explore the rich heritage of Advent. All three readings focus on the coming of light out of darkness, the coming of Christ in glory, and on the last judgment.)

- *The Collect* (BCP 184/236): God's Son came into the world to destroy the works of the devil and to make us children of God and heirs of eternal life.
- *Joshua 24:1–3a, 14–25:* Joshua calls all the tribes of Israel to put away the foreign gods and worship the one, true God who led them out of slavery and darkness.
- *Psalm 78:1–7:* A historical psalm regarding teaching and inspiring faithfulness to future generations.
- *1 Thessalonians 4:13–18:* Paul explains that the congregation in Thessalonica should not grieve for those who have died as Christians. Paul's vision of the coming of Christ is dramatic; both the living and the dead will be united in Christ at the Lord's coming.
- *Matthew 25:1–13:* Jesus told a parable based on the wedding customs of the day to show the need for preparedness for the coming of the Kingdom. He concluded, "Keep awake therefore, for you know neither the day nor the hour."

ALTERNATIVE READINGS

- Amos 5:18–24
- Canticle: Wisdom 6:17–20: A Song of Love and Wisdom
- Psalm 70

KEY WORDS, IDEAS, AND CONCEPTS TO EXPLORE
- Darkness and light
- The coming of the Lord
- Judgment day
- Justice
- Empty worship practices
- Parable

STORIES TO TELL
- Joshua leading the tribes of Israel across the Jordan River into the Promised Land.
- The parable of the ten bridesmaids.

CHRISTIAN PRACTICE AND LITURGICAL TRADITION
- The Apostles' Creed and the Nicene Creed affirm the resurrection of the dead and the final judgment: "He will come again in glory to judge the living and the dead, and his kingdom will have no end" (BCP 359).
- "The Christian Hope" section of An Outline of the Faith (BCP 861–862) discusses the final things.
- The joy of the resurrection is reflected in the traditions of Christian burial. See the rubric that begins, "The liturgy for the dead is an Easter liturgy. It finds all its meaning in the resurrection. Because Jesus was raised from the dead, we, too, shall be raised" (BCP 507).

FORMATION IN BAPTISMAL DISCIPLESHIP
The congregation lives in the light of the resurrection and the final judgment. Hope and judgment characterize the outlook of the church as it proclaims Christ to the world.

LESSER FEASTS AND FASTS
- Leo the Great, Bishop of Rome, 461 (November 10)
- Martin, Bishop of Tours, 397 (November 11)
- Charles Simeon, Priest, 1836 (November 12)
- Consecration of Samuel Seabury, First American Bishop, 1784 (November 14)

Proper 28, Year A (The Sunday Closest to November 16)

THEME OF THE LECTIONS
Being ready for the final judgment.

- *The Collect* (BCP 184/236): God caused all Holy Scripture to be written for our learning. We ask that we may hear, read, take careful notice of, learn, and make the scriptures our own.
- *Judges 4:1–7*: Deborah, a prophetess and judge, prepares for battle against those who worship false gods.
- *Psalm 123*: A song of ascent that reflects the pilgrims' experience of hostile environments while expressing trust in a sovereign God who cares for them.
- *1 Thessalonians 5:1–11*: Paul reminds the Thessalonians that the Day of the Lord Jesus Christ will come unexpectedly. They are to live in faith and love, knowing that God has not destined them for the terrors of his wrath but to receive salvation.
- *Matthew 25:14–30*: The parable of the talents.

ALTERNATIVE READINGS
- Zephaniah 1:7, 12–18
- Psalm 90:1–8, (9–11), 12

KEY WORDS, IDEAS, AND CONCEPTS TO EXPLORE
- Judges in the Old Testament
- The day of the Lord
- Judgment day
- Wrath
- Justice

STORIES TO TELL
- The story of Deborah.
- The parable of the talents.

CHRISTIAN PRACTICE AND LITURGICAL TRADITION
Today's Collect addresses how God continues to speak to us through the Bible. In "An Outline of the Faith" (BCP 853), we have the church's explanation of what we believe the Bible to be—the Word of God.

FORMATION IN BAPTISMAL DISCIPLESHIP
- Church living requires action and risk, not passivity.
- We have the responsibility to use our talents to mirror God's creative action in the world. What we do shows forth the glory of God, no matter how insignificant we think our actions might be. We must face the consequences of our failure to mirror God's creation, whether through our fear or rebellion. We face these consequences individually and as a nation and society.

LESSER FEASTS AND FASTS

- Margaret, Queen of Scotland, 1093 (November 16)
- Hugh, Bishop of Lincoln, 1200 (November 17)
- Hilda, Abbess of Whitby, 680 (November 18)
- Elizabeth, Princess of Hungary, 1231 (November 19)
- Edmund, King of East Anglia, 870 (November 20)
- C. S. Lewis, Apologist and spiritual writer, 1963 (November 22)

Proper 29, Year A (The Sunday Closest to November 23)

THEME OF THE LECTIONS

This day is often referred to as the Sunday of Christ the King, or The Reign of Christ. Christ's sovereignty is the major theme in the lections for all three years.

- *The Collect* (BCP 185/236): It is God's will to restore all things in Jesus Christ, who is King of kings and Lord of lords.
- *Ezekiel 34:11–16, 20–24*: The Lord will be a shepherd to his people. He will find them, no matter where they are, and bring them back home. There will be judgment between one sheep and another.
- *Psalm 100*: A psalm of thanksgiving, recognizing God's sovereign role as shepherd to his people.
- *Ephesians 1:15–23*: Christ as head of the church, sitting at God's right hand, the most honored position.
- *Matthew 25:31–46*: Jesus describes the final judgment, when the Son of Man will come in glory and all the people will be gathered before him. He will welcome those who have been ready for him because they fed the hungry, welcomed the stranger, and clothed the needy. "Truly I tell you, just as you did it to one of the least of these who are members of my family, you did it to me."

ALTERNATIVE READINGS

- Psalm 95:1–7a
- Ephesians 1:15–23

KEY WORDS, IDEAS, AND CONCEPTS TO EXPLORE

- Christ as king or sovereign
- Kingdom of God
- The work of a shepherd

STORIES TO TELL

- The story of the king sitting in judgment from Matthew.

CHRISTIAN PRACTICE AND LITURGICAL TRADITION

- Some of the traditions associated with worship in the Episcopal Church have their origins in the royal court: for example, purple, the color for Advent and Lent, was the color associated with royalty and became linked to the coming of Christ as king.
- The psalms and prayers of the church are filled with imagery of the ruler.

FORMATION IN BAPTISMAL DISCIPLESHIP

The earliest Christian creed, "Jesus is Lord," means that Jesus stands above all other earthly power and authority. All through history and into the present moment, choosing God above earthly authority has caused persecution and conflict in the life of the church. The congregation and wider church must witness always to the authority of Jesus Christ, realizing that there will be times when conflict will be the direct result of such a witness.

LESSER FEASTS AND FASTS

- Clement, Bishop of Rome, c. 100 (November 23)
- James Otis Sargent Huntington, Priest and Monk, 1935 (November 25)
- Kamehameha and Emma, King and Queen of Hawaii, 1864, 1885 (November 28)

A Summary of the Lectionary Text

Year B

THE SUNDAYS OF ADVENT

The First Sunday of Advent, Year B

THEME OF THE LECTIONS

The day will come when God's wisdom and presence will be fully revealed. It will be a time of both tremendous hope and promise, but it will also be a time of judgment. God's people must live in readiness for that great day to come.

- *The Collect:* See Year A.
- *Isaiah 64:1–9:* A prayer for forgiveness, justice, and mercy.
- *Psalm 80:1–18:* A plea for restoration to life with God: "Let your face shine, that we shall be saved."
- *1 Corinthians 1:1–9:* Paul writes to "all those who in every place call on the name of Jesus Christ," giving thanks for the grace of God that was given in Christ Jesus so that believers do not lack any spiritual gift as we wait for the coming of our Lord.
- *Mark 13:24–37:* Jesus tells Peter, James, John, and Andrew that the time of the coming of the Son of Man at the end of history is known only to God; and he cautions all people to be alert and watchful.

KEY WORDS, IDEAS, AND CONCEPTS TO EXPLORE

- Judgment
- Grace
- Spiritual gifts
- "Day of our Lord Jesus Christ"
- Being watchful

STORIES TO TELL

- Stories about the Prophets, such as Isaiah, Micah, Jeremiah, and Hosea.

CHRISTIAN PRACTICE AND LITURGICAL TRADITION

Christians are called out to be the watchmen for an ever-evolving new age in which the world and presence of God can be actualized in the lives of the people. Martin Luther King, Jr. (*Lesser Feasts and Fasts*, April 4) is a classic example of a dreamer who took the Advent readings seriously and moved to seek fulfillment of the word in his own life and in the lives of others.

FORMATION IN BAPTISMAL DISCIPLESHIP

See Advent 1, Year A. The church has been given the grace and gifts to minister in the name of Christ.

The Second Sunday of Advent, Year B

THEME OF THE LECTIONS

John the Baptist announces the coming of the long expected day pointed to in the Hebrew Scriptures. The "good tidings" of Isaiah 40 become the "good news" announced in the opening words of the gospel according to Mark. Repentance is a part of accepting that good news.

- *The Collect:* See Year A.
- *Isaiah 40:1–11:* In these beautiful words we hear the promise of the coming of the Lord to a world where the way has been prepared, and in which the rough places have been made smooth.
- *Psalm 85:1–2, 8–13:* A song of hope and promise for the coming of salvation.
- *2 Peter 3:8–15a, 18:* Advent, when we are "waiting for and hastening the coming of the day of God," is a most appropriate time for us to think of the sort of persons we ought to be "in leading lives of holiness and godliness."
- *Mark 1:1–8:* As promised by the prophet Isaiah, John the Baptist appeared in the wilderness where he taught about the need for repentance. People confessed their sins and were baptized by John in the River Jordan. John told them that the Lord was coming and that he would baptize with the Holy Spirit.

KEY WORDS, IDEAS, AND CONCEPTS TO EXPLORE

- God is like a shepherd
- New heavens and a new earth
- Gospel

- Baptism
- Apocalyptic literature
- Baptism with the Holy Spirit

STORIES TO TELL

- The story of John the Baptist, including the narrative details from the gospel of Luke (Luke 1:5–80).

CHRISTIAN PRACTICE AND LITURGICAL TRADITION

- The beautiful text from Isaiah may be familiar from Handel's Messiah.
- The origin of the word "gospel" comes from the Isaiah text and from Mark's opening words. "Gospel" means "good news."

FORMATION IN BAPTISMAL DISCIPLESHIP

The radical call for repentance informs the preparation given for those preparing for their baptism (see also Luke 3:1–20).

The Third Sunday of Advent, Year B

THEME OF THE LECTIONS

The promised day of God is dawning. John is the herald of that day.

- *The Collect:* See Year A.
- *Isaiah 61:1–4, 8–11:* All that God had promised regarding the rebuilding and restoration of Jerusalem would shortly be fulfilled.
- *Psalm 126:* A song of rejoicing in the Lord, in the expectation that the Lord will keep his promises, and do great things for his people (Canticle 3 or 15 is the Magnificat).
- *1 Thessalonians 5:16–24:* Paul closes a letter to the church in Thessalonica with advice to live thankfully, to pray, to test everything, and to hold to what is good.
- *John 1:6–8, 19–28:* Priests and Levites came from Jerusalem to ask John the Baptist who he was. They pressed him with questions. He told them that he was not the Messiah, nor Elijah, nor any other prophet. They wanted to know why he was baptizing. John replied, "I baptize with water. Among you stands one whom you do not know. . . ." John was aware that he had been sent to prepare the Way of the Lord.

KEY WORDS, IDEAS, AND CONCEPTS TO EXPLORE

- John the Baptist
- The vision of the perfect Day of the Lord that is to come

- Prayer
- The "coming of our Lord Jesus Christ" (or the "Second Coming")
- Christ (Messiah)
- Role of Elijah (from Malachi 4:5)
- Baptism

STORIES TO TELL

- John the Baptist (continued from Advent 2).
- Stories of saints from *Lesser Feasts and Fasts*.

CHRISTIAN PRACTICE AND LITURGICAL TRADITION

- The tradition of lighting Advent candles comes from references to the light and to the dawning of a new day expressed in this Sunday's gospel reading.

FORMATION IN BAPTISMAL DISCIPLESHIP

- Who in our history or in contemporary life have followed the role of John the Baptist?
- Those preparing for their baptism on the First Sunday after the Epiphany (The Baptism of our Lord) need to look carefully at the beautiful poetic description of God's coming day of perfect peace. Using their own words and imagery, how would candidates for baptism (or their parents and sponsors) describe God's intentions fully realized in the day that is coming? How can the church live in such a way that the dream is expressed in the lives of the people?

The Fourth Sunday of Advent, Year B

THEME OF THE LECTIONS

God's promise of favor to the house of David and to the people is fulfilled in Jesus. A mystery is revealed. The promise now includes the Gentiles.

- *The Collect:* See Year A.
- *2 Samuel 7:1–11, 16:* The Lord gives the prophet Nathan a message for David, who reigns as king in Jerusalem. The Lord will establish David's descendants as a lasting kingdom to rule over his people Israel forever.
- *Psalm 89:1–4, 19–26:* A royal psalm, containing praise for God's steadfast love and faithfulness.
- *Romans 16:25–27:* At the close of Paul's letter to the Romans we find a benediction referring to "the revelation of the mystery that was kept secret for long ages but now disclosed, and through the prophetic writings is made known to all the Gentiles, according to the command of the eternal God."

- *Luke 1:26–38:* Jesus' miraculous birth is promised. This reading emphasizes what the child is to be named and the titles by which he will be described: "Son of the Most High, and the Lord God will give to him the throne of his ancestor David. He will reign over the house of Jacob for ever, and of his kingdom there will be no end."

KEY WORDS, IDEAS, AND CONCEPTS TO EXPLORE

- Significance of the house of David
- The "revelation of the mystery"
- Gospel
- Son of God
- Elizabeth, mother of John the Baptist

STORIES TO TELL

- The stories from Matthew and Luke leading up to Jesus' birth.

CHRISTIAN PRACTICE AND LITURGICAL TRADITION

- The references in the liturgy of the church to the House of David and the honor given to King David find their significance in today's lections.
- The honor given Mary stems from her willingness to respond to God's call.
- The tradition of The Jesse Tree, "A shoot shall come out from the stock of Jesse, and a branch shall grow out of his roots."

FORMATION IN BAPTISMAL DISCIPLESHIP

As Mary did, we are called to an open response to God's word and presence.

THE SUNDAYS AFTER THE EPIPHANY

The Second Sunday after the Epiphany, Year B

THEME OF THE LECTIONS

Responding to God's call to be a "light to the nations."

- *The Collect:* See Year A.
- *1 Samuel 3:1–10 (11–20):* Eli recognizes that it is the Lord who is calling Samuel; and he tells Samuel to answer, "Speak, Lord, for your servant is listening."
- *Psalm 139:1–5, 12–17:* The psalmist asserts that he or she is fully known—actions, thoughts, lifestyle, and speech by God, implying our vulnerability and connection to God.

- *1 Corinthians 6:12–20:* Paul speaks against a misunderstanding of Christian freedom; and emphasizes that our bodies are a place of the indwelling Holy Spirit; and the spirit is God's gift to us through baptism. (This Sunday begins a serialized reading of 1 Corinthians 6–9 and 2 Corinthians 1–3; therefore, the epistle reading may not be in thematic harmony with the Old Testament, psalm, and gospel lections.)
- *John 1:43–51:* Jesus calls Philip to be his disciple. Philip goes to Nathaniel and tells him that Jesus of Nazareth is the person who was spoken of by Moses in the Law. Nathaniel questions that the promised Messiah could come from the little town of Nazareth. Jesus surprises Nathaniel when they meet and promises him a heavenly vision.

KEY WORDS, IDEAS, AND CONCEPTS TO EXPLORE
- The temple and the ark of God
- Our bodies are "temples of the Holy Spirit"
- Baptism as being sanctified and washed
- The disciples Philip, Andrew, Simon Peter, and Nathaniel
- The title "rabbi"
- Overview of Paul's correspondence to the Corinthians

STORIES TO TELL
During the early Sundays after the Epiphany, we hear the stories of Jesus calling his disciples. Explore these stories from all three years of the lectionary.

CHRISTIAN PRACTICE AND LITURGICAL TRADITION
The baptismal rite includes elements of being called that reflect Jesus' call to the first disciples: "I present N. to receive the sacrament of baptism . . . Do you renounce Satan . . . Do you turn to Jesus?"

FORMATION IN BAPTISMAL DISCIPLESHIP
Christians see their baptism as a calling into discipleship. Christ calls people into servanthood today as the first disciples were called on lakeshore and in the counting house.

The Third Sunday after the Epiphany, Year B

THEME OF THE LECTIONS
The calling of the disciples, yesterday and today.
- *The Collect:* See Year A.
- *Jonah 3:1–5, 10:* Jonah is sent to Nineveh, where they repent and are saved.

- *Psalm 62:6–12:* God is our rock, and our hope rests finally on the foundation of God's steadfast love.
- *1 Corinthians 7:29–31:* Expecting the end soon created a sense of urgency that changed all relationships—domestic, personal, and economic. A world passing away does not make demands like a world thought to last forever.
- *Mark 1:14–20:* Jesus' early ministry in Galilee, calling his hearers to repentance and God's forgiveness. Simon and his brother Andrew are invited to follow Jesus; and later Jesus calls the sons of Zebedee, James and John, who leave their father and come with Jesus.

KEY WORDS, IDEAS, AND CONCEPTS TO EXPLORE
- Calling of the disciples
- Our calling into discipleship (at baptism)
- Salvation
- Repentance

STORIES TO TELL
- The stories of Jesus calling his disciples continue
- The story of Jonah

CHRISTIAN PRACTICE AND LITURGICAL TRADITION
The Baptismal liturgy asks us to be disciples of Christ. We must make a commitment to change and to grow in Christ's way. This means turning away from evil and separation. We renounce evil and accept Christ.

FORMATION IN BAPTISMAL DISCIPLESHIP
Discipleship includes repentance and commitment.

The Fourth Sunday after the Epiphany, Year B

THEME OF THE LECTIONS
God's word, spoken and embodied in Jesus, is power.
- *The Collect:* See Year A.
- *Deuteronomy 18:15–20:* Moses called all Israel together and told them that God would raise up for them a prophet like Moses. God will reveal his will to the prophet and the prophet will say only what God commands.
- *Psalm 111:* A song of rejoicing for God's marvelous works. "The fear of the Lord is the beginning of wisdom."

- *1 Corinthians 8:1–13:* Paul gives advice to the church at Corinth. Do not use your freedom in the gospel to tempt others to sin who are not so strong in their faith. Act always in love.
- *Mark 1:21–28:* Jesus and his disciples came to Capernaum, and on the Sabbath Jesus taught in the synagogue. A man was suffering from an unclean spirit that recognized Jesus as the Holy One of God. The spirit obeyed Jesus' command to leave the man. "He commands even the unclean spirits, and they obey him."

KEY WORDS, IDEAS, AND CONCEPTS TO EXPLORE
- Prophets
- Idols and false gods
- Scribes
- Unclean spirits
- Exorcism
- Tempting others to sin
- Defeating the power of evil

CHRISTIAN PRACTICE AND LITURGICAL TRADITION
- Jesus had the power to drive out evil from the lives of people. Eucharistic Prayer B states, "In him, you have delivered us from evil, and made us worthy to stand before you"—a vivid reminder that Christ's presence in the Eucharist stands between evil and us today.
- In the Lord's Prayer we ask to be delivered from evil.
- The Baptismal Covenant calls for the faithful to "persevere in resisting evil" (BCP 304).

FORMATION IN BAPTISMAL DISCIPLESHIP
The Christian is called to confront personal and societal evil as a part of the Baptismal Covenant: "Will you persevere in resisting evil, and, whenever you fall into sin, repent and return to the Lord?" (BCP 304).

The Fifth Sunday after the Epiphany, Year B

THEME OF THE LECTIONS
God's power to heal is revealed in the life of the prophets and, above all, in the ministry of Jesus.
- *The Collect:* See Year A.
- *Isaiah 40:21–31:* The very stars adhere to the divine places set for them at creation.

- *Psalm 147:1–12, 21c:* This song of praise features God's activity in the creation and redemption of the world.
- *1 Corinthians 9:16–23:* Whatever he has to do to make it possible for people to hear and understand the gospel, Paul will do. He tries to become all things to all people for the sake of the gospel.
- *Mark 1:29–39:* In the early days of Jesus' ministry there are accounts of his healing many people who were ill or troubled. In today's gospel, Jesus heals Peter's mother-in-law.

KEY WORDS, IDEAS, AND CONCEPTS TO EXPLORE

- The power of God to heal and restore life

STORIES TO TELL

- The healing stories from Mark.

CHRISTIAN PRACTICE AND LITURGICAL TRADITION

- We pray for healing in the Ministration to the Sick (BCP 453–461).
- In the Prayers of the People we pray for those in need of any kind of healing (BCP 383–393).

FORMATION IN BAPTISMAL DISCIPLESHIP

Congregations are called by their baptism into Christ, who heals and restores to life, to the ministry of healing. Intercessions at the Eucharist are embodied by the baptized as they care for one another and as they witness to Christ's healing among them.

The Sixth Sunday after the Epiphany, Year B

THEME OF THE LECTIONS

God's promise of wholeness is revealed in acts of healing.

- *The Collect:* See Year A.
- *2 Kings 5:1–15:* Naaman, commander of the Syrian army, is a leper. He learns though a slave who had been carried off in a raid on Israel that there is a prophet in Samaria who can heal Naaman. The king of Syria sends Naaman to the king of Israel, who knows that he does not possess the power to cure Naaman and fears a plot. Elisha heals Naaman, who says, "Now I know there is no God in all the earth except in Israel."
- *Psalm 30:* A song of thanksgiving that may have been used originally by someone who had been healed from illness.

- *1 Corinthians 9:24–27:* To emphasize the importance of discipline in the Christian life, Paul uses the analogy of runners who compete for a prize—the race for an imperishable crown.
- *Mark 1:40–45:* Jesus heals a leper and tells him not to say anything about his cure, but to go to the priest and make the offering that Moses commanded. The leper spread the word in spite of Jesus' command; and Jesus could not go freely into the towns but had to stay in the country with people coming to him from every direction.

KEY WORDS, IDEAS, AND CONCEPTS TO EXPLORE
- Healing as a sign of God's power
- Elisha the prophet
- Self-control

STORIES TO TELL
- The story of Naaman from 2 Kings.
- The story from Mark of Jesus cleansing a leper.

CHRISTIAN PRACTICE AND LITURGICAL TRADITION
It is the cleansing power which is mediated in the sacrament of absolution and experienced in the Eucharist.

FORMATION IN BAPTISMAL DISCIPLESHIP
The healing power of Jesus' love and word is an instrument of healing that we too can share as Christians. As we see our healing mission as disciples, we too spread the light.

The Seventh Sunday after the Epiphany, Year B

THEME OF THE LECTIONS
The power of God's forgiveness.
- *The Collect:* See Year A.
- *Isaiah 43:18–25:* God speaks of his faithful care for his people Israel, though they have not responded to his love and forgiveness. "I am he who blots out your transgressions for my own sake, and I will not remember your sins."
- *Psalm 41:* The psalmist is upheld by trusting God and will remain in God's presence forever because God always considers the poor.
- *2 Corinthians 1:18–22:* God is faithful and consistent. All the promises of God come straight from Jesus.

- *Mark 2:1–12:* Four men lower a paralytic through a roof into Jesus' presence. Jesus speaks to the paralytic, "Son, your sins are forgiven." In Jesus' time physical and mental illness were thought to be the result of sin, and healing was related to forgiveness.

KEY WORDS, IDEAS, AND CONCEPTS TO EXPLORE
- God's promise
- Healing
- Authority
- Forgiveness

STORIES TO TELL
- The gospel story of the healing of the paralytic.

CHRISTIAN PRACTICE AND LITURGICAL TRADITION
The formal prayers of the church are always offered "through Jesus Christ," reflecting the reading from 2 Corinthians.

FORMATION IN BAPTISMAL DISCIPLESHIP
The church is called to be a healing community.

The Eighth Sunday after the Epiphany, Year B

THEME OF THE LECTIONS
Marriage as a metaphor describing the relationship between God and the faithful.
- *The Collect:* See Year A.
- *Hosea 12:14–20:* Israel is described by the prophet as a faithless wife whom God loves and will once more make his own. God will show his compassion, and the land will answer with grain, wine, and oil.
- *Psalm 103:1–13, 22:* A song of blessing to God for his grace and forgiveness.
- *2 Corinthians 3:1–6:* Christ whose Spirit lives within human hearts is the content of the letter.
- *Mark 2:18–22:* Jesus answers the criticism that his followers do not fast by comparing his time with his disciples to the presence of the bridegroom at a marriage feast.

KEY WORDS, IDEAS, AND CONCEPTS TO EXPLORE
- Glory
- "Unveiled faces"

- Marriage customs in biblical times that shed light on today's lessons
- The use of wineskins
- Fasting as a discipline
- Marriage as a symbol for the Body of Christ

CHRISTIAN PRACTICE AND LITURGICAL TRADITION

The "Exhortation" in the marriage rite (BCP 423) expresses the meaning behind today's lessons.

FORMATION IN BAPTISMAL DISCIPLESHIP

If the congregation is to reflect the gospel, then it will function more like a family than an institution. To come into the church at baptism is to enter into a marriage-like relationship between the baptized and Christ as present in the church. Marriage, in turn, becomes a metaphor to understand Christian relationships between all people who reveal Christ's love for each other.

The Last Sunday after the Epiphany, Year B

THEME OF THE LECTIONS

The Transfiguration of our Lord.
- *The Collect:* See Year A.
- *2 Kings 2:1–12:* Elijah passes his mantle onto Elisha and then ascends in a whirlwind into heaven on a chariot of fire.
- *Psalm 50:1–6:* A divine speech is introduced with an appearance of God.
- *2 Corinthians 4:3–6:* Paul expects the Lord's coming soon, and judgment will be a time of unveiling secrets.
- *Mark 9:2–9:* The Transfiguration account from Mark's gospel.

KEY WORDS, IDEAS, AND CONCEPTS TO EXPLORE

- Transfiguration
- Moses and Elijah
- Theophany
- Holy Mountain

STORIES TO TELL

- The story of God and Elijah and Elisha in 2 Kings.
- The story of Jesus' transfiguration.

CHRISTIAN PRACTICE AND LITURGICAL TRADITION

The Sundays after the Epiphany are framed by both the Feast of the Epiphany, with its star in the heavens, and Jesus' face shining like the sun at the Transfiguration. The light of God's revelation in Jesus becomes clearer in the ensuing weeks as disciples are called and the word is proclaimed.

FORMATION IN BAPTISMAL DISCIPLESHIP

Each Sunday Christians gather "on the mountain top" in the assembly for the revelation of God so that we can see more clearly the way of Christ in our lives.

THE SUNDAYS OF LENT

The First Sunday in Lent, Year B

THE BAPTISMAL RITE

The need for conversion is expressed in the baptismal entrance rite as well as in the renunciations of evil:

- There is one Body and one Spirit. There is one hope in God's call to us (BCP 299).
- Do you renounce Satan and all the spiritual forces of wickedness that rebel against God? (BCP 302).

BAPTISMAL THEME EXPRESSED IN THE LECTIONARY READINGS

- Noah and the ark: Turning away from evil and accepting the covenant of salvation.
- Jesus' temptations: What tempts us away from our baptismal ministry?

THEME OF THE LECTIONS

- *The Collect:* See Year A.
- *Genesis 9:8–17:* The covenant with Noah in which God promises Noah that never again shall the Creation be destroyed by a flood; and designates the rainbow as a sign of divine reassurance to Noah.
- *Psalm 25:1–9:* The Lord is faithful to those who keep his covenant.
- *1 Peter 3:18–22:* To be baptized is to enter into the ark and be "saved" from the swirling waters of death. Note that the word "nave," denoting the place where the congregation gathers, is related to the Latin word for "ship" (navy).
- *Mark 1:9–15:* A description of Jesus' baptism and his acknowledgment by God as his Son, followed by a brief account in which Jesus, led by the

Spirit, is in conflict with the powers of evil and receives the ministrations of angels.

The Second Sunday in Lent, Year B

THE BAPTISMAL RITE

In our baptism we offer ourselves to God in Christ, for in the water of baptism "we are buried with Christ in his death" (BCP 306). This sacrifice of self is reinforced at every celebration of the Eucharist, where we offer "our selves, our souls and bodies, to be a reasonable, holy, and living sacrifice" to God (BCP 336). Each Eucharistic prayer makes some reference to self-offering.

BAPTISMAL THEME EXPRESSED IN THE LECTIONARY READINGS

Saying "yes" to Jesus Christ and offering our lives to God in Christ.

THEME OF THE LECTIONS

- *The Collect:* See Year A.
- *Genesis 17:1–7, 15–16:* Abraham's faith in God is tested, and Abraham demonstrates his readiness to sacrifice his son Isaac in obedience to God's command.
- *Psalm 22:22–30:* God is present to all, including the afflicted. The payment of vows was part of a ritual of gratitude, probably involving a sacrificial meal.
- *Romans 4:13–25:* The promise of many descendants through Isaac is experienced through the righteousness of faith, not through the law (of Moses).
- *Mark 8:31–38:* Jesus was preparing his disciples for his suffering, rejection, and death. When Peter protested, Jesus reproved Peter and spoke to the people as well as the disciples and told them, "If any want to become my followers, let them deny themselves and take up their cross and follow me." Discipleship includes the possibility of really dying.

The Third Sunday in Lent, Year B

THE BAPTISMAL RITE

The Baptismal Covenant (BCP 304–305).

BAPTISMAL THEME EXPRESSED IN THE LECTIONARY READINGS

We are called into a covenant relationship with God at baptism. In Christ there is a new covenant symbolized by Jesus' action of cleansing the temple. In the new covenant, Jesus' body becomes the meeting place between God and creation, rather than the temple in Jerusalem. Paul reminds his readers that the former covenant does not bring life, but only frustration and anguish.

THEME OF THE LECTIONS

- *The Collect:* See Year A.
- *Exodus 20:1–17:* Moses gave the people of Israel the Ten Commandments that can be viewed as a synopsis of the 613 commandments of the Torah. We are called into a covenantal relationship with God.
- *Psalm 19:* The psalmist praises God's law and prays to be saved from secret faults.
- *Corinthians 1:18–25:* The cross, seen as God's folly by the Jews and the Greeks, locates God at the intersection of human foolishness and weakness, overcoming them all.
- *John 2:13–22:* Jesus enters the temple and cleanses it. He speaks of the destruction of the temple and his being able to raise it in three days, symbolically speaking of his own death and resurrection.

The Fourth Sunday in Lent, Year B

THE BAPTISMAL RITE

THE PRAYERS FOR THE CANDIDATES

Deliver them, O Lord, from the way of sin and death. Open their hearts to your grace and truth. Fill them with your holy and life-giving Spirit. Keep them in the faith and communion of your holy Church. Teach them to love others in the power of the Spirit. Send them into the world in witness to your love. Bring them to the fullness of your peace and glory (BCP 305–306).

BAPTISMAL THEME EXPRESSED IN THE LECTIONARY READINGS

God continues to call people back from exile. Salvation (salving/healing) comes as a gift of grace. The Eucharist is the proclamation that Christ sustains us on our journey back from exile. It points to the heavenly banquet where all the faithful will gather with those who have gone before to sing praises to God: "Holy, holy, holy Lord, God of power and might. . . "

THEME OF THE LECTIONS

- *The Collect:* See Year A.
- *Numbers 21:4–9:* The account of Israel's complaint and rebellion against Moses and God while wandering in the wilderness. Snakes then plague the people, and upon Moses' plea to God, the people are healed.

- *Psalm 107:1–3, 17–22:* God delivers the people from their distress, showing his steadfast love for them.
- *Ephesians 2:1–10:* A ringing proclamation that we have been saved through God's grace and not by anything we may have done.
- *John 3:14–21:* God's love is revealed in the giving of his unique Son. The coming of Jesus as the light of the world creates a choice for us to be born of God or to be a child of darkness.

The Fifth Sunday in Lent, Year B

THE BAPTISMAL RITE

THE THANKSGIVING OVER THE WATER

> We thank you, Father, for the water of Baptism. In it we are buried with Christ in his death. By it we share in his resurrection. (BCP 306)

THIS BAPTISMAL TEXT COMES STRAIGHT FROM ST. PAUL

> Therefore we have been buried with (Christ) by baptism into death, so that, just as Christ was raised from the dead by the glory of the Father, so we too might walk in newness of life. (Rom. 6:4)

The Easter Vigil is a liturgical enactment of that process of entering into Christ's death so that we may have life.

> Almighty God, whose most dear Son went not up to joy but first he suffered pain, and entered not into glory before he was crucified: Mercifully grant that we, walking in the way of the cross, may find it none other than the way of life and peace; through Jesus Christ our Lord. (BCP 272)

BAPTISMAL THEME EXPRESSED IN THE LECTIONARY READINGS

In Jesus' death and resurrection and through our baptism, we have a covenant with God written on our hearts.

THEME OF THE LECTIONS

- *The Collect:* See Year A.
- *Jeremiah 31:31–34:* Jeremiah's ringing words of promise are shared. The day will come when God will make a new covenant with the people written on their hearts rather than on stone.
- *Psalm 51:1–13:* A prayer for the gift of a clean heart and the renewal of a right spirit; OR

- *Psalm 119:9–16:* Framed by God's word, the psalmist humbly suggests that there is always more to learn.
- *Hebrews 5: 5–10:* Christ is the eternal high priest who acts as the perfect mediator between God and all people.
- *John 12:20–33:* Jesus speaks in words that reflect his obedience to his Father's will. By losing his life, Jesus brings life for others. A follower of Jesus must look at death and life in the same way.

Refer to Year A for Holy Week and Easter lections.

THE SUNDAYS OF EASTER

The Weeks of Easter, Year B

As in Year A, in Year B we read selections from the Acts of the Apostles for the six weeks of Easter following Easter Sunday because we need to hear the story of the first-century church in order to understand our mission in the world today.

For the epistle lections in Year B we read selections from 1 John. This writing seems to have come out of the community that was influenced by the Gospel of John. The concern of 1 John is to clarify the testimony given about Jesus in the Gospel of John. Heresies were beginning to influence the church, and 1 John was written partly as a corrective to false teachings. In the Easter season, this sequential reading of 1 John provides us with reflections about our faith in Christ that guide us through this period of *mystagogia*.

Selections from the Hebrew Scriptures are provided as alternatives in all three years. When the Hebrew Scriptures are used, they replace either the selection from Acts or the selection from 1 John.

Easter Sunday (Principle Service)

THEME OF THE LECTIONS

The Resurrection of Jesus the Christ is proclaimed.

- *The Collect:* See Year A.
- *Acts of the Apostles 10:34–43:* See First Sunday after the Epiphany, Year A.
- *Isaiah 25:6–9:* See Easter Evening, Year A.
- *Psalm 118:1–2, 14–24:* See Easter Sunday, Year A.
- *1 Corinthians 15:1–11:* An early summary of the teachings of the passion story; Jesus died, was buried, was raised, and appeared, all according to the Scriptures.

- *John 20:1–18:* See Year A; OR
- *Mark 16:1–8:* Three women friends of Jesus came to the tomb early Sunday morning to find the huge stone that had been placed in front of the door rolled away. They went into the tomb and saw a young man, who told them that Jesus had risen. They were to tell his disciples that Jesus would go ahead of them to Galilee. The women were petrified with terror and said nothing to anyone.

The Second Sunday of Easter, Year B

THEME OF THE LECTIONS

We know the risen Christ through faith. "Blessed are those who have not seen and yet have come to believe" (John 20:29b). We may not see the risen Christ but we will know the risen Christ as we gather in faith-filled community on the "eighth day."

- *The Collect:* See Year A.
- *Acts of the Apostles 4:32–35:* Luke's picture of common ownership expresses a vision of the practices of the community of the resurrection.
- *Psalm 133:* A Song of Ascent, featuring imagery of family, Zion, and blessing for the people of God.
- *1 John 1:1–2:2:* Walking in God's light is a common life which we share with the Father and the Son. God is light, and if we claim to share his life while we live in the dark, our lives are a lie. We can admit our sins, because God is just and can be trusted to forgive us.
- *John 20:19–31:* The story of Jesus appearing to Thomas; see Year A.

The Third Sunday of Easter, Year B

THEME OF THE LECTIONS

We know Christ in sacramental life. Jesus appears to the disciples and in eating with them he is able to show that he appears not as a ghost but as the risen Christ. Then he opens "their minds to understand the scriptures" (Luke 36:45), relating what they have experienced with him to what they know of the Hebrew Scriptures. This lection has a focus similar to the Emmaus story in Year A (see Easter 3, Year A).

- *The Collect:* See Year A.
- *Acts of the Apostles 3:12–19:* A prophetic speech to the Jews; Peter shares how Jesus is the fulfillment of the Scriptures.
- *Psalm 4:* A profession of faith.
- *1 John 3:1–7:* The love that the Father has shown for us in Jesus Christ

makes every Christian a child of God; but what we shall become as children of God remains a mystery.

- *Luke 24:36b–48:* The risen Lord comes to his disciples; they cannot believe the evidence of their senses. He invites them to touch him; he eats a piece of fish they had cooked. He explains that everything that has happened was part of God's intention for him, and that they are witnesses.

The Fourth Sunday of Easter, Year B

THEME OF THE LECTIONS

The risen Christ is known through the ministry of the church modeled by Jesus, the Good Shepherd.

- *The Collect:* See Year A.
- *Acts of the Apostles 4:5–12:* Peter confronts the Jewish rulers and elders about the authority of the Holy Spirit and Jesus' role as messiah and savior.
- *Psalm 23:* See Year A.
- *1 John 3:16–24:* Love must be genuine and must show itself in action. God has commanded us to believe in his Son Jesus Christ and to love one another as Jesus commanded.
- *John 10:11–18:* Jesus describes himself as the Good Shepherd who lays down his life for his sheep. The Good Shepherd has other sheep (non-Jews) whom he must bring to the Father, and these sheep will also listen to his voice. The Good Shepherd lays down his life of his own free will in obedience to the Father, and he will receive it again.

The Fifth Sunday of Easter, Year B

THEME OF THE LECTIONS

A new community is formed out of the resurrection; the indwelling of the Holy Spirit is the life of that community. Jesus promises his followers that those who love him will be guided by the Holy Spirit and will also see him. Jesus reminds his followers that though he will soon leave them in death, he will send them the Holy Spirit. Those who follow the commandments of love will find new life in intimate association with Jesus and the Father.

- *The Collect:* See Year A.
- *Acts of the Apostles 8:26–40:* Philip baptizes the Ethiopian eunuch and proclaims the good news beyond Jerusalem.
- *Psalm 22:24–30:* All will participate in the saving grace of God.

- *1 John 4:7–21:* The command has come to us from Christ, that if we love God we must also love one another. "God is love" is not a way of defining God; it describes God's redeeming action through Christ.
- *John 15:1–8:* Jesus tells his disciples that he is the true vine, those who believe in him are its branches, and his Father is the gardener who prunes and tends the vine. The union of vine and branches speaks powerfully of Christians being part of Jesus and of one another.

The Sixth Sunday of Easter, Year B

THEME OF THE LECTIONS

The theme of the new community formed out of the resurrection and the indwelling of the Holy Spirit in the life of that community is grounded in love.

- *The Collect:* See Year A.
- *Acts of the Apostles 10:44–48:* The Holy Spirit is given to all who hear the word, including the Gentiles.
- *Psalm 98:* God's gift of life to the people reveals God's steadfast love and faithfulness.
- *1 John 5:1–6:* Faith is the basis for love and becomes the victory that conquers the world.
- *John 15:9–17:* Jesus speaks of his great love for his disciples, which has come to him from the Father, and calls upon them to show the same love toward each other. This love has formed his followers into a new community in relationship with Jesus and the Father, no longer servants but friends.

The Seventh Sunday of Easter, Year B

THEME OF THE LECTIONS

The church is consecrated as the Body of Christ. The Holy Spirit empowers and sanctifies the church. The Body of Christ becomes a living sacrament to the world, an "outward and visible sign" of Christ's redeeming presence in history. "Sanctify them in the truth; your word is truth. As you have sent me into the world, so I have sent them into the world. And for their sakes I sanctify myself, so that they also may be sanctified in truth" (John 17:17–19).

- *The Collect:* See Year A.
- *Acts of the Apostles 1:15–17, 21–26:* Peter tells about the death of Judas and the need to choose someone to fill Judas' place among the twelve

apostles. The choice fell upon Matthias, who had been with them from Jesus' baptism and had witnessed his resurrection.

- *Psalm 1:* Happy are those who are open to a relationship with God.
- *1 John 5:9–13:* God has given us eternal life, and this life is found in Christ Jesus his Son. If we believe in the Son we truly have life. If we refuse to accept God's own witness to his Son, we will not have eternal life.
- *John 17:6–19:* In his final time with his disciples, Jesus intercedes for them with the Father, through prayer.

PENTECOST

The Day of Pentecost, Year B

THEME OF THE LECTIONS

- *The Collect:* See Year A.
- *Acts of the Apostles 2:1–21:* See Year A.
- *Numbers 11:24–30:* The Spirit descends upon Moses and the seventy elders whom God called to assist Moses with the people as they wandered in the wilderness.
- *Psalm 104:25–35, 37:* See Year A.
- *1 Corinthians 12:3b–13:* All Christians are brought into one body by baptism, in the one Spirit. We have been given varieties of gifts but the same Spirit. There are varieties of service, but the same Lord.
- *John 20:19–23:* An account of the evening of the first Easter when Jesus appeared to his disciples behind locked doors, greeting them, "Peace be with you." He breathed on them, saying, "Receive the Holy Spirit"; OR
- *John 7:37–39:* The Spirit that flows out through Jesus, as water flowed out of the rock for the Israelites.

TRINITY SUNDAY

Trinity Sunday, Year B

THEME OF THE LECTIONS

The God of history is revealed in three persons: Father, Son, and Spirit.

- *The Collect:* See Year A.
- *Isaiah 6:1–8:* Isaiah had a vision of the Lord high on a throne, surrounded

by seraphim that sang praises to God. It is in this vision that Isaiah receives and accepts his call with "Here am I; send me!"

- *Psalm 29:* An enthronement psalm glorifying the heavenly beings OR Canticle 2 OR Canticle 13.
- *Romans 8:12–17:* If we are led by the Spirit of God we are children of God. When we cry, "Abba! Father!" the Spirit bears witness that we are children and heirs of God and fellow-heirs of Christ. We must share the sufferings of Christ to share his glory.
- *John 3:1–17:* Nicodemus, a member of the Jewish Council, comes in the light to talk to Jesus about how it is possible to be born again. Jesus tells him that this gift comes through water and the Spirit (baptism) and through God loving the world so much that he gave his only Son so that everyone who has faith in him would have eternal life.

KEY WORDS, IDEAS, AND CONCEPTS TO EXPLORE

- Trinity
- Seraphim and cherubim
- Names of God
- Abba
- Heirs with Christ

STORIES TO TELL

- The story of the call of Isaiah.
- The story of God of Nicodemus.

CHRISTIAN PRACTICE AND LITURGICAL TRADITION

Part of the text of the Sanctus, which is sung or said at every Eucharist, is taken from Isaiah 6 (Holy, Holy, Holy).

FORMATION IN BAPTISMAL DISCIPLESHIP

Christians are called to be holy, as God is holy.

THE SEASON AFTER PENTECOST

Proper 4, Year B (The Sunday Closest to June 1)

THEME OF THE LECTIONS

Jesus has ultimate authority, even over the commandments of the Torah.

- *The Collect:* See Year A.

- *1 Samuel 3:1–10, (11–20):* The call of Samuel as a boy in the Temple.
- *Psalm 139:1–5, 12–17:* God searches and knows his creation. God's presence and spirit are inescapable.
- *2 Corinthians 4:5–12:* For Paul, participating in Christ's death means living in a way that Jesus' presence is experienced in the lives of the faithful. We are called to proclaim Jesus Christ as Lord.
- *Mark 2:23–3:6:* Jesus' explanation of how the Sabbath should be observed, counter to rabbinic law of the day.

ALTERNATIVE READINGS
- Deuteronomy 5:12–15
- Psalm 81:1–10

KEY WORDS, IDEAS, AND CONCEPTS TO EXPLORE
- Call
- Sabbath
- Ultimate authority of Jesus
- Treasure in earthen vessels
- Bearing the cross of Christ
- This week begins a six-week reading of 2 Corinthians. Take time in the educational setting to provide an overview of the epistle.

STORIES TO TELL
- The call of Samuel.

CHRISTIAN PRACTICE AND LITURGICAL TRADITION
The practice of Sabbath is counter-cultural in today's world. The Ten Commandments remind us to set aside a day to keep holy and give thanks to God each week.

FORMATION IN BAPTISMAL DISCIPLESHIP
The sense of covenant that incorporates demands for faithfulness with the promise of abundant life lies at the heart of Christian life; at the same time, the church lives by grace and not by law.

Proper 5, Year B (The Sunday Closest to June 8)

THEME OF THE LECTIONS
Doing the will of God.
- *The Collect:* See Year A.

- *1 Samuel 8:4–11, (12–15), 16–20, (11:14–15):* The people of Israel cry out to Samuel to give them a king to rule over them such as the other nations. Saul is chosen to be their first king.
- *Psalm 138:* God alone is to be worshipped; celebrate God's steadfast love and faithfulness.
- *2 Corinthians 4:13–5:1:* We know that God who raised the Lord Jesus to life will raise us too. Our eyes are fixed on the things that are unseen; what is seen passes away; the unseen is eternal. Faith leads to hope even in the face of adversity.
- *Mark 3:20–35:* Jesus tells his accusers that we sin against the Holy Spirit when we do not see that Satan may be present in our judgments of others. All who do the will of God is brother, sister, mother to Christ.

ALTERNATIVE READINGS
- Genesis 3:8–15
- Psalm 130

KEY WORDS, IDEAS, AND CONCEPTS TO EXPLORE
- Disobedience
- Hubris (wanting to be like God)
- Faith
- Thanksgiving
- Satan
- Beelzebub
- Demons
- Being brothers and sisters of Christ

STORIES TO TELL
- Samuel's selection of Saul as Israel's first king.

CHRISTIAN PRACTICE AND LITURGICAL TRADITION
In Old Testament times, anointing involved smearing a person's head with scented oil as a way of designating the person for a particular office. We are "anointed" or "sealed" with oil (Chrism) at Baptism and marked as Christ's own forever (BCP 308).

FORMATION IN BAPTISMAL DISCIPLESHIP
An awareness of the need for humility in the face of God's ultimate wisdom and authority must inform the life of the congregation and the individual Christian.

Proper 6, Year B (The Sunday Closest to June 15)

THEME OF THE LECTIONS

The kingdom of God arrives through God's grace, not by human striving for power.

- *The Collect:* See Year A.
- *1 Samuel 15:34–16:13:* he anointing of David by Samuel to become king of Israel over Saul.
- *Psalm 20:* The anointed is the king, the earthly agent of God's rule.
- *2 Corinthians 5:6–10, (11–13), 14–17:* Paul realizes that his destiny is yet to come. Looking to the future, he longs for the time when human suffering will end and our lives will be laid open before Christ.
- *Mark 4:26–34:* Jesus taught the people parables about the kingdom of God: how seed, scattered on the land in secret, grows until it has produced a crop and harvest time has come; or the tiny mustard seed, which once planted grows taller and larger than other plants and forms branches to make shade for the birds.

ALTERNATIVE READINGS

- Ezekiel 17:22–24
- Psalm 92:1–4, 11–14

KEY WORDS, IDEAS, AND CONCEPTS TO EXPLORE

- Anointing
- Kingdom of God
- Parable
- The mustard plant
- Harvest
- Hubris

STORIES TO TELL

- The anointing of David.
- The parables of the growing seed and mustard seed.

CHRISTIAN PRACTICE AND LITURGICAL TRADITION

The traditions associated with Rogation Days emphasize God's presence in the mystery of creation and growth in the natural world. The proper for Rogation Days includes the text from today's gospel (BCP 930).

214

FORMATION IN BAPTISMAL DISCIPLESHIP

God plants his kingdom in us and in creation. Sometimes growth comes so slowly that it is imperceptible. We may become discouraged, but God's kingdom is happening nevertheless.

Proper 7, Year B (The Sunday Closest to June 22)

THEME OF THE LECTIONS

God's power to still the storms of nature and of evil is revealed in Jesus.

- *The Collect:* See Year A.
- *1 Samuel 17:(1a, 4–11, 19–23), 32–49:* David, youngest son of Jesse, defeats the Philistine, Goliath, with a shepherd's sling. King Saul then honors him.
- *Psalm 9:9–20:* God's justice will be manifest as the wicked destroy themselves.
- *2 Corinthians 6:1–13:* Paul calls the Corinthians to work together as ministers of God despite their hardships and disagreements.
- *Mark 4:35–41:* When a storm came up on the lake and frightened the disciples, Jesus rebuked the wind and commanded the sea to be still. His followers were filled with awe and asked, "Who then is this, that even the wind and the sea obey him?"

ALTERNATIVE READINGS

- 1 Samuel 17:57–18:5, 10–16
- Psalm 133
- Job 38:1–11
- Psalm 107:1–3, 23–32

KEY WORDS, IDEAS, AND CONCEPTS TO EXPLORE

- God's power of evil
- Ministers of God
- Role of deacons

STORIES TO TELL

- David and Goliath.
- The story of Jesus stilling the storm.

CHRISTIAN PRACTICE AND LITURGICAL TRADITION

- Candidates renounce evil at their baptism (BCP 302).

- We ask God to "deliver us from evil" every time we offer the Lord's Prayer.
- Eucharistic Prayer B includes the phrase, "You have delivered us from evil, and made us worthy to stand before you" (BCP 368).

FORMATION IN BAPTISMAL DISCIPLESHIP

The passing of the peace in the liturgy dramatizes the role of the Christian in the world. Reconciliation is expressed as an essential component in congregational life, which is precisely why the peace is shared every time Christians gather for Eucharist. Evil is taken seriously in the liturgy, in counseling, and in social witness.

Proper 8, Year B (The Sunday Closest to June 29)

THEME OF THE LECTIONS

God's power to heal and bring life even out of death is revealed in Jesus.
- *The Collect:* See Year A.
- *2 Samuel 1:1, 17–27:* David's lament over the deaths of Saul and Jonathan, calling the Israelites to mourn the loss.
- *Psalm 130:* A plea for deliverance from a chaotic situation, to which one's sins have contributed.
- *2 Corinthians 8:7–15:* God accepts what we have to give. Paul is trying to bring about a relationship of mutual responsibility among the churches in Corinth to be generous in their giving.
- *Mark 5:21–43:* Jairus, a leader in one of the synagogues, came to Jesus and begged him to save the life of his daughter. While Jairus was pleading with Jesus, a messenger came to say that the child was dead. Jesus told Jairus not to be afraid but to have faith. Jesus went to his home, and healed the child.

ALTERNATIVE READINGS

- Wisdom of Solomon 1:13–15; 2:23–24
- Canticle: Lamentations 3:21–33: A Song of God's Mercy
- Psalm 30

KEY WORDS, IDEAS, AND CONCEPTS TO EXPLORE

- Mourning
- Life and death
- Healing
- Raising to life
- Stewardship

- Generosity
- Charity
- Alms

STORIES TO TELL
- David and Jonathan.
- The healing of Jairus' daughter.

CHRISTIAN PRACTICE AND LITURGICAL TRADITION
- The offertory at the Eucharist is a weekly call to generosity. Tithes and gifts are offered for the needs of others.
- The dismissal from the Eucharist includes the exhortation to "Go in peace to love and serve the Lord."

FORMATION IN BAPTISMAL DISCIPLESHIP
Acts 2:43–47 describes a church in which everything was held in common and distributed to each person as needed. This vision of congregational life, as idealistic as it may seem, must shape the church's understanding of community, stewardship, and the Baptismal Covenant, which calls for the Christian to "seek and serve Christ in all persons" (BCP 305).

Proper 9, Year B (The Sunday Closest to July 6)

THEME OF THE LECTIONS
Jesus' rejection by his own people, but God's grace overcomes all.
- *The Collect:* See Year A.
- *2 Samuel 5:1–5, 9–10:* The people of Israel claim David as one of their own even though he was from Judah. He is anointed king and begins to build up the Jerusalem, the City of David.
- *Psalm 48:* A song of Zion, it affirms that Jerusalem symbolizes God's universal sovereignty.
- *2 Corinthians 12:2–10:* Paul has been granted visions and revelations. He realizes that his weakness is turned into strength through God's grace.
- *Mark 6:1–13:* Jesus heals and teaches in his hometown, Nazareth. The people are offended by his actions. He is dismayed by the lack of faith of the people there.

ALTERNATIVE READINGS
- Ezekiel 2:1–5
- Psalm 123

KEY WORDS, IDEAS, AND CONCEPTS TO EXPLORE

- Jerusalem
- The role of a king
- Prophet
- Rejection of God's word
- Grace
- Power known in weakness

STORIES TO TELL

- David's reign as king.

CHRISTIAN PRACTICE AND LITURGICAL TRADITION

The role of the prophets is central to the biblical story. We read the words of Jesus in the gospels to see what he might be saying to us "in the flesh" of our human experience. The gospel readings are offered as a way of moving us to discover how Christ is encountering us personally in our daily lives.

FORMATION IN BAPTISMAL DISCIPLESHIP

The church that follows Christ will experience rejection and alienation.

Proper 10, Year B (The Sunday Closest to July 13)

THEME OF THE LECTIONS

New life following a time of death and mourning.

- *The Collect:* See Year A.
- *2 Samuel 6:1–5, 12b–19:* David brings the Ark of the Covenant to Jerusalem. It is viewed as the throne of the Lord; God is now in the midst of the people.
- *Psalm 24:* An entrance liturgy, it was probably used originally in a procession of worshippers accompanied by the Ark of the Covenant into the Temple. The preparation of one's self and profession of faith anticipates God's sovereignty.
- *Ephesians 1:3–14:* Paul's letter to the church at Ephesus begins with a prayer of praise to God for all that he has done for us in Christ.
- *Mark 6:14–29:* Mark recounts the death of John the Baptist in a flashback, after Herod wonders if Jesus is the baptizer now risen from the dead.

ALTERNATIVE READINGS

- Amos 7:7–15
- Psalm 85:8–13

KEY WORDS, IDEAS, AND CONCEPTS TO EXPLORE

- Ark of the Covenant
- Cherubim
- Burnt offerings
- Praise
- Anointing
- Herod
- This week begins an eight-week, semi-continuous reading of Ephesians. Take time to introduce the epistle as an educational offering.

STORIES TO TELL

- David's dancing.
- The life and ministry of John the Baptist.

CHRISTIAN PRACTICE AND LITURGICAL TRADITION

- Music, song, and dance are central ways we praise God in our worship today.
- Ephesians 1:13 ("marked with the seal of the promised Holy Spirit") and other texts lie behind the anointing at baptism: "You are sealed by the Holy Spirit in Baptism and marked as Christ's own for ever" (BCP 308).

FORMATION IN BAPTISMAL DISCIPLESHIP

Adoration is a form of prayer in which we lift up our hearts and minds to God, asking nothing but to enjoy God's presence.

Proper 11, Year B (The Sunday Closest to July 20)

THEME OF THE LECTIONS

God dwells with us through Jesus.

- *The Collect:* See Year A.
- *2 Samuel 7:1–14a:* David desires to build a temple for the Lord. God declares that he doesn't desire a dwelling place, but will make David a "house," a great name and dynasty for generations to come.
- *Psalm 89:20–37:* The promises of the covenant with David and his children.
- *Ephesians 2:11–22:* The law of the Jewish people stood like a "dividing wall" between the Jews and the Gentiles. Paul reminds the congregation at Ephesus that Christ is our peace. The Christian is the living temple of God in the world.
- *Mark 6:30–34, 53–56:* Jesus is recognized wherever he goes by the people. They follow him and are healed by his touch.

ALTERNATIVE READINGS
- Jeremiah 23:1–6
- Psalm 23

KEY WORDS, IDEAS, AND CONCEPTS TO EXPLORE
- Covenant
- House of David
- Peace
- Household of God
- Foundation of the apostles
- Dwelling place of God in the Spirit
- The Temple as the meeting place between God and the people

STORIES TO TELL
- Jesus' healing stories.

CHRISTIAN PRACTICE AND LITURGICAL TRADITION
- Our churches are sanctuaries for prayer and healing.
- The Ministration of the Sick is a service that includes the Laying on of Hands and Anointing. Many call these "healing services" (BCP 453–461).

FORMATION IN BAPTISMAL DISCIPLESHIP
Christ has compassion for the people of the church and the world who hunger for God's word and healing.

Proper 12, Year B (The Sunday Closest to July 27)

THEME OF THE LECTIONS
Jesus' compassion for the people leads him to respond with food for mind and body. The feeding of the five thousand expresses the significance of the Holy Eucharist. This Eucharistic theme will be carried on in Propers 13, 14, 15, and 16, Year B. God's power is revealed in Jesus as the waters are parted and calmed.
- *The Collect:* See Year A.
- *2 Samuel 11:1–15:* David plots to make Bathsheba his wife.
- *Psalm 14:* An indictment to those who are evildoers, while those who are righteous are favored by God.
- *Ephesians 3:14–21:* A prayer for Christ to dwell in our hearts through faith, followed by the doxology, "to him be glory in the church and in Christ Jesus to all generations, for ever and ever. Amen."

- *John 6:1–21:* The feeding of the five thousand, followed by Jesus' rejection of the attempt to make him king. Jesus also shows his control over nature by walking on the water and stilling the storm.

ALTERNATIVE READINGS

- 2 Kings 4:42–44
- Psalm 145:10–19

KEY WORDS, IDEAS, AND CONCEPTS TO EXPLORE

- Sin
- God as king
- Eucharist
- God's power over the waters (beginning with Genesis 1)

STORIES TO TELL

- The story David and Bathsheba.
- The story of the Feeding of the Five Thousand.
- The story of Jesus walking on the water.

CHRISTIAN PRACTICE AND LITURGICAL TRADITION

"Grace is God's favor towards us, unearned and undeserved. By grace God forgives our sins, enlightens our minds, stirs our hearts, and strengthens our wills" (BCP 858). The Eucharist is one of the means by which we receive God's grace.

FORMATION IN BAPTISMAL DISCIPLESHIP

To accept the reality of Christ's presence in the bread of the sacrament is to be open to a whole new dimension of life. It is the Lord who is the source of our life and strength. It is he who quiets the waters and winds around us if we have the faith to perceive his presence. Our eyes become open to the events that happen around us as we see the Lord feeding us in the sacrament.

Proper 13, Year B (The Sunday Closest to August 3)

THEME OF THE LECTIONS

A continuation of the Eucharistic theme from Proper 12, Year B. Jesus is the bread of heaven. (See Propers 12, 14, 15, and 16, Year B.)

- *The Collect:* See Year A.
- *2 Samuel 11:26–12:13a:* Nathan brings a legal case before David. As king he was responsible for ensuring the rights of the poor. David recognizes himself in the story, acknowledges his transgressions, and receives God's punishment.

- *Psalm 51:1–13:* A prayer for help, acknowledging one's personal sinfulness.
- *Ephesians 4:1–16:* Paul calls the Christians in Ephesus to be humble, patient, and loving toward one another. The variety of individual gifts that equip God's people for mission in his service contributes to the unity of the church. Christians are all part of the one Body and the one Spirit in Christ.
- *John 6:24–35:* The crowds continue to follow Jesus looking for food. He appeals to them to seek the food of eternal life.

ALTERNATIVE READINGS

- Exodus 16:2–4, 9–15
- Psalm 78:23–29

KEY WORDS, IDEAS, AND CONCEPTS TO EXPLORE

- Eucharistic actions (took bread, blessed, broke, gave)
- Manna
- Bread of life
- Put on the new nature of Christ
- Spiritual gifts
- Unity of the church

STORIES TO TELL

- The prophecies and teachings of Nathan.
- The feeding of the Israelites in the wilderness.

CHRISTIAN PRACTICE AND LITURGICAL TRADITION

In the Eucharist we are given the bread "which comes down from heaven and gives life to the world" (John 6:33).

FORMATION IN BAPTISMAL DISCIPLESHIP

In celebrating the Holy Eucharist week by week we both participate in and receive the Body of Christ.

Proper 14, Year B (The Sunday Closest to August 10)

THEME OF THE LECTIONS

A continuation of the Bread of Life theme. (See Propers 12, 13, 15, and 16, Year B.)

- *The Collect:* See Year A.
- *2 Samuel 18:5–9, 15, 31–33:* The death of Absalom and David's grief following his hearing the results of the battle against him.

- *Psalm 130:* A pleading for deliverance from a chaotic situation followed by evidence of God's forgiveness and steadfast love.
- *Ephesians 4:25–5:2:* Paul explains that falsehood, anger, dishonesty, and bad language have no part in the life of a Christian. He urges not to grieve the Holy Spirit, the seal with which we are marked in our baptism, but to be generous, tenderhearted, and forgiving.
- *John 6:35, 41–51:* Jesus tells his listeners that he is the living bread, which has come down from heaven; those who eat this bread will live forever. The bread Jesus gives is his own flesh and he gives it for the life of the world.

ALTERNATIVE READINGS
- 1 Kings 19:4–8
- Psalm 34:108

KEY WORDS, IDEAS, AND CONCEPTS TO EXPLORE
- Grief
- Forgiveness
- God's steadfast love
- Manna
- Jesus, the Bread of Life
- "Sealed by the Holy Spirit"
- The "I am" statements of Jesus

STORIES TO TELL
- David and Absalom.

CHRISTIAN PRACTICE AND LITURGICAL TRADITION
The ancient rite of anointing in baptism reflects the epistle for today: "N., *you are sealed by the Holy Spirit in Baptism and marked as Christ's own for ever*" (BCP 308).

FORMATION IN BAPTISMAL DISCIPLESHIP
The letter to the Ephesians reminds us that Christians are called to "live in love, as Christ loved us," to be kind and tenderhearted in our forgiveness of one another. Paul gives us instruction about communal life in the church.

Proper 15, Year B (The Sunday Closest to August 17)

THEME OF THE LECTIONS

A continuation of the Bread of Life theme. (See Propers 12, 13, 14, and 16, Year B). God's Word (Logos, Wisdom) brings the life-giving knowledge of God. God's Word is the very bread of life.

- *The Collect:* See Year A.
- *1 Kings 2:10–12; 3:3–14:* David's death and burial. Solomon becomes king and God grants his request for wisdom and promises him wealth as well.
- *Psalm 111:* A psalm of praise for God's works and actions.
- *Ephesians 5:15–20:* Paul cautions the congregations to try to discern the will of the Lord and to act like sensible people. They are to let the Holy Spirit fill them and to give daily thanks for everything to God in the Lord Jesus Christ's name. Live as a new people, giving up your old ways.
- *John 6:51–58:* Jesus describes the central significance of the Eucharist—he is truly the bread of heaven, and whoever eats his flesh and drinks his blood shall receive eternal life.

ALTERNATIVE READINGS

- Proverbs 9:1–6
- Psalm 34:9–14

KEY WORDS, IDEAS, AND CONCEPTS TO EXPLORE

- God's wisdom
- *Logos*
- Psalms, hymns, spiritual songs
- Bread of heaven
- The flesh and blood of Christ

STORIES TO TELL

- Solomon as king.

CHRISTIAN PRACTICE AND LITURGICAL TRADITION

- The wonderful heritage of hymnody is expressed in the reading from Ephesians.
- The writer of the Gospel of John sees Jesus as the incarnation of God's Wisdom, who came to humanity in the flesh of Jesus to reveal God's Word by living it fully among people: *In the beginning was the Word, and the Word was with God, and the Word was God . . . And the Word became flesh and lived among us* (John 1:1, 14a).

FORMATION IN BAPTISMAL DISCIPLESHIP
To know Christ is to know God's wisdom. To know that wisdom is like being fed at a banquet table.

Proper 16, Year B (The Sunday Closest to August 24)

THEME OF THE LECTIONS
The conclusion of the Bread of Life theme from Propers 12,13,14, and 15, Year B, with the disciples' response to Jesus' pronouncement that he is the "bread of life."
- *The Collect:* See Year A.
- *1 Kings 8:(1, 6, 10–11), 22–30, 41–43:* Solomon's prayer praising God and requesting the continuation of the covenant with Israel.
- *Psalm 84:* The source of happiness is centered in God's presence and sovereignty.
- *Ephesians 6:10–20:* A call to arms and prayer for strength to proclaim the truth. "Put on the whole armor of God."
- *John 6:56–69:* Jesus continues to speak of himself as the bread of heaven, and of the life of the spirit, but many of his hearers were taking what he said literally.

ALTERNATIVE READINGS
- Joshua 24:1–2a, 14–18
- Psalm 34:15–22

KEY WORDS, IDEAS, AND CONCEPTS TO EXPLORE
- Discipleship
- Bread of life
- Calling into covenant relationship

STORIES TO TELL
- Solomon's kingship.

CHRISTIAN PRACTICE AND LITURGICAL TRADITION
The baptismal rite expresses the sense of call and the theme of choice (*"Do you desire to be baptized?"*). To be baptized is to enter into an eternal covenant with God.

FORMATION IN BAPTISMAL DISCIPLESHIP
Christians are called in baptism into an eternal covenant with God.

Proper 17, Year B (The Sunday Closest to August 31)

THEME OF THE LECTIONS

Putting the love of God and neighbor above pious empty practices.

- *The Collect:* See Year A.
- *Song of Solomon 2:8–13:* A women's love poem.
- *Psalm 45:1–2, 7–10:* A love song, perhaps to a king or at a wedding.
- *James 1:17–27:* God's person and gifts are pure. True believers keep themselves pure, unstained by the world. We are to be doers of the word, not only hearers.
- *Mark 7:1–8, 14–15, 21–23:* The Pharisees and scribes asked Jesus why his disciples did not live in accordance with tradition, but ate without washing their hands. Jesus said to those who were listening that it is not what goes into a person that makes them unclean, it is the evil that comes out of their heart that defiles them.

ALTERNATIVE READINGS

- Deuteronomy 4:1–2, 6–9
- Psalm 15

KEY WORDS, IDEAS, AND CONCEPTS TO EXPLORE

- God's steadfast love
- Purity laws
- Ceremonial traditions of the Pharisees
- This week begins a four-week, semi-continuous reading of James. Take time to set the stage for the hearing of this epistle.

CHRISTIAN PRACTICE AND LITURGICAL TRADITION

The history of liturgical change through the reform of the Book of Common Prayer has shown how the church has sought to be faithful to our theological and ethical convictions. In essence, liturgy is the work of the people. As Episcopalians, we use reason to connect Scripture and tradition to culture, changing human experience, and new knowledge. From the first Book of Common Prayer of 1549 to our current 1979 book, as well as *Book of Occasional Services* and supplemental texts, such as *Enriching Our Worship*, we continue to be cognizant of how we worship.

FORMATION IN BAPTISMAL DISCIPLESHIP

In a church that finds meaning in ceremonial ritual worship, it is important always to examine those practices in the light of this Sunday's lessons.

Proper 18, Year B (The Sunday Closest to September 7)

THEME OF THE LECTIONS

Faith is shown by one's actions, especially in showing compassion. Jesus is a sign of the dawning of God's reign.

- *The Collect:* See Year A.
- *Proverbs 22:1–2, 8–9, 22–23:* Words of the wise offering a professional ethic of care for the poor.
- *Psalm 125:* Trust in the Lord, who wills peace over the wicked.
- *James 2:1–10, (11–13), 14–17:* No special treatment is to be given to the rich; the law to be observed is given in Scripture: "Love your neighbor as yourself." Faith that does not lead to action has no life.
- *Mark 7:24–37:* Jesus' healing of the Syrophoenician woman's daughter and the deaf man with a speech impediment.

ALTERNATIVE READINGS

- Isaiah 35:4–7a
- Psalm 146

KEY WORDS, IDEAS, AND CONCEPTS TO EXPLORE

- "Doers of the word"
- First fruits
- The kingdom of God
- Healing
- Care for the poor

STORIES TO TELL

- The healing of the Syrophoencian woman's daughter.
- The healing of the deaf man with a speech impediment.

CHRISTIAN PRACTICE AND LITURGICAL TRADITION

We pray for God's kingdom to come every time we pray the Lord's Prayer.

FORMATION IN BAPTISMAL DISCIPLESHIP

One of the statements we affirm in the Baptismal Covenant, with God's help, is *"to seek and serve Christ in all persons, loving your neighbor as yourself."*

Proper 19, Year B (The Sunday Closest to September 14)

THEME OF THE LECTIONS

Peter recognizes Jesus as the Christ. The cost of discipleship includes bearing the cross.

- *The Collect:* See Year A.
- *Proverbs 1:20–33:* Woman Wisdom warns the simple (whom seem to have previously rejected teaching) that she will not be there when the inevitable disaster comes upon them. However, there is always a new chance to accept her.
- *Psalm 19:* The all-encompassing importance of God's instruction OR
- Canticle—*Wisdom 7:26–8:1:* A Song in Praise of Wisdom.
- *James 3:1–12:* James urges control over the mouth as it can speak both blessing and curse. However, one cannot bless God and curse others.
- *Mark 8:27–38:* In response to a question from Jesus, Peter answered that Jesus was the Messiah. Jesus began to speak plainly to them about his coming suffering, rejection, and death. Peter protested and was rebuked by Jesus. "If any want to become my followers, let them deny themselves and take up their cross and follow me."

ALTERNATIVE READINGS

- Isaiah 50:4–9a
- Psalm 116:1–8

KEY WORDS, IDEAS, AND CONCEPTS TO EXPLORE

- "Doers of the word"
- Faith and works
- Christ/Messiah
- The power of words and speech
- Taking up the cross

STORIES TO TELL

- Peter as an apostle of Jesus.

CHRISTIAN PRACTICE AND LITURGICAL TRADITION

Stories of persons from *Lesser Feasts and Fasts* who have participated in the suffering of others to bring healing into their lives are part of our tradition. Stories of doctors, nurses, researchers in medical science who risked their lives, social workers among the poor and oppressed, political leaders and others who have attempted to enter the struggle of suffering would be appropriate to study.

FORMATION IN BAPTISMAL DISCIPLESHIP

Christian congregations must practice hospitality to all people, with an imperative to reach out to the poor. The call to respond to human need comes directly from Scripture and the Baptismal Covenant.

Proper 20, Year B (The Sunday Closest to September 21)

THEME OF THE LECTIONS

Jesus predicts his passion a second time and reminds his disciples that to be great in the kingdom of God is to be the servant of all.

- *The Collect:* See Year A.
- *Proverbs 31:10–31:* Within the house are all the blessings of wisdom— wealth, justice, generosity to the poor, reputation, children, and a good spouse. The pursuit of wisdom has brought every blessing.
- *Psalm 1:* Happy are those who are open to God's teaching.
- *James 3:13–4:3, 7–8a:* True wisdom is peace-loving, considerate, and reasonable. Jealousy and ambition bring disorder and evil. The church must live by the values of the gospel, not of the world.
- *Mark 9:30–37:* Jesus' disciples argue about which of them is the greatest. "Whoever wants to be first must be last of all and servant of all." Jesus then puts his arm around a child saying, "Whoever welcomes one such child in my name welcomes me, and whoever welcomes me welcomes not me but the one who sent me."

ALTERNATIVE READINGS

- Wisdom of Solomon 1:16–2:1, 12–22
- Jeremiah 11:18–20
- Psalm 54

KEY WORDS, IDEAS, AND CONCEPTS TO EXPLORE

- Servant of all
- Son of Man
- Wisdom
- Envy and selfish ambition
- Friendship with the world

STORIES TO TELL

- The story of Jesus welcoming a child.

CHRISTIAN PRACTICE AND LITURGICAL TRADITION

- The tradition of foot washing on Maundy Thursday dramatizes Jesus' words in today's gospel text about servanthood.
- Jesus' passion, suffering, and death are remembered every time the Holy Eucharist is celebrated. The Eucharist proclaims Jesus' servant ministry as a way of life.

FORMATION IN BAPTISMAL DISCIPLESHIP

The first in God's kingdom will be least of all and servant of all. Jesus' life of witness to God's way raises hostility among those who feel judged by his life. God's wisdom often runs counter to the world's wisdom.

Proper 21, Year B (The Sunday Closest to September 28)

THEME OF THE LECTIONS

Jesus' power breaks out in spontaneous acts of healing that cannot be confined to the church.

- *The Collect:* See Year A.
- *Esther 7:1–6, 9–10, 9:20–22:* Queen Esther petitions for the life of herself and her people.
- *Psalm 124:* A communal song of thanksgiving for God's deliverance.
- *James 5:13–20:* Pray for those who are sick and anoint them with oil in the name of the Lord for healing.
- *Mark 9:38–50:* When Jesus' disciple John said to him, "Teacher, we saw someone casting out demons in your name, and we tried to stop him," Jesus told John to accept those people who tried to do good in his name.

ALTERNATIVE READINGS

- Numbers 11:4–6, 10–16, 24–29
- Psalm 19:7–14

KEY WORDS, IDEAS, AND CONCEPTS TO EXPLORE

- Millstone
- The power of Jesus' name
- Living righteously
- Judgment
- Submission to God
- Receiving power and authority for ministry

STORIES TO TELL

- Queen Esther and the Jewish celebration of Purim.

CHRISTIAN PRACTICE AND LITURGICAL TRADITION

- The passing of the peace calls the church to live out God's forgiveness in the life of the community.
- At the Eucharist all confess their sin and separation before God and all receive forgiveness; it is God who judges and forgives.

FORMATION IN BAPTISMAL DISCIPLESHIP

The Holy Spirit is present wherever healing is happening, peace is proclaimed, justice is fought for, or suffering is lifted up in love.

Proper 22, Year B (The Sunday Closest to October 5)

THEME OF THE LECTIONS

The sanctity of human relationships.

- *The Collect:* See Year A.
- *Job 1:1, 2:1–10:* Job continues to be blameless and upright despite Satan's harm to him.
- *Psalm 26:* A lament from one who has been falsely accused of wrongdoing, asking for God's redemption.
- *Hebrews 1:1–4; 2:5–12:* Because Christ shared so completely in everything that we suffer, Christ is the perfect high priest who "made us worthy to stand" before God (Eucharistic Prayer B, BCP 368).
- *Mark 10:2–16:* Jesus' teaching on marriage and divorce.

ALTERNATIVE READINGS

- Genesis 2:18–24
- Psalm 8

KEY WORDS, IDEAS, AND CONCEPTS TO EXPLORE

- Christ as high priest
- Temple sacrifices
- Marriage
- The sacredness of human relationships
- A four-week, semi-continuous reading of the book of Job begins this Sunday.
- A seven-week, semi-continuous reading of the first ten chapters of Hebrews

begins this Sunday. Take time to introduce this epistle, and to provide an understanding of the temple priesthood and sacrificial system.

STORIES TO TELL

- The story of Job.

CHRISTIAN PRACTICE AND LITURGICAL TRADITION

- The Celebration and Blessing of a Marriage (BCP 423–434) reflects the principles set forth in today's gospel. Though marriage is a sacred relationship, the church recognizes the necessity of divorce where a couple cannot live into the commitment they made. It is expected that counseling, continuing concern, and repentance will be a part of Christian divorce.
- The Eucharistic prayers of the Book of Common Prayer reflect the sacrificial language of Hebrews: *You . . . sent Jesus Christ . . . to share our human nature, to live and die as one of us, to reconcile us to you, the God and Father of all. He stretched out his arms upon the cross, and offered himself, in obedience to your will, a perfect sacrifice for the whole world.* (BCP 362).

FORMATION IN BAPTISMAL DISCIPLESHIP

The sacredness of relationships in today's lections and in the marriage rite of the Book of Common Prayer expresses the sacredness of all relationships before God: "God is love, and those who abide in love abide in God, and God abides in them" (1 John 4:16b).

Proper 23, Year B (The Sunday Closest to October 12)

THEME OF THE LECTIONS

The desire for wealth can lead to injustice, lack of compassion, and estrangement from God.

- *The Collect:* See Year A.
- *Job 23:1–9, 16–17:* Job persistently seeks to find God for answers, despite his friends urging him to seek God for forgiveness.
- *Psalm 22:1–15:* Feeling abandoned by God, the psalmist seeks God to help in times of despair as God has done in the past.
- *Hebrews 4:12–16:* God knows the secrets of the heart. We approach God with boldness so that we may receive mercy and find grace.
- *Mark 10:17–31:* Jesus insists all honor be directed to God. In his conversation with the rich man, Jesus states that riches distract and cause self-glorification. All should be given to the poor, as we will have riches in heaven.

ALTERNATIVE READINGS

- Amos 5:6–7, 10–15
- Psalm 90:12–17

KEY WORDS, IDEAS, AND CONCEPTS TO EXPLORE

- Justice and the acquisition of wealth
- Stewardship
- Total commitment to God

STORIES TO TELL

- The trials and tribulations of Job.

CHRISTIAN PRACTICE AND LITURGICAL TRADITION

The monastic tradition models a total dedication to God by requiring its members to live simply and hold all goods in common.

FORMATION IN BAPTISMAL DISCIPLESHIP

Stewardship is a life lived for God rather than for social and economic advantage.

Proper 24, Year B (The Sunday Closest to October 19)

THEME OF THE LECTIONS

God calls the Christian into servant ministry, which means sharing in the suffering of others in order to bring life and healing.

- *The Collect:* See Year A.
- *Job 38:1–7, (34–41):* The Lord finally appears to Job to answer his plea and deliver more demands and admonishments.
- *Psalm 104:1–9, 24, 37b:* A song of praise to God who has created the cosmos and exerted control over chaos.
- *Hebrews 5:1–10:* Jesus' suffering led to his perfection, his role being that of high priest who offers sacrifice (himself) for the people.
- *Mark 10:35–45:* James, John, and the other disciples argue over who will be sitting at the side of Jesus in the Kingdom of God. Jesus tells them that whoever would be great must be a servant, because the Son of Man had not come to be served but to serve, and to give his life as a ransom for many.

ALTERNATIVE READINGS

- Isaiah 53:4–12
- Psalm 91:9–16

KEY WORDS, IDEAS, AND CONCEPTS TO EXPLORE

- Suffering
- Servant ministry
- "Life as a ransom for many"
- Jesus as high priest

STORIES TO TELL

- Job's case against God.

CHRISTIAN PRACTICE AND LITURGICAL TRADITION

The role of deacon expresses the servant ministry of all the baptized. At ordination, the candidate hears these words from the bishop: *In the name of Jesus Christ, you are to serve all people, particularly the poor, the weak, the sick, and the lonely . . . You are to interpret to the Church the needs, concerns, and hopes of the world.* (BCP 543).

FORMATION IN BAPTISMAL DISCIPLESHIP

The congregation must take seriously its role to be servant to the world. Members need to be trained and encouraged to engage in servant ministry through their work and in their community.

Proper 25, Year B (The Sunday Closest to October 26)

THEME OF THE LECTIONS

Jesus comes to proclaim God's new day where people who are physically and metaphorically blind to injustice will see clearly the way of God.

- *The Collect:* See Year A.
- *Job 42:1–6, 10–17:* God declares Job the winner in his lengthy disputation about divine wisdom and justice. Acting at God's command, Job intercedes for his friends.
- *Psalm 34:1–8, (19–22):* God's deliverance, interspersed with invitations for others to look to and experience the wisdom and goodness of God.
- *Hebrews 7:23–28:* The priesthood of Jesus is forever, and he is able to save those who draw near to God through him, because he lives to intercede for them. He did this once and for all when he sacrificed his own life.
- *Mark 10:46–52:* Jesus heals a blind beggar, Bartimaeus, on the road outside of Jericho.

ALTERNATIVE READINGS

- Jeremiah 31:7–9
- Psalm 126

KEY WORDS, IDEAS, AND CONCEPTS TO EXPLORE
- Healing
- Seeking maturity in faith
- Blindness as a metaphor for turning from God's covenant

STORIES TO TELL
- The conclusion of the story of Job.
- The healing of blind Bartimaeus.

CHRISTIAN PRACTICE AND LITURGICAL TRADITION
The hymn "Amazing Grace" in *The Hymnal 1982* (671) and *Lift Every Voice and Sing* (181) by John Newton expresses a turning point in his life and his dependence on God.

FORMATION IN BAPTISMAL DISCIPLESHIP
A congregation needs to ask constantly where it is blind to human need and to God's call to live by the Baptismal Covenant.

Proper 26, Year B (The Sunday Closest to November 2)

THEME OF THE LECTIONS
Loving God and neighbor are the greatest commandments.
- *The Collect:* See Year A.
- *Ruth 1:1–18:* Famine, death, and childlessness begin the story of Ruth and Naomi.
- *Psalm 146:* The Lord watches over prisoners, strangers, the orphaned and widowed.
- *Hebrews 9:11–14:* Christ's death is the perfect atonement for the sins of all, once and for all.
- *Mark 12:28–34:* Jesus' recitation of the *Shema*, summarizing it as loving God and neighbor. To fulfill these commandments is far more than burnt offerings or sacrifices.

ALTERNATIVE READINGS
- Deuteronomy 6:1–9
- Psalm 119:1–8

KEY WORDS, IDEAS, AND CONCEPTS TO EXPLORE
- High priest
- Loving God and neighbor

- The *Shema* (from Deuteronomy)
- The story of Ruth is told in this week and next week's Old Testament readings.

STORIES TO TELL
- The story of Ruth and Naomi.

CHRISTIAN PRACTICE AND LITURGICAL TRADITION
- The commandment to love God and neighbor is part of the optional penitential order before the Eucharist (BCP 319, 351; see also 324).
- The "loving neighbor as self" commandment is also reflected in the Baptismal Covenant: "Will you seek and serve Christ in all persons, loving your neighbor as yourself?" (BCP 305).

FORMATION IN BAPTISMAL DISCIPLESHIP
The commandments to love God and neighbor serve as a way of measuring a congregation's faithfulness to the gospel.

Proper 27, Year B (The Sunday Closest to November 9)

THEME OF THE LECTIONS
The offering of several women is a witness to true faith in God. (Note: The themes of the season of Advent begin to be expressed this week, offering an opportunity to explore the rich heritage of Advent. This week the readings focus on the coming of Christ in glory and on the last judgment.)
- *The Collect:* See Year A.
- *Ruth 3:1–5; 4:13–17:* Naomi's security is sealed by the birth of a male child to Ruth and Boaz. Boaz designates the child, Obed, as the redeemer of her land.
- *Psalm 127:* Children are a gift from God.
- *Hebrews 9:24–28:* Christ has not entered a sanctuary made by human hands, which is only a symbol of the reality, but heaven itself, where he appears before God on our behalf. Christ will appear again to bring salvation to those who are waiting for him.
- *Mark 12:38–44:* Jesus admonishes those who are rich and give little out of their affluence, while a poor widow gives out of her poverty, and offers all that she has to live on.

ALTERNATIVE READINGS
- 1 Kings 17:8–16
- Psalm 146

KEY WORDS, IDEAS, AND CONCEPTS TO EXPLORE
- House of David and genealogy of Jesus
- High priest
- Offering
- Offertory at the Eucharist
- Stewardship

STORIES TO TELL
- The story of Naomi, Ruth, and Boaz.
- The poor widow in the gospel text.

CHRISTIAN PRACTICE AND LITURGICAL TRADITION
- The child of Ruth and Boaz (Obed) is the father of Jesse, who is the father of David.
- The offertory at the Eucharist expresses the theme of self-offering in today's lections. The call for total self-offering is reflected in the Eucharistic prayers of the prayer book: *And here we offer and present unto thee, O Lord, our selves, our souls and bodies, to be a reasonable, holy, and living sacrifice unto thee"* (BCP 336).

FORMATION IN BAPTISMAL DISCIPLESHIP
- Stewardship is a way of life, not a fundraising campaign.

Proper 28, Year B (The Sunday Closest to November 16)

THEME OF THE LECTIONS
The coming day of glory and judgment is ushered in by a time of frightening upheaval and persecution.
- *The Collect:* See Year A.
- *1 Samuel 1:4–20:* God answers Hannah's prayer for a son.
- *Canticle—1 Samuel 2:1–10:* The Song of Hannah.
- *Hebrews 10:11–14, (15–18), 19–25:* Jesus sits at God's right hand and waits to have all enemies under his feet. The church is told to uphold traditional virtues: faith, hope, and love.
- *Mark 13:1–8:* Jesus predicts the destruction of Jerusalem and the end times.

ALTERNATIVE READINGS
- Daniel 12:1–3
- Psalm 16

KEY WORDS, IDEAS, AND CONCEPTS TO EXPLORE

- Apocalyptic literature is heard during this pre-Advent and the Advent season. This style of literature uses poetry and rich imagery to emphasize that suffering and struggle lead to God's final intervention at the end of the present age. God will come to usher in the kingdom of God, a time when God's full sovereignty is known "on earth as in heaven." Apocalyptic literature gives hope to a church under persecution, for the struggles of the present moment are a sign that God's reign is indeed coming. Persecution and suffering are not the end, but the beginning. God's kingdom brings the promise of judgment and salvation. It may arrive at any time, so the church must always be ready. See *An Outline of the Faith*, "The Christian Hope" section (BCP 861–862).
- Stories of barren women who give birth to sons is a recurrent theme in Scripture (Sarah, Rebekah, Hannah, Elizabeth).

STORIES TO TELL

- The story of Hannah and birth of Samuel.

CHRISTIAN PRACTICE AND LITURGICAL TRADITION

The creeds and prayers of The Book of Common Prayer express the theme of God's coming promise and judgment:

- *He will come again to judge the living and the dead* (Apostles' Creed, BCP 96).
- *He will come again in glory to judge the living and the dead, and his kingdom will have no end* (Nicene Creed, BCP 359).
- *Therefore we proclaim the mystery of faith: Christ has died. Christ is risen. Christ will come again* (BCP 363).

FORMATION IN BAPTISMAL DISCIPLESHIP

The congregation lives in the light of the resurrection and the final judgment. Hope and judgment characterize the outlook of the church as it proclaims Christ to the world.

Proper 29, Year B (The Sunday Closest to November 23)

THEME OF THE LECTIONS

This day is often referred to as the Sunday of Christ the King, or Reign of Christ. Christ's sovereignty is the major theme in the lections for all three years.

- *The Collect:* See Year A.
- *2 Samuel 23:1–7:* The last words of David refer to the everlasting covenant of the Lord's promise of an eternal dynasty for David's house.

- *Psalm 132:1–13, (14–19):* A recollection of David's rebuilding of Jerusalem and the temple as well as the covenant made to David that an anointed one would come in the future.
- *Revelation 1:4b–8:* Jesus Christ is coming with the clouds. Every eye shall see him; everyone who pierced him and all the peoples of the world shall cry out in remorse. "'I am the Alpha and the Omega', says the Lord God, who is and who was and who is to come, the Almighty.'"
- *John 18:33–37:* Pilate asks Jesus, "Are you the King of the Jews?" Jesus answers, "You say that I am a king. For this I was born, and for this I came into the world, to testify to the truth. Everyone who belongs to the truth listens to my voice."

ALTERNATIVE READINGS
- Daniel 7:9–10, 13–14
- Psalm 93

KEY WORDS, IDEAS, AND CONCEPTS TO EXPLORE
- Christ as king or sovereign
- Everlasting dominion
- Testifying to the truth

CHRISTIAN PRACTICE AND LITURGICAL TRADITION
- Some of the traditions associated with worship in the Episcopal Church have their origins in the royal court: for example, purple, the color for Advent and Lent, was the color associated with royalty and became linked to the coming of Christ as king.
- The psalms and prayers of the church are filled with imagery of the ruler.

FORMATION IN BAPTISMAL DISCIPLESHIP
"Jesus is Lord" (the earliest Christian creed) means that Jesus stands above all other earthly power and authority. All through history and into the present moment, choosing God above earthly authority has caused persecution and conflict in the life of the church. The congregation and wider church must witness always to the authority of Jesus Christ, realizing that there will be times when conflict will be the direct result of such a witness.

A Summary of the Lectionary Text

Year C

THE SUNDAYS OF ADVENT

The First Sunday of Advent, Year C

THEME OF THE LECTIONS

God's day is coming when all of the world will know the power and authority of God. Poetry best describes this mystery. The whole earth, in earthquake and other natural phenomena, will proclaim that great day.

- *The Collect:* See Year A.
- *Jeremiah 33:14–16:* God promises to restore the kingship and the priesthood and to reunite the peoples of Israel and Judah.
- *Psalm 25:1–9:* A lament, it offers petition and praise to God while offering up one's life as trust in God.
- *1 Thessalonians 3:9–13:* Paul closes a letter to the people of the church in Thessalonica with thanks for the joy they have given him by their faith and love, and a prayer that when Christ comes again they may stand firm and faultless before him.
- *Luke 21:25–36:* Jesus told of the signs of his coming again with power and great glory, and said that when these things begin to happen, people will know that the kingdom of God is near.

KEY WORDS, IDEAS, AND CONCEPTS TO EXPLORE

- The Day of the Lord
- Judgment
- "Son of man coming in a cloud"
- The kingdom of God

CHRISTIAN PRACTICE AND LITURGICAL TRADITION

Today's reading from Jeremiah (33:15) could be used to introduce the Jesse Tree tradition in which Jesus' family tree is represented by the symbols of the stories of his heritage, instead of the names of his ancestors. Representations of Jacob's ladder, Noah's ark, the apple of Adam, and other Old Testament symbols can be used.

FORMATION IN BAPTISMAL DISCIPLESHIP

See Advent 1, Year A above.

The Second Sunday of Advent, Year C

THEME OF THE LECTIONS

John the Baptist proclaims the coming of Jesus and calls people into repentance through baptism.

- *The Collect:* See Year A.
- *Baruch 5:1–9:* "For God shall lead Israel with joy in the light of his glory, with the mercy and righteousness that come from him"; OR
- *Malachi 3:1–4:* A messenger is being sent to prepare the way for the coming of the Lord.
- *Canticle 4* (BCP 50) OR *Canticle 16* (BCP 92): The Song of Zechariah.
- *Philippians 1:3–11:* Paul writes lovingly to the members of the new church in Philippi, praying that when the Lord comes to be our judge, they will be filled with the righteousness that comes through Jesus Christ.
- *Luke 3:1–6:* Luke places the ministry of John the Baptist in its context in history and reminds us that the prophet Isaiah had foretold that John would come to prepare the way of the Lord.

KEY WORDS, IDEAS, AND CONCEPTS TO EXPLORE

- Timothy, a disciple of Paul
- John the Baptist
- A baptism of repentance
- Forgiveness of sins

STORIES TO TELL

- The story of John the Baptist.

CHRISTIAN PRACTICE AND LITURGICAL TRADITION

Repentance is a part of conversion; it means to turn in a new direction. In the baptismal rite, candidates first reject evil and then turn to accept Jesus Christ as Savior and Lord. In the early church and in the Orthodox tradition today, those to be baptized faced west as they denounced evil and then turned around to face east as they accepted Jesus.

FORMATION IN BAPTISMAL DISCIPLESHIP

The radical call for repentance guides the preparation given of those who will be baptized. This week's gospel lection needs to be read in the context of next week's gospel, Luke 3:7–18.

The Third Sunday of Advent, Year C

THEME OF THE LECTIONS

God's new day is dawning in Jesus. It will be a day in which God's compassion for the weak and oppressed is fully realized. In the meantime, Christians must act in accordance with God's intentions for the kingdom.
- *The Collect:* See Year A.
- *Zephaniah 3:14–20:* A call to rejoicing, celebrating the kingship of the Lord, whose care will provide security for his people. The future will be bright.
- *Canticle 9* (BCP 86): The First Song of Isaiah, a song of praise for salvation, for the great one in the midst of you is the Holy One of Israel.
- *Philippians 4:4–7:* "The Lord is near . . . And the peace of God, which surpasses all understanding, will guard your hearts and your minds in Christ Jesus."
- *Luke 3:7–18:* John the Baptist warned the people that they must repent. When the people asked what they must do, he told them to share what they had, to collect no more than was due, to be content with what they earned.

KEY WORDS, IDEAS, AND CONCEPTS TO EXPLORE
- The coming Day of the Lord (or "Second Coming")
- John the Baptist
- Repentance
- Ethics of the gospel
- The Baptismal Covenant calls us to service and justice.

STORIES TO TELL

- John the Baptist (continued from Advent 2).

CHRISTIAN PRACTICE AND LITURGICAL TRADITION

The Advent season combines a sense of joyous hope in God's coming with the power in the fullness of time, as well as the radical call for repentance (a life turned around) that goes with the vision. Hope and judgment are the twin themes of the Advent season.

FORMATION IN BAPTISMAL DISCIPLESHIP

The radical lifestyle of the repentant Christian is outlined in the words of John the Baptist heard in the gospel. Those preparing for their baptism on the First Sunday after the Epiphany (The Baptism of our Lord), and the parents and sponsors of candidates, must discern how those radical words will affect them in their covenant life.

The Fourth Sunday of Advent, Year C

THEME OF THE LECTIONS

God's promise of favor to the house of David and to the people is fulfilled in Jesus. A mystery is revealed. The promise now includes the Gentiles.

- *The Collect:* See Year A.
- *Micah 5:2–5a:* "Bethlehem in Ephratha" was David's city. The ancient prophecy promises that a new ruler for Israel whose roots are far back in the past will come from this city.
- *Psalm 80:1–7:* A cry to the Shepherd of Israel, that he will forgive and restore his people.
- *Hebrews 10:5–10:* Jesus, through the offering of his body for our salvation, does away with ritual sacrifices and offerings that are made in obedience to law and creates a new sort of obedience.
- *Luke 1:39–45 (46–55):* Mary goes to visit her relative Elizabeth in the uplands of Judah. Elizabeth is expecting a child who is to be John the Baptist. Elizabeth is filled with joy at Mary's coming, and cries, "And why has this happened to me, that the mother of my Lord comes to me?" The Song of Mary follows.

KEY WORDS, IDEAS, AND CONCEPTS TO EXPLORE

- Bethlehem as the birthplace of Jesus
- The meeting of Mary and Elizabeth

STORIES TO TELL

- The stories from Matthew and Luke leading up to Jesus' birth.

CHRISTIAN PRACTICE AND LITURGICAL TRADITION

"The Song of Mary" (The Magnificat) is often said or sung at Evening Prayer, or as an option in place of the psalm during several weeks of Advent. (Notice the radical nature of Mary's song: the poor shall be raised up and the powerful will be brought down.)

FORMATION IN BAPTISMAL DISCIPLESHIP

The words of the Christmas story are so familiar and so filled with nostalgic memories that we can easily forget their power to call our lives into question. Christ calls for radical change in our individual lives and in society. His call is a part of the Christmas proclamation and is the reason for the penitential tone of Advent.

THE SUNDAYS AFTER THE EPIPHANY

The Second Sunday after the Epiphany, Year C

THEME OF THE LECTIONS

To be baptized is to have new life and to know the risen Christ.

- *The Collect:* See Year A.
- *Isaiah 62:1–5:* New names given by the Lord to Jerusalem point to God's favor, and the relationship is compared to a marriage between God and his people.
- *Psalm 96:* A celebration of God's steadfast love (*hesed*).
- *1 Corinthians 12:1–11:* All are empowered through baptism with spiritual gifts. (This Sunday begins a serialized reading of 1 Corinthians beginning at the twelfth chapter; therefore, the epistle reading will not usually be in thematic harmony with the Old Testament, psalm, and gospel lections.)
- *John 2:1–11:* The miracle of water changed to wine at the marriage feast at Cana points to Jesus' death and glorification when everything will be transformed.

KEY WORDS, IDEAS, AND CONCEPTS TO EXPLORE

- The significance of names
- *"Hesed"*
- Spiritual gifts

- "Jesus is Lord," the first creed of the church
- Wedding customs in biblical times
- Marriage as a metaphor of relationship with God
- Overview of 1 Corinthians

STORIES TO TELL

- The wedding at Cana.

CHRISTIAN PRACTICE AND LITURGICAL TRADITION

The wedding of Cana is mentioned in the opening exhortation of the Celebration and Blessing of a Marriage (BCP 423).

FORMATION IN BAPTISMAL DISCIPLESHIP

Baptism is not membership in the church. It is a calling into intimate relationship with God that can be expressed through the images of marriage, adoption, and birth into a family. The church emphasizes the ministry of the baptized, recognizing that everyone has been empowered by the Holy Spirit with spiritual gifts.

The Third Sunday after the Epiphany, Year C

THEME OF THE LECTIONS

Scripture is to be heard, interpreted, and embodied in the lives of God's people.

- *The Collect:* See Year A.
- *Nehemiah 8:1–3, 5–6, 8–10:* Ezra the scribe assembled the people of Israel in Jerusalem to hear the book of the law of Moses and to instruct the people in what was read.
- *Psalm 19:* The proclamation of the all-encompassing importance of God's "torah."
- *1 Corinthians 12:12–31a:* Paul reminds the congregation at Corinth that they are the Body of Christ and individually members of the Body. Every person is needed as part of that Body and no one can be discarded. They are joined as parts of the whole.
- *Luke 4:14–21:* Filled with the power of the Holy Spirit, Jesus went back into Galilee. In the synagogue in Nazareth Jesus read from the book of Isaiah the good news of salvation. When he had read he closed the book and said, "Today this scripture has been fulfilled in your hearing."

KEY WORDS, IDEAS, AND CONCEPTS TO EXPLORE
- The book of the law (Torah)
- The role of priests and Levites in biblical times
- The Body of Christ
- The synagogue in Jewish life
- The power of the Spirit

STORIES TO TELL
- The story of Ezra gathering the people together to hear the reading of the Torah. These were people who had lived in Babylonian exile and who needed to hear the story again in order to renew their identity as God's people.
- The story of Jesus reading and interpreting the words of Isaiah.

CHRISTIAN PRACTICE AND LITURGICAL TRADITION
The ritual of reading the gospel at the Eucharist comes out of the ancient rite described in today's first reading. Notice that the role of the Levite is to help the people understand the law. This describes the role of preacher and teacher in the church today.

FORMATION IN BAPTISMAL DISCIPLESHIP
As Jesus embodied the scripture in his life ("Today this scripture has been fulfilled in your hearing"), so the church is to embody God's word in the life of the congregation and each individual Christian.

The Fourth Sunday after the Epiphany, Year C

THEME OF THE LECTIONS
To speak God's word is to risk rejection from those around us.
- *The Collect:* See Year A.
- *Jeremiah 1:4–10:* Jeremiah is called to speak for God. He says, "'Ah, Lord God! Truly I do not know how to speak, for I am only a boy.' But the Lord said to me, 'Do not say, "I am only a boy"; for you shall go to all to whom I send you, and you shall speak whatever I command you. . . . See, today I appoint you over nations and over kingdoms. . .'"
- *Psalm 71:1–6:* The psalmist prays for God's continuing protection.
- *1 Corinthians 14:12b–20:* Paul cautions the congregation at Corinth about the use of the gift of speaking in tongues. "One who speaks in a tongue should pray for the power to interpret."
- *Luke 4:21–32:* The people in the synagogue knew Jesus' family and were

puzzled and angered by his words. He spoke of Elijah and Elisha and their miraculous help to a widow and a leper who were not Israelites. The people led Jesus to a hill intending to throw him over the edge. He walked into the crowd and away from them, and went to Capernaum where he continued to teach.

KEY WORDS, IDEAS, AND CONCEPTS TO EXPLORE

- The role of prophets
- Spiritual gifts
- The gift of speaking in tongues

STORIES TO TELL

- The story of Jesus' visit to Nazareth in Luke 4:14–30, pointing out the striking contrast between the way the people first receive Jesus and then their anger at him.
- The stories that lie behind Jesus' references in the gospel reading: the widow of Zarephath (1 Kings 17:8-24); the healing of Naaman the Syrian (2 Kings 5:1–19).

CHRISTIAN PRACTICE AND LITURGICAL TRADITION

As Jesus proclaimed the word of God from Isaiah, he confronted the sinful pride of his own people. In the Eucharistic liturgy, confession follows the hearing of the word. God's word confronts us, which leads to our acknowledgment of the gap between God's call and our response.

FORMATION IN BAPTISMAL DISCIPLESHIP

The readings for today confront the terrible cost of discipleship. To speak and act in God's name sets one apart.

The Fifth Sunday after the Epiphany, Year C

THEME OF THE LECTIONS

The calling of the disciples to mission.

- *The Collect:* See Year A.
- *Isaiah 6:1–8 (9–13):* The call and commission of the prophet Isaiah.
- *Psalm 138:* A song of thanksgiving that celebrates God's steadfast love and faithfulness.
- *1 Corinthians 15:1–11:* Paul reminds the congregation at Corinth that the scriptures are fulfilled in Christ's resurrection appearances. Paul speaks of five appearances and of his own experience of seeing the Lord.

- *Luke 5:1–11:* Jesus tells Simon Peter to go on the lake and put down nets. Peter protests that they have fished all night and have caught nothing, but he will do what Jesus says. The nets enclose a school of fish, and James and John in the other boat help with the enormous catch. They take their boats to shore, leave everything, and follow Jesus.

KEY WORDS, IDEAS, AND CONCEPTS TO EXPLORE

- The gospel
- Resurrection appearances
- God's call to Isaiah, to the disciples, and to the church today

STORIES TO TELL

- The call and ministry of Isaiah.
- The calling of Peter, James, and John.

CHRISTIAN PRACTICE AND LITURGICAL TRADITION

The baptismal rite enacts the calling narratives heard in this week's readings. God calls disciples into baptism. Each Christian responds and turns to accept Jesus and reject evil. We hear God's word, accept the covenant, and receive the empowerment of the Holy Spirit for ministry in the world.

FORMATION IN BAPTISMAL DISCIPLESHIP

At baptism every Christian is called into ministry. Simon Peter's call is the call of every Christian: "Follow me."

The Sixth Sunday after the Epiphany, Year C

THEME OF THE LECTIONS

The Sermon on the Plain: God's way demands that the Christian makes choices that often put the faithful in conflict with those around them. (Note that a reading of Luke's equivalent to Matthew's Sermon on the Mount begins this Sunday.)

- *The Collect:* See Year A.
- *Jeremiah 17:5–10:* Draws contrasts between those who trust in their own strength and those who trust in the Lord.
- *Psalm 1:* Contrasts between the righteous and the wicked.
- *1 Corinthians 15:12–20:* Paul raises the questions that surround Christ's resurrection. If there is to be no resurrection, we have no hope as Christians; but we know in fact that Christ was raised from the dead.

- *Luke 6:17–26:* Jesus heals the sick and troubled people who come to him. He teaches his followers that the hungry, the poor, and those who are reviled for his sake are blessed in God's eyes. Those who live in self-centered comfort will experience affliction.

KEY WORDS, IDEAS, AND CONCEPTS TO EXPLORE
- The way of the righteous and the way of the wicked
- Proverbial sayings
- Resurrection
- "First fruits"
- The Sermon on the Plain
- Blessedness
- Judgment results in a reversal of fortune

CHRISTIAN PRACTICE AND LITURGICAL TRADITION
The "Song of Mary" sung or said at Evening Prayer speaks of God bringing down the powerful and lifting up the lowly.

FORMATION IN BAPTISMAL DISCIPLESHIP
God's word is radical, and calls for a radical response. The words that Jesus spoke turned the world upside down for those who accepted them as God's word for them. The poor receive a kingdom. The hungry are satisfied. The life of the baptized must be formed in words and actions that "turn the world upside down" for the gospel of Jesus Christ. (See Isaiah 55:8–9: "For my thoughts are not your thoughts, nor are your ways my ways, says the Lord.")

The Seventh Sunday after the Epiphany, Year C

THEME OF THE LECTIONS
The Sermon on the Plain: God's mercy must be expressed in the life of the Christian.
- *The Collect*: See Year A.
- *Genesis 45:3–11, 15:* Joseph declares his identity to his brothers and asks if their father is still living. Joseph believes that all that happened to him at the hands of his brothers was God's will and that God sent him to Egypt to preserve life there.
- *Psalm 37:1–12, 41–42:* The psalmist counsels patience, though the wicked seem to prosper. The Lord will uphold the righteous.

- *1 Corinthians 15:35–38, 42–50:* Further instruction to the people of Corinth about resurrection after death. Paul explains that earthly bodies will be transformed into spiritual beings.
- *Luke 6:27–38:* Jesus teaches: love your enemies, do good to those who hate you, bless those who curse you, pray for those who abuse you. Do not judge and you will not be judged. Forgive, and you will be forgiven. The measure you give will be the measure you receive.

KEY WORDS, IDEAS, AND CONCEPTS TO EXPLORE

- God's mercy
- Forgiveness
- Resurrection
- The Sermon on the Plain
- The ethics of Jesus

STORIES TO TELL

- The story of Joseph forgiving his brothers from Genesis.

CHRISTIAN PRACTICE AND LITURGICAL TRADITION

- The passing of the peace expresses a forgiving community at worship.
- The resurrection is at the heart of Christian teaching, prayer, and creed.

FORMATION IN BAPTISMAL DISCIPLESHIP

The Christian congregation aspires to live the higher standards of the gospel. Enmity and harsh judgments have no place in the assembly.

The Eighth Sunday after the Epiphany, Year C

THEME OF THE LECTIONS

The Sermon on the Plain: Our actions must match our words in response to God's covenant.

- *The Collect:* See Year A.
- *Sirach 27:4–7:* Correct speech is important. (Speech represents the embodiment of one's wisdom.)
- *Isaiah 55:10–13:* The power of the divine word given by the prophet will make certain that it accomplishes its purposes.
- *Psalm 92:1–5, 11–14:* A song of thanks, comparing the faithful and righteous to trees that flourish in the courts of the Lord.
- *1 Corinthians 15:51–58:* Through our Lord Jesus Christ, God has given us victory over sin and death.

- *Luke 6:39–49:* Jesus teaches the meaning of discipleship, and asks, "Why do you call me 'Lord, Lord,' and not do what I tell you?" Those who hear his words and do them are like those who build on foundations of rock. Those who hear and do not do Jesus' words are like those who build without foundations.

KEY WORDS, IDEAS, AND CONCEPTS TO EXPLORE

- The Sermon on the Plain
- Word
- Resurrection
- Sowing seed
- Building on a foundation
- God's victory revealed in Jesus

STORIES TO TELL

- The gospel story of the wise man and foolish man building houses on rocks and sand.

CHRISTIAN PRACTICE AND LITURGICAL TRADITION

- The centrality of self-examination and confession in the life of the church is expressed in prayer book worship. The Litany of Penitence for Ash Wednesday (BCP 267–269) offers a striking illustration of today's lessons.
- Prayers for those who have died are a constant reminder that these relationships go on beyond the grave.

FORMATION IN BAPTISMAL DISCIPLESHIP

The Baptismal Covenant stresses continuing in *"the apostles' teaching and fellowship"* (BCP 304). The centrality of living in a community centered on God's word lies at the heart of Christian formation.

The Last Sunday after the Epiphany, Year C

THEME OF THE LECTIONS

The Transfiguration of our Lord.

- *The Collect:* See Year A.
- *Exodus 34:29–35:* After Moses had received the Ten Commandments from God, his face shone with a radiant light. The people of Israel were afraid, and Moses veiled his face when he spoke with the people.
- *Psalm 99:* God deserves worship, because God wills and works for justice and righteousness among the people.

- *2 Corinthians 3:12–4:2:* Those who view God with unveiled faces gradually acquire God's glory as a gift of the Spirit.
- *Luke 9:28–36, (37–43a):* Luke's account of Christ's Transfiguration—Peter, James, and John saw his dazzling white clothing, his shining face, his conversation with Moses and Elijah, and heard the voice from the cloud proclaiming Jesus as the Son and God's Chosen.

KEY WORDS, IDEAS, AND CONCEPTS TO EXPLORE
- Transfiguration
- New covenant
- Gifts of the Spirit

STORIES TO TELL
- The story of Jesus' transfiguration.
- The story of Moses speaking with God.

CHRISTIAN PRACTICE AND LITURGICAL TRADITION
The Sundays after the Epiphany are framed by both the Feast of the Epiphany, with its star in the heavens, and Jesus' face shining like the sun at the Transfiguration. The light of God's revelation in Jesus becomes clearer in the ensuing weeks as disciples are called and the word is proclaimed.

FORMATION IN BAPTISMAL DISCIPLESHIP
The ministry of the baptized is expressed in the epistle lesson. Paul thinks of each covenant (the old covenant given by Moses and the new covenant given by Jesus) as a ministry (*diakonia*) in which one serves. We experience Christ's life-giving Spirit in the new covenant.

THE SUNDAYS OF LENT

The First Sunday in Lent, Year C

In Year C we begin an exploration of five great themes related to baptism.

BAPTISMAL THEME: CREED
The Apostles' Creed, in which belief leads to faithfulness:
> I believe in God, the Father almighty, creator of heaven and earth . . . (BCP 304)

BAPTISMAL THEMES EXPRESSED IN THE LECTIONARY READINGS

Belief and acceptance of Jesus as Lord. The ancient creed outlining God's mighty acts for Israel spoken at the time of offering the first fruits of the harvest is matched in this week's readings by the simple statement from Romans, "Jesus is Lord." Jesus responded to temptation by his own "creed" taken from Deuteronomy 4:4, 8, 12: ". . . One does not live by bread alone . . . Worship the Lord your God, and serve only him . . . Do not put the Lord your God to the test."

THE LECTIONARY READINGS

- *The Collect*: See Year A.
- *Deuteronomy 26:1–11:* The text describes an ancient liturgical rite pre-scribed for the offering of the first fruits of the harvest. The statement forms a creed that is to be proclaimed by the faithful recounting of what God has done for Israel.
- *Psalm 91:1–2, 9–16:* The Lord will protect and deliver those who trust in him.
- *Romans 10:8b–13:* If through faith we confess that Jesus is Lord and be-lieve that God has raised Jesus from the dead, we will be saved. There is no distinction among people because the same Lord is Lord of all. The three simple words "Jesus is Lord" are the church's earliest creed.
- *Luke 4:1–13:* Following his baptism, the Spirit led Jesus into the wilderness. For forty days he had nothing to eat and he encountered the devil, who tempted Jesus to take care of his own needs, to demonstrate supernatural gifts, and to become ruler of the kingdoms of the earth. Jesus rejected them all, and the devil left Jesus, waiting to take up the contest at a later time.

The Second Sunday in Lent, Year C

BAPTISMAL THEME: COVENANT

The Baptismal Covenant: *Let us join with those who are committing themselves to Christ and renew our own baptismal covenant* (BCP 303).

BAPTISMAL THEME EXPRESSED IN THE LECTIONARY READINGS

The Baptismal Covenant in the Book of Common Prayer includes the Apostles' Creed followed by five statements of our commitment to live according to our beliefs. The response to each statement of commitment is the same: "I will, with God's help." Keeping covenant means making right choices (the narrow road), and joining Jesus "on the way" to Jerusalem.

THE LECTIONARY READINGS

- *The Collect*: See Year A.
- *Genesis 15:1–12,17–18:* Abram (Abraham) grieved that he had no son to be his heir. God promised that he would have a son of his own and that his descendents would be as numerous as the stars in the sky. Abraham's faith is what made him righteous before God. The covenant-making rite described in this text indicates the serious nature of the relationship being established between Abraham and Sarah's descendants and God.
- *Psalm 27:* The psalmist believes that no matter what troubles come to him, the Lord will be with him; and he will wait patiently for the Lord.
- *Philippians 3:17–4:1:* Paul announces the true citizenship of the faithful in Philippi: they are citizens of heaven. That is, they live in the world with a different vision and set of values than the people around them. Their total commitment is to God's plan rather than to the momentary satisfaction of "the belly." Paul sets the example for Christian life.
- *Luke 13: 31–35:* (Verses 22–30 heighten the point Jesus was making and are important to share with catechumens and those who are reaffirming their baptismal vows.) Jesus describes how difficult it will be to be saved— to enter the kingdom of God. He scorns Herod's threat against his life, and turns his face to Jerusalem, where suffering and death are waiting for him. He grieves for the city of Jerusalem, which rejects and destroys the prophets sent by God.

The Third Sunday in Lent, Year C

BAPTISMAL THEME: CALLING

The welcome given to the newly baptized:

> *We receive you into the household of God. Confess the faith of Christ crucified, proclaim his resurrection, and share with us in his eternal priesthood.* (BCP 308)

BAPTISMAL THEME EXPRESSED IN THE LECTIONARY READINGS

Baptism is a calling into ministry. For the Christian, baptism is the "burning bush" experience that makes sense of the rest of one's life in Christ. The fact that baptism comes for many at infancy means that the church must constantly look back to baptism to reaffirm the sacred calling to participate with God in continuing acts of salvation. The gospel reading is a solemn reminder that with the call comes accountability. God expects the Christian and the church to bear fruit: "If it bears fruit next year, well and good; but if not, you can cut it down" (Luke 13:9).

THE LECTIONARY READINGS

- *The Collect*: See Year A.
- *Exodus 3:1–15:* God cared about the Israelites in slavery in Egypt and revealed himself to Moses in a burning bush that did not burn. Jehovah, the God of their forefathers, had sent Moses to them, to lead them out of Egypt.
- *Psalm: 63:1–8:* A song of thanksgiving or psalm of trust, it narrates the experience and results of the psalmist's encounter with God in the Temple.
- *1 Corinthians 10:1–13:* The Exodus story is to be a lesson for all Christians, Paul wrote. Though all the Hebrew people passed through the Sea of Reeds, not all of them were faithful. We cannot take our baptism (our Sea of Reeds experience) for granted. Our response to the event of our baptism is the test of our righteousness before God.
- *Luke 13:1–9:* In the gospel reading Jesus stresses the need for repentance through the parable of the fig tree. We never know when a final accounting will be called for.

The Fourth Sunday in Lent, Year C

BAPTISMAL THEME: EUCHARIST

The Holy Eucharist is the sacrament of baptismal renewal and reconciliation, and a foretaste of the Reign of God:

> *Offer to God a sacrifice of thanksgiving, and make good your vows to the Most High.* (Offertory sentence at the Eucharist, BCP 376)

BAPTISMAL THEME EXPRESSED IN THE LECTIONARY READINGS

"Holy Baptism is appropriately administered within the Eucharist as the chief service on a Sunday or other feast" (BCP 298). It has been said that the Eucharist is the only "repeatable" part of the baptismal rite. Those made sons and daughters of God at their baptism are welcomed to the feast of the Eucharist as the prodigal son was welcomed by his father with sandals, a ring, and feasting. Christians are fed for the journey both as a remembrance and as a promise.

THE LECTIONARY READINGS

- *The Collect*: See Year A.
- *Joshua 5:9–12:* After the people of Israel crossed the Jordan and at last entered the Promised Land, they kept the Passover at Gilgal. They ate

their unleavened cakes, and there was no more manna. That year they ate the food that had grown in the land of Canaan. [Read Joshua 4:1–5:12 to see the context of the assigned reading on this fourth Sunday in Lent. The daily feeding of manna was replaced with the harvested crops available in the new land. The first Passover was celebrated as the Israelites prepared to leave Egypt a generation earlier. Now as the people pass through the Jordan River, Passover was celebrated again. Exodus 12:14 commands that it be celebrated "as a festival to the Lord; throughout your generations you shall observe it as a perpetual ordinance." In the reading for this fourth Sunday, there is a liturgical feeling to the scene described. A procession moves across the Jordan. Stones are erected as a memorial. Bread is shared both as a remembrance and as a promise. The Jewish Passover lies at the heart of the Christian Eucharist: "Christ our Passover is sacrificed for us" (BCP 364). Jesus is the manna for the Christian: "I am the bread of life. Your ancestors ate the manna in the wilderness, and they died . . . Whoever eats of this bread will live forever; and the bread that I will give for the life of the world is my flesh. (John 6:48–49, 51b)]

- *Psalm 32:* In a song of thanksgiving, the psalmist associates deliverance with God's steadfast love and suggests that the essences of trust and the source of joy is found in confession and forgiveness.
- *2 Corinthians 5:16–21:* Christians are a whole new creation and must see themselves as "ambassadors of Christ" in the world. So if anyone is in Christ, there is a new creation: everything old has passed away; see, everything has become new! All this is from God, who reconciled us to himself through Christ, and has given us the ministry of reconciliation. Baptism makes us that new creation. We are "born again." The ministry of reconciliation points ahead to the gospel reading and the Eucharist.
- *Luke 15:1–3, 11b–32:* The parable of the prodigal son. As the younger son was welcomed by the father and invited to the banquet, so we are welcomed as daughters and sons and invited to the Eucharist. At the passing of the peace we repeat the act of the father toward his son: "But while he was still far off, his father saw him and was filled with compassion; he ran and put his arms around him and kissed him." As the epistle reading so beautifully reminds us, this simple act of reconciliation is to be our ministry in the world as well.

The Fifth Sunday in Lent, Year C

BAPTISMAL THEME: PROMISE

The Thanksgiving over the Water:

> *We thank you Father, for the water of Baptism. In it we are buried with Christ in his death. By it we share in his resurrection. Through it we are reborn by the Holy Spirit. Therefore in joyful obedience to your Son, we bring into his fellowship those who come to him in faith, baptizing them in the Name of the Father, and of the Son, and of the Holy Spirit.* (BCP 306–307)

BAPTISMAL THEME EXPRESSED IN THE LECTIONARY READINGS

God did a "new thing" as Moses led the slaves of Egypt through the water of the Sea of Reeds into the wilderness of Sinai. God did a "new thing" as Joshua led the people across the Jordan River and celebrated Passover in the Promised Land. God promises a "new thing," a "new Exodus" when water will flow in the desert for God's people. God does a "new thing" in leading Christians into the waters of baptism where they are "buried with Christ" so that they may "share in his resurrection."

THE LECTIONARY READINGS

- *The Collect*: See Year A.
- *Isaiah 43:16–21:* A new Exodus is promised to God's people living in Babylonian exile. The Lord tells his people that he is doing a new thing. He gives water in the wilderness and rivers in the desert so that his special people may drink and live.
- *Psalm 126:* A joyous song of praise to the Lord. Salvation is described in terms of water in the desert.
- *Philippians 3:4b–14:* There is nothing more important to Paul than his relationship with Christ. Everything that he considered important before his turning to Christ now means nothing. Paul wants to know Christ and the power of faith in Christ's resurrection so he may share Christ's sufferings.
- *John 12:1–18:* Jesus shares dinner with Lazarus, Mary, and Martha at their home in Bethany. Mary anoints Jesus' feet, foreshadowing the events to come as Jesus is about to enter Jerusalem for the last time.

The Sundays of Easter

THE WEEKS OF EASTER, YEAR C

As in Year A and Year B, we read selections from the Acts of the Apostles for the six weeks of Easter following Easter Sunday because we need to hear the story of the first-century church in order to understand our mission in the world today.

The second readings during the Great Fifty Days of Easter in Year C come from the Revelation to John, providing glimpses of God's coming reign, when Christ's work of reconciliation is fully realized. The readings from the Hebrew Scriptures can be substituted for the first or second reading during Easter, though the tradition is to read only from the Christian Scriptures during this season.

Easter Sunday, Year C

THEME OF THE LECTIONS

The Resurrection of Jesus the Christ is proclaimed.
- *The Collect:* See Year A.
- *Acts of the Apostles 10:34–43:* See First Sunday After the Epiphany, Year A; OR
- *Isaiah 65:17–25:* The prophet recalls God's promises. God is still in control of human history.
- *Psalm 118:1–2, 14–24:* See Year A.
- *1 Corinthians 15:19–26:* Christ, Adam, and the future resurrection.
- *John 20:1–18:* See Year A; OR
- *Luke 24:1–10:* As the women followers of Jesus came to the tomb very early Sunday morning, bringing spices, they found the tomb open and empty. "Two men in dazzling garments" suddenly appeared and asked the women why they were looking among the dead for some who was living. The women went back and told the remaining eleven disciples all they had seen.

The Second Sunday of Easter, Year C

THEME OF THE LECTIONS

Knowing the risen Christ through faith. "Blessed are those who have not seen and yet have come to believe" (John 20:29b). We may not see the risen Christ but we will know the risen Christ as we gather in faith-filled community on the "eighth day."

- *The Collect*: See Year A.
- *Acts of the Apostles 5:27–32:* Peter and the apostles stand before the Jewish council and witness to the power of the Holy Spirit.
- *Psalm 118:14–29:* A song of thanksgiving proclaiming that this is the day on which the Lord has acted to save his people; OR
- *Psalm 150:* An expression of praise to be completed by the participation of everything that breathes.
- *The Revelation to John 1:4–8:* John's announcement of the revelation of Jesus Christ concluding with a doxology that echoes the Exodus story of deliverance.
- *John 20:19–31:* The story of Jesus appearing to Thomas. See Year A.

The Third Sunday of Easter, Year C

THEME OF THE LECTIONS

Knowing Christ in sacramental life. Jesus appears to the disciples and in eating with them he is able to show that he appears not as a ghost but as the risen Christ. This lection has a focus similar to the Emmaus story (see Easter 3, Year A).

- *The Collect*: See Year A.
- *Acts of the Apostles 9:1–6, 7–20:* A dramatic account of Saul's encounter on the road to Damascus and Saul's conversion to the belief that Jesus is the Son of God.
- *Psalm 30:* A song of thanksgiving from misplaced confidence in the self to humble gratitude and praise that will endure forever.
- *The Revelation to John 5:11–14:* John has a vision of the Lamb, symbolizing Christ, a Redeemer who receives the same sort of worship as God the Creator.
- *John 21:1–19:* Jesus' third resurrection appearance, this time to the seven disciples by the Sea of Tiberias where they were fishing. Casting their nets where Jesus told them to, their nets overflowed. Later, they shared a meal on the beach, with fish and bread.

The Fourth Sunday of Easter, Year C

THEME OF THE LECTIONS

Ministry as a way of revealing the risen Christ. The risen Christ is known through the ministry of the church modeled by Jesus, the Good Shepherd, who gives eternal life.

- *The Collect:* See Year A.
- *Acts of the Apostles 9:36–43:* Peter heals a female disciple named Tabitha (Dorcas) in Joppa from the dead.
- *Psalm 23:* The Lord is my shepherd.
- *The Revelation to John 7:9–17:* A vision of the saints and martyrs who are with God. The Lamb who is in the midst of the throne will be their shepherd and will guide them to the water of life, and God will wipe away all tears from their eyes.
- *John 10:22–30:* On a festival day Jesus was walking in the temple at Jerusalem. Jews asked him to tell them plainly if he was the Messiah. Jesus said he had told them, but because they were not his sheep they did not believe. His own sheep know his voice and follow him, and he gives them eternal life.

The Fifth Sunday of Easter, Year C

THEME OF THE LECTIONS

The new community formed out of the resurrection will be known by the love its members have for one another.

- *The Collect:* See Year A.
- *Acts of the Apostles 11:1–18:* Peter shares a vision in which he recognizes that God's gift to the Gentiles is the repentance that leads to life. God is the primary agent of the mission to all people.
- *Psalm 148:* An all-inclusive invitation to all of God's creation to praise God.
- *The Revelation to John 21:1–6:* A vision of the new creation, given for all.
- *John 13:31–35:* Part of Jesus' final message to his friends. "Where I am going, you cannot come. I give you a new commandment, that you love one another. Just as I have loved you, you also should love one another."

The Sixth Sunday of Easter, Year C

THEME OF THE LECTIONS

The theme of the new community formed out of the resurrection continues from Easter 5. Jesus promises the Holy Spirit, who will come to be their counselor and dwell with them in their life together.

- *The Collect:* See Year A.
- *Acts of the Apostles 16:9–15:* Paul has a vision and travels to Philippi in Macedonia, where he meets Lydia. She proclaims her faith and is baptized.

- *Psalm 67*: A hymn of praise for a generous harvest, asking for God's blessing.
- *The Revelation to John 21:10, 22–22:5*: A vision of a city of light where there will be no need of the sun, and where the river of the water of life flows from the throne of God and of the Lamb. The Lord God will be their light, and God and the Lamb shall reign forever and ever.
- *John 14:23–29*: Jesus, in preparing his disciples for his death, promises that the Holy Spirit will come to them. He gives them the gift of his peace, and tells them not to be afraid. He has told them in advance, so that when it happens they may have faith; OR
- *John 5:1–9*: Jesus' arrival in Jerusalem for a festival, where he heals the sick on the Sabbath.

The Seventh Sunday of Easter, Year C

THEME OF THE LECTIONS

The unity of the church. We hear the conclusion of Jesus' great "priestly prayer," in which he calls for unity within the church so that Christians can witness to the presence of God in their lives.

- *The Collect*: See Year A.
- *Acts of the Apostles 16:16–34*: Paul and Silas were beaten and put in prison because Paul had healed a woman slave who had been possessed by a spirit, and whose owners were angry at the cure. In the night, an earthquake broke open the doors of the prison and unfastened the bonds of the prisoners. The terrified jailer led Paul and Silas from the prison and asked what he must do to be saved. He and his whole family were baptized at once, and the jailer took Paul and Silas to his home.
- *Psalm 97*: Righteousness and justice are the foundation of God's throne. The appropriate response given is one of joy and gratitude.
- *The Revelation to John 22:12–14, 16–17, 20–21*: A detailed portrait of the New Jerusalem, a great city where the glory of God will be shared with all.
- *John 17:20–26*: Jesus intercedes with God for future Christians as well as for the first disciples. The unity of those who believe will teach the world that Jesus' mission is from the Father.

PENTECOST

The Day of Pentecost, Year C

THEME OF THE LECTIONS

- *The Collect:* See Year A.
- *Acts of the Apostles 2:1–21:* See Year A.
- *Genesis 11:1–9:* The Tower of Babel and the confusion of human language created by God due to human pride and presumption.
- *Psalm 104:25–35, 37:* See Year A.
- *Romans 8:14–17:* We are heirs of Christ through adoption by the Spirit.
- *John 14:8–17, (25–27):* Jesus' explanation that he is the Father and all things will be done if asked in his name.

TRINITY SUNDAY

Trinity Sunday, Year C

THEME OF THE LECTIONS

The glory of the Lord is revealed in three persons through the Spirit of truth.

- *The Collect:* See Year A.
- *Proverbs 8:1–4, 22–31:* The speech of Wisdom (Sophia in Greek) who was at the beginning of Creation and is now present with God.
- *Psalm 8:* A song of praise, proclaiming God's worldwide reign; OR Canticle 2 OR Canticle 13.
- *Romans 5:1–5:* The Holy Spirit is given to believers as the tangible expression of God's love.
- *John 16:12–15:* Jesus tells his friends he will be leaving them so that the Spirit of truth whom he will send from the Father will come to them. The Spirit of truth will judge the sin of the world, affirm that Jesus is with the Father, and prove that God condemns the powers of evil.

KEY WORDS, IDEAS, AND CONCEPTS TO EXPLORE

- Trinity
- Names of God
- Glory
- Holy
- Spirit of truth

FORMATION IN BAPTISMAL DISCIPLESHIP

The mutual and equal relationships among the three persons of the Trinity provide the basic model for understanding the church as community. As God is known in a communion of three persons, so the church is to be known as the community of God's people.

The Season after Pentecost

Proper 4, Year C (The Sunday Closest to June 1)

THEME OF THE LECTIONS

God's power and presence are revealed.

- *The Collect:* See Year A.
- *1 Kings 18:20–21, (22–29), 30–39:* The contest between Elijah and Ahab, husband of Jezebel. The people recognize that Yahweh is the true God, who controls all things.
- *Psalm 96:* Among all authorities, the Lord is preeminent.
- *Galatians 1:1–12:* Paul writes to the church at Galatia. He speaks of himself as an apostle independent of human authority, having been commissioned by God and Jesus Christ. He emphasizes that anyone who preaches a gospel of variance with the Gospel of Christ is to be considered an outcast.
- *Luke 7:1–10:* Jesus heals the servant of a Centurion who had shown great faith, despite not being a Jew.

ALTERNATIVE READINGS

- 1 Kings 8:22–23, 41–43
- Psalm 96:1–9

KEY WORDS, IDEAS, AND CONCEPTS TO EXPLORE

- Altar sacrifices
- Authority
- God's "dwelling place"
- Faith
- Healing
- Grace
- Gospel
- This week begins a six-week, semi-continuous reading of Galatians. Provide an overview of the epistle to provide a context.

STORIES TO TELL

- Stories associated with Ahab and Jezebel.
- The healing of the centurion's servant.

CHRISTIAN PRACTICE AND LITURGICAL TRADITION

Intercessions are a part of every worship service.

FORMATION IN BAPTISMAL DISCIPLESHIP

The church is a people called into prayer. Personal prayer flows out of public (liturgical) prayer. The church gathers in prayer and then goes out into the world to enact the prayers in actions of service and justice.

Proper 5, Year C (The Sunday Closest to June 8)

THEME OF THE LECTIONS

God comes to bring life even out of death.

- *The Collect:* See Year A.
- *1 Kings 17:8–16, (17–24):* Elijah is shown as a miracle-working man of God. He continues to provide food for a widow and later heals the woman's son.
- *Psalm 146:* We entrust our life to God who is Creator.
- *Galatians 1:11–24:* Paul defends his authority as an apostle. The gospel he preaches comes from God, revealed by Jesus Christ, and not from any human agency.
- *Luke 7:11–17:* Jesus brings back to life a boy after he meets a mother weeping in a funeral procession. The people were filled with awe and proclaim, "God has shown his care for his people."

ALTERNATIVE READINGS

- 1 Kings 17:17–24
- Psalm 30

KEY WORDS, IDEAS, AND CONCEPTS TO EXPLORE

- Healing
- Raising to life
- Word of the Lord
- Funeral practices of biblical times
- Prophecy
- Grace

- Preaching
- Jerusalem as first center of apostolic authority
- Trace Paul's activities on a map or through photos or images of the geographical area.

STORIES TO TELL

- The story of Elijah and the widow of Zarephath.
- The story of Jesus healing the son of the woman of Nain.

CHRISTIAN PRACTICE AND LITURGICAL TRADITION

The Burial of the Dead and the church's prayers for those who have died recognize a "raising up" into the resurrection life. We pray with hope (BCP 507).

FORMATION IN BAPTISMAL DISCIPLESHIP

Christians are formed through prayer and devotion to an awareness of the communion of saints, the "whole family of God, the living and the dead" (BCP 862).

Proper 6, Year C (The Sunday Closest to June 15)

THEME OF THE LECTIONS

The forgiveness of sins.

- *The Collect:* See Year A.
- *1 Kings 21:1–10, (11–14), 15–21a:* Jezebel plots to obtain the vineyard of Naboth for her husband, Ahab. Elijah then prophesies the destruction of Ahab and his house, including Jezebel. Ahab asks for forgiveness and is spared, but others in his household are not.
- *Psalm 5:1–8:* A lament, asking God's forgiveness.
- *Galatians 2:15–21:* Paul argues with Cephas (Peter) over eating with Gentile Christians, saying that God's acceptance comes through faith in Christ rather than by works of the law.
- *Luke 7:36–83:* While he is eating dinner in a Pharisee's home, a woman who was leading an immoral life kisses Jesus' feet and wets them with her tears and dries them with her hair. She anoints his feet with myrrh. Jesus forgives the woman her sins, saying, "Your faith has saved you; go in peace."

ALTERNATIVE READINGS

- 2 Samuel 11:26–12:10, 13–15
- Psalm 32

KEY WORDS, IDEAS, AND CONCEPTS TO EXPLORE

- Sin
- Forgiveness
- Repentance
- Justification
- "Crucified with Christ"
- "Christ lives in me"
- Customs associated with hospitality in biblical times

STORIES TO TELL

- Naboth's vineyard.
- A woman anoints the feet of Jesus.

CHRISTIAN PRACTICE AND LITURGICAL TRADITION

- The traditions associated with the foot washing on Maundy Thursday provide an experience of servant ministry.
- The understanding that "Christ dwells in us" expressed in the prayer book comes, in part, from the Galatians text: that we may be made "one body with him, that he may dwell in us, and we in him" (BCP 336).

FORMATION IN BAPTISMAL DISCIPLESHIP

Congregations practice hospitality as a way of welcoming stranger and visitor into the forgiving fellowship of the church.

Proper 7, Year C (The Sunday Closest to June 22)

THEME OF THE LECTIONS

The commanding word of Jesus and power of God to search out the needy.

- *The Collect:* See Year A.
- *1 Kings 19:1–4, (5–7), 8–15a:* Elijah flees the wrath of Jezebel and goes into hiding. The Lord comes to Elijah, not in wind, fire, or earthquake but a still, small voice.
- *Psalm 42 and Psalm 43:* A cry to God for help.
- *Galatians 3:23–29:* We were held prisoners of the law until Christ came to us. Baptized into union with Christ, there is no such thing as Jew or Greek, slave or free, male or female. All are one people in Jesus Christ.
- *Luke 8:26–39:* Jesus heals the Gerasene demoniac.

ALTERNATIVE READINGS

- Isaiah 65:1–9
- Psalm 22:18–27

KEY WORDS, IDEAS, AND CONCEPTS TO EXPLORE

- God searching us out
- Living by faith rather than by law
- God's power over evil

CHRISTIAN PRACTICE AND LITURGICAL TRADITION

A Public Service of Healing can be found in *The Book of Occasional Services*.

FORMATION IN BAPTISMAL DISCIPLESHIP

Jesus' mind is set, already, on where he is ultimately headed. He knows, even as he is teaching and traveling, his physical and spiritual destination. On what is your face set, and how does it influence how you live your life each day?

Proper 8, Year C (The Sunday Closest to June 29)

THEME OF THE LECTIONS

Leaving everything to follow Christ.

- *The Collect:* See Year A.
- *2 Kings 2:1–2, 6–14:* Elijah gives his mantle to Elisha, who then watches Elijah ascend in a whirlwind into heaven.
- *Psalm 77:1–2, 11–20:* The psalmist's memory of old inspires hope and a renewed faith that will be effective even when God's way is unseen.
- *Galatians 5:1, 13–25:* The harvest of the Spirit is love, joy, peace, patience, goodness, kindness, faithfulness, and self-control. Paul urges Christians to walk by the Spirit without conceit or envy of one another.
- *Luke 9:51–62:* Traveling to Jerusalem, Jesus and his friends are refused accommodations in a Samaritan village. Jesus explains that discipleship means putting the kingdom of God ahead of every other responsibility or relationship.

ALTERNATIVE READINGS

- 1 Kings 19:15–16, 19–21
- Psalm 16

KEY WORDS, IDEAS, AND CONCEPTS TO EXPLORE

- Mantle

- Discipleship
- Rejection of God's word
- Freedom of the gospel
- Living by the Spirit
- Fruits of the Spirit
- We will be walking with Jesus on the way to Jerusalem and the cross from this week through Proper 26.

STORIES TO TELL
- Elisha and Elijah.

CHRISTIAN PRACTICE AND LITURGICAL TRADITION
At the ministration of communion the congregation moves to the Holy Table to receive the sacrament. In a sense, this movement expresses the call of the gospel to follow Christ. In some traditions, worship includes an "altar call" when people are invited to come forward to dedicate their lives to Christ. Episcopalians have a weekly "altar call" at the ministration of the Eucharist.

FORMATION IN BAPTISMAL DISCIPLESHIP
The congregation is called to look ahead to the coming reign of God rather than back with nostalgia to the past.

Proper 9, Year C (The Sunday Closest to July 6)

THEME OF THE LECTIONS
The power of God to defeat evil and bring about a new creation.
- *The Collect:* See Year A.
- *2 Kings 5:1–14:* Naaman, commander of the Syrian army, is a leper. He learns that there is a prophet in Samaria who can heal him. Elisha heals Naaman, who in a later verse says, "I know there is no God in all the earth but in Israel" (2 Kings 5:15).
- *Psalm 30:* A song of thanksgiving by someone who has been healed.
- *Galatians 6:(1–6), 7–16:* Because circumcision would bring Christians under the protection of the Jewish law and they would escape persecution, pressure was brought to bear on uncircumcised Gentiles. Paul said that circumcision doesn't matter; all that matters is the new creation in Christ.
- *Luke 10:1–11, 16–20:* Jesus chose seventy people to carry on the mission and sent them in pairs to the towns he would visit himself. He spoke

to them of the demands of discipleship and how they should visit the people of the towns. The seventy were given the power to defeat the forces of evil and their names are written in heaven.

ALTERNATIVE READINGS
- Isaiah 66:10–14
- Psalm 66:1–8

KEY WORDS, IDEAS, AND CONCEPTS TO EXPLORE
- God's peace
- Kingdom (or reign) of God
- Discipline of the disciple
- Judgment
- Circumcision
- The "marks of Jesus" (suffering for the sake of the gospel)
- God's "motherly" comfort

STORIES TO TELL
- The healing of Naaman the leper.

CHRISTIAN PRACTICE AND LITURGICAL TRADITION
The image of God as mother is found in a variety of our church's traditions, including the writings of Julian of Norwich.

FORMATION IN BAPTISMAL DISCIPLESHIP
Paul becomes a model for the church, bearing the marks of the cross by accepting suffering in proclaiming the gospel.

Proper 10, Year C (The Sunday Closest to July 13)

THEME OF THE LECTIONS
Doing God's word.
- *The Collect:* See Year A.
- *Amos 7:7–17:* The Lord showed Amos a vision of a man beside a wall with a plumb line and told Amos he was setting a plumb line to test his people of Israel, and that they would rise against Jeroboam (the king of Israel). Despite being warned to go away and never prophesy again, Amos speaks of how the Lord ordered him to prophesy to the people of Israel.
- *Psalm 82:* An indictment to the leaders to give justice to the weak on behalf of God.

- *Colossians 1:1–14:* A prayer of hope that God will give wisdom and insight into his will, and strength and power to meet whatever comes with patience and joy.
- *Luke 10:25–37:* A lawyer puts a question to Jesus, "What must I do to inherit eternal life?" Jesus responds with the two great commandments—love for God and love for your neighbor. "Who is my neighbor?" Jesus replies with the story of the Good Samaritan.

ALTERNATIVE READINGS
- Deuteronomy 30:9–14
- Psalm 25:1–9

KEY WORDS, IDEAS, AND CONCEPTS TO EXPLORE
- Plumb line
- Commandments
- God's word
- Priests and Levites
- Neighbor
- Prayer
- Spiritual wisdom
- Bearing fruit
- This week begins a four-week, semi-continuous reading of Colossians. Take time to introduce the epistle as an educational offering.

STORIES TO TELL
- Amos, a farmer of sycamore trees called to prophesy.
- The parable of the Good Samaritan.

CHRISTIAN PRACTICE AND LITURGICAL TRADITION
Many hospitals and congregations are named "Good Samaritan," reflecting the compassion expressed in the gospel story.

FORMATION IN BAPTISMAL DISCIPLESHIP
Acts of mercy inform the life and prayers of the congregation. As the despised Samaritan responded to the man in need, the church recognizes God's presence in the lives of those often considered its enemies.

Proper 11, Year C (The Sunday Closest to July 20)

THEME OF THE LECTIONS

God calls us to take time for Sabbath.

- *The Collect:* See Year A.
- *Amos 8:1–12:* Amos' visions reveal a coming judgment on Israel, especially its merchants, and political and religious leaders for economic abuses and deceitful practices.
- *Psalm 52:* A prophetic announcement of judgment and instructions for the righteous.
- *Colossians 1:15–28:* Paul writes of the reconciled community, which must continue in the faith and hope of the gospel. The sufferings with which Paul is afflicted are to be endured for the sake of Christ's body, the church.
- *Luke 10:38–42:* Mary and Martha were sisters in whose home Jesus visited. Mary sat at Jesus' feet, listening to his teaching, while Martha was doing all the tasks of preparation for guests.

ALTERNATIVE READINGS

- Genesis 18:1–10a
- Psalm 15

KEY WORDS, IDEAS, AND CONCEPTS TO EXPLORE

- Sabbath
- Judgment
- Suffering in Christ's name
- Mystery
- "Christ in you"
- Hope of glory

STORIES TO TELL

- Mary and Martha's visit with Jesus.

CHRISTIAN PRACTICE AND LITURGICAL TRADITION

The Great Fifty Days of Easter have traditionally been called *mystagogia*, a time when the mysteries of the faith are revealed to those who have been baptized at the Easter Vigil. Paul wrote about the "mystery" being revealed at last (Romans 16:25), and in Eucharistic Prayer A we say, "Therefore we proclaim the mystery of faith. . ." (BCP 363).

FORMATION IN BAPTISMAL DISCIPLESHIP

The church is called to hold leaders accountable for injustices directed toward the poor and those without a voice.

Proper 12, Year C (The Sunday Closest to July 27)

THEME OF THE LECTIONS

Being faithful to God in Christ; the importance and power of prayer.

- *The Collect:* See Year A.
- *Hosea 1:2–10:* Hosea's message of faithlessness is directed against abuses in Israelite religious practices using the image of marriage infidelity.
- *Psalm 85:* Steadfast love and faithfulness are at the essence of God.
- *Colossians 2:6–15, (16–19):* Paul warns the congregation at Colossae against false teaching, tells them to be rooted in Christ, firm in the faith they have been taught, and to let their hearts overflow with thankfulness for what God has done for us in Christ Jesus.
- *Luke 11:1–13:* Jesus teaches his disciples to pray and tells them to ask, and they will receive, to knock, and the door will be opened to them. If they, who are sinful human beings, know how to give their children good gifts, how much more will their heavenly Father give the Holy Spirit to those who ask?

ALTERNATIVE READINGS

- Genesis 18:20–32
- Psalm 138

KEY WORDS, IDEAS, AND CONCEPTS TO EXPLORE

- Faithfulness
- Prayer
- Intercession
- The Lord's Prayer (compare the two versions of the Lord's Prayer found in this Sunday's gospel and Matthew 6:9–13)
- Receiving and living in Christ

STORIES TO TELL

- The parable of the persistent friend.

CHRISTIAN PRACTICE AND LITURGICAL TRADITION

The origin of the Lord's Prayer is heard in today's gospel lection.

FORMATION IN BAPTISMAL DISCIPLESHIP

Intercessory prayer must be at the heart of congregational life; a life of prayer leads to acts of prayer.

Proper 13, Year C (The Sunday Closest to August 3)

THEME OF THE LECTIONS

One cannot place hope in wealth and status.

- *The Collect:* See Year A.
- *Hosea 11:1–11:* God shows compassion for Israel and promises to restore its people to their homes.
- *Psalm 107:1–9, 43:* Deliverance occurs after the needy have cried to the Lord.
- *Colossians 3:1–11:* Set one's hope and mind on things in Christ, not on earthly things. We are all one in Christ.
- *Luke 12:12–21:* Jesus refuses to be judge in division of a family property. He tells the parable of a man who gathered wealth for himself, but was a pauper in the sight of God.

ALTERNATIVE READINGS

- Ecclesiastes 1:2, 12–14; 2:18–23
- Psalm 49:1–11

KEY WORDS, IDEAS, AND CONCEPTS TO EXPLORE

- God's chosen ones
- God's wisdom
- Vanity
- Parable
- "Rich toward God"
- Stewardship

STORIES TO TELL

- The parable of the rich fool.

CHRISTIAN PRACTICE AND LITURGICAL TRADITION

The ancient custom of clothing the newly baptized in white garments had the symbolic significance of stripping off the old self and being clothed with a new self (Colossians 3:9–14). Later this symbol of being clothed in Christ became associated with the vesting of the priest in preparation for the celebration of the Eucharist.

FORMATION IN BAPTISMAL DISCIPLESHIP

Colossians provides a picture of the ideal communal life of the church, forming people into the Body of Christ.

Proper 14, Year C (The Sunday Closest to August 10)

THEME OF THE LECTIONS

Being righteous through faith.

- *The Collect:* See Year A.
- *Isaiah 1:1, 10–20:* Criticisms of the Temple rituals and prayers show that without justice and compassion they are meaningless to God, who ignores them.
- *Psalm 50:1–8, 23–24:* Those that follow the covenant will receive the promise of salvation.
- *Hebrews 11:1–3, 8–16:* The writer of the letter to the Hebrews calls the followers of Christ to faith and describes faith as that which gives assurance to our hopes and convinces us of realities we do not see. The story of Abraham and Sarah is used as an example of such faith and righteousness.
- *Luke 12:32–40:* Jesus tells his little community of followers that their Father in heaven has chosen to give them the kingdom. Therefore, they can trust themselves wholly to God. They are to hold themselves ready, because the Son of Man will come when they least expect him.

ALTERNATIVE READINGS

- Genesis 15:1–6
- Psalm 33:12–22

KEY WORDS, IDEAS, AND CONCEPTS TO EXPLORE

- Temple practices
- Righteousness through faith
- Inheritance
- Treasure
- This Sunday begins a four week, semi-continuous reading of Hebrews 11–13. Provide a background in the educational setting for this epistle. Hebrews can be difficult for the contemporary hearer to understand with its frequent allusions to temple practices and priesthood.

STORIES TO TELL

- The story of Abraham and Sarah.

CHRISTIAN PRACTICE AND LITURGICAL TRADITION

Texts such as the gospel for today led, in part, to the monastic tradition of taking a vow of poverty as an expression of total commitment to Christ.

FORMATION IN BAPTISMAL DISCIPLESHIP

Value formation is at the heart of today's readings. Possessions are not inherently evil. We lose our sense of wholeness with God, however, when we begin to think that we can control our destiny through what we have.

Proper 15, Year C (The Sunday Closest to August 17)

THEME OF THE LECTIONS

The cost of discipleship means choosing God above all others even when it creates conflict and division.

- *The Collect:* See Year A.
- *Isaiah 5:1–17:* The parable of the unfruitful vineyard is used to describe Israel and Judah. Greed, manipulation of justice, violence, and dishonesty will receive divine judgment.
- *Psalm 80:1–2, 8–18:* A community lament asking God to restore the people.
- *Hebrews 11:29–12:2:* We are surrounded by a cloud of witnesses who help us persevere in following Christ, the perfect example of faithful obedience to God.
- *Luke 12:49–56:* Jesus says that he has come to bring the fire of judgment to the earth. He knows that martyrdom lies ahead for him. Before there can be peace, there will be divisions, even among members of families.

ALTERNATIVE READINGS

- Jeremiah 23:23–29
- Psalm 82

KEY WORDS, IDEAS, AND CONCEPTS TO EXPLORE

- Cloud of witnesses
- Communion of saints
- Discipline
- Judgment
- Casting fire upon earth
- Apocalyptic literature

CHRISTIAN PRACTICE AND LITURGICAL TRADITION

The role of confession and penitence in the life of the church is heightened by texts such as those we hear this day.

FORMATION IN BAPTISMAL DISCIPLESHIP

The church lives expectantly ("Christ will come again"), constantly judging its life not by the norms of the present time, but by the ethic of the coming reign of God.

Proper 16, Year C (The Sunday Closest to August 24)

THEME OF THE LECTIONS

Jesus brings God's new covenant to the world.
- *The Collect:* See Year A.
- *Jeremiah 1:4–10:* Jeremiah is called to speak for God. He says, "I do not know how to speak, for I am only a boy." The Lord responds, ". . . for you shall go to all to whom I send you, and you shall speak whatever I command you. . . today I appoint you over nations and over kingdoms. . . "
- *Psalm 71:1–6:* The psalmist prays for God's continuing protection.
- *Hebrews 12:18–29:* Christians must remember that they stand in the light of the new covenant and not in the blazing fire of the old covenant. Christ's blood means reconciliation and forgiveness and not revenge. The new covenant makes possible the true worship of God.
- *Luke 13:10–17:* Jesus heals a bent-over, crippled woman on the Sabbath.

ALTERNATIVE READINGS
- Isaiah 58:9b–14
- Psalm 103:1–8

KEY WORDS, IDEAS, AND CONCEPTS TO EXPLORE
- Judgment
- Sabbath
- New Covenant

STORIES TO TELL
- The call of Jeremiah.
- The healing of the bent woman.

CHRISTIAN PRACTICE AND LITURGICAL TRADITION

Sabbath and Jubilee continue to be important principles for Christians. When is keeping Sabbath most important and when is observing Jubilee important? What are the modern-day parallels to the story of the bent-over woman in today's text, and what wisdom will be required to apply the right biblical principles at the right time?

FORMATION IN BAPTISMAL DISCIPLESHIP

The New Covenant is explained in *An Outline of the Faith* (BCP 850–851).

Proper 17, Year C (The Sunday Closest to August 31)

THEME OF THE LECTIONS

A call to compassion and a warning against pride.

- *The Collect:* See Year A.
- *Jeremiah 2:4–13:* Israel is reminded how they had followed the Lord in their "youth" but have since strayed from God's ways.
- *Psalm 81:1, 10–16:* God desires that the current hearers listen and do not repeat the mistakes of their ancestors who forgot God's law.
- *Hebrews 13:1–8, 15–16:* Christians are urged to love their fellow Christians; to show hospitality; to remember those in prison or those who are being mistreated; to keep the marriage bond intact; to be content with what they have; to honor their leaders and teachers and to follow their examples; and to remember that Jesus Christ is the same yesterday, today, and forever.
- *Luke 14:1, 7–14:* Jesus tells a parable that illustrates humility. He also says, "When you give a banquet, invite the poor, the crippled, the lame, and the blind." We will be blessed, because they cannot repay.

ALTERNATIVE READINGS

- Sirach 10:12–18
- Proverbs 25:6–7
- Psalm 112

KEY WORDS, IDEAS, AND CONCEPTS TO EXPLORE

- Biblical customs of hospitality
- Pride
- Exaltation and humility
- Compassion

STORIES TO TELL

- The parable of the banquet.

CHRISTIAN PRACTICE AND LITURGICAL TRADITION

The Prayer of Humble Access is said as a prayer of preparation before receiving
Holy Communion in the Rite I liturgy (BCP 337).

> We do not presume to come to this thy Table, O merciful
> Lord, trusting in our own righteousness, but in thy mani-
> fold and great mercies. We are not worthy so much as to
> gather up the crumbs under they Table. But thou are the
> same Lord whose property is always to have mercy. Grant
> us therefore, gracious Lord, so to eat the flesh of thy dear
> Son Jesus Christ, and to drink his blood, that we may ever-
> more dwell in him, and he in us. Amen.

FORMATION IN BAPTISMAL DISCIPLESHIP

Hospitality must be the hallmark of the Christian congregation. The stranger is
greeted and brought into its life, and those in need are heard and responded to
in the name of Jesus Christ.

Proper 18, Year C (The Sunday Closest to September 7)

THEME OF THE LECTIONS

Counting the cost of discipleship.

- *The Collect:* See Year A.
- *Jeremiah 18:1–11:* Jeremiah's visit to the potter becomes a symbol of
  God's plan for Israel and offers a final invitation to repent.
- *Psalm 139:1–5, 12–17:* We are fully known (our actions, thoughts, life-
  style, and speech) by God. We are vulnerable and dependent on God's
  presence in our lives.
- *Philemon 1–21:* Paul asks for the release of a runaway slave, Onesimus.
  As Christians, we are now brothers in Christ.
- *Luke 14:25–33:* Jesus describes the cost of discipleship to those who are
  following him. No one who does not put Jesus' work ahead of everything, even ahead of his own life, can be his disciple. No one can be his
  disciple without giving up all that he has.

ALTERNATIVE READINGS

- Deuteronomy 30:15–20
- Psalm 1

KEY WORDS, IDEAS, AND CONCEPTS TO EXPLORE

- Potter's clay
- Vulnerability
- Discipleship
- Bearing the cross
- This week Paul's brief letter to Philemon is read. Discuss the background of the letter.

STORIES TO TELL

- Jeremiah at the potter's house.

CHRISTIAN PRACTICE AND LITURGICAL TRADITION

The cross has long been the definitive symbol of Christianity and its founder. As early as the 50s of the first century, Paul used "the cross" as a recognized symbol of a much larger set of ideas and beliefs:

> For Christ did not send me to baptize but to proclaim the gospel, and not with eloquent wisdom, so that the cross of Christ might not be emptied of its power. For the message about the cross is foolishness to those who are perishing, but to us who are being saved it is the power of God. For it is written, "I will destroy the wisdom of the wise, and the discernment of the discerning I will thwart." (1 Corinthians 1:17–19)

FORMATION IN BAPTISMAL DISCIPLESHIP

Christians must become aware of the radical nature of discipleship. "Bearing the cross" means bearing the pain of injustice and suffering that is so evident in the world. The church and individual Christians are called to be involved in the struggles for wholeness and justice.

Proper 19, Year C (The Sunday Closest to September 14)

THEME OF THE LECTIONS

Jesus seeks out the lost sinners and rejoices at finding them.

- *The Collect:* See Year A.
- *Jeremiah 4:11–12, 22–28:* The coming desolation, which causes God anguish, despite having brought the enemy to besiege the land.

- *Psalm 14:* Failure to entrust life to God causes terror. The oppressed find refuge in God.
- *I Timothy 1:12–17:* Paul thanks God for judging him as trustworthy in spite of his persecution of God's people in former days. Paul feels that the grace of the Lord has been given to him.
- *Luke 15:1–10:* Jesus is challenged for welcoming and eating with sinners. He tells two parables, in each of which there is rejoicing over something that had been lost and was found again.

ALTERNATIVE READINGS
- Exodus 32:7–14
- Psalm 51:1–11

KEY WORDS, IDEAS, AND CONCEPTS TO EXPLORE
- Grace
- Mercy
- Forgiveness
- Pharisees and scribes
- Today begins a seven-week reading of 1 and 2 Timothy. Introduce the two epistles, along with Titus. The three epistles together are called the "pastoral epistles" because they deal with pastoral oversight of the New Testament church.

STORIES TO TELL
- The parable of the lost sheep.
- The parable of the lost coin.

CHRISTIAN PRACTICE AND LITURGICAL TRADITION
The Timothy text mentioned above is included in the "comfortable words" following the absolution in Rite I (BCP 332).

FORMATION IN BAPTISMAL DISCIPLESHIP
The congregation engages in evangelism not merely to draw new members into the church, but to reach out to those burdened with their own sense of sin and alienation.

Proper 20, Year C (The Sunday Closest to September 21)

THEME OF THE LECTIONS

Living in preparation for the judgment that is coming. (The parable heard in the gospel this week seems to praise the steward's dishonesty. Read the parable with Jesus' sense of humor in mind. The dishonest steward is better prepared than Jesus' disciples!)

- *The Collect:* See Year A.
- *Jeremiah 8:18–9:1:* God joins with the people and the earth in expressing vulnerability, pain, and grief over the invasion that will destroy life in the land.
- *Psalm 70:1–9:* A prayer for help. God stands with the poor and needy.
- *1 Timothy 2:1–7:* Paul urges that prayers be offered for all persons and for all in high office. It is God's will that all should find salvation and come to know the truth.
- *Luke 16:1–13:* Jesus tells the story of a rich man who had a steward who was discharged for bad management of his master's property. Jesus' disciples must be able to act when need arises, and must know the uses of wealth, but never be enslaved by it.

ALTERNATIVE READINGS

- Amos 84–7
- Psalm 113

KEY WORDS, IDEAS, AND CONCEPTS TO EXPLORE

- Intercessory prayer
- Nature of parables
- Steward or manager
- Living in readiness for judgment

STORIES TO TELL

- The parable of the dishonest steward.

CHRISTIAN PRACTICE AND LITURGICAL TRADITION

The rubrics on page 383 of the Book of Common Prayer set forth the topics for intercessory prayer. The church must pray for "the Nation and all in authority," "the welfare of the world," and other people, places, and institutions each time we gather to celebrate the Eucharist.

FORMATION IN BAPTISMAL DISCIPLESHIP

Intercessory prayer for the church and for the world must inform the life of the congregation. The church prays through its acts of healing and justice as well as through its words.

Proper 21, Year C (The Sunday Closest to September 28)

THEME OF THE LECTIONS

God judges those who neglect the poor and suffering.

- *The Collect:* See Year A.
- *Jeremiah 32:1–3a, 6–15:* Jeremiah is a model of obedient hopefulness in the face of tragedy and despair.
- *Psalm 91:1–6, 14–16:* A song of trust in God's deliverance.
- *1 Timothy 6:6–19:* Paul reminds Timothy of his calling to run the race of faith and take hold of eternal life. Timothy is to speak to those who are wealthy, and to tell them to fix their hopes on God rather than on money, to give away and to share, so that they may grasp the life that is truly life.
- *Luke 16:19–31:* Jesus told a story of a very rich man and a poor man (Lazarus) who was ill and lay hungry at the rich man's gate.

ALTERNATIVE READINGS

- Amos 6:1a, 4–7
- Psalm 146

KEY WORDS, IDEAS, AND CONCEPTS TO EXPLORE

- Awareness of those who suffer from sickness, hunger, oppression
- Seeking Christ in serving those in need
- Social justice
- Warning to the wealthy

STORIES TO TELL

- The story of the rich man and Lazarus.

CHRISTIAN PRACTICE AND LITURGICAL TRADITION

The Baptismal Covenant calls each Christian to be aware of suffering and injustice:

- *Will you seek and serve Christ in all persons, loving your neighbor as yourself?*

- *Will you strive for justice and peace among all people, and respect the dignity of every human being?* (BCP 305)

FORMATION IN BAPTISMAL DISCIPLESHIP

The congregation must constantly ask, who is the Lazarus at our gate, and how can we respond?

Proper 22, Year C (The Sunday Closest to October 5)

THEME OF THE LECTIONS

Living in faith knowing that we are following the teachings of God.
- *The Collect:* See Year A.
- *Lamentations 1:1–6:* A poet laments Jerusalem.
- *Canticle: Lamentations 3:19–26:* A Song of Waiting OR *Psalm 137:* A recollection of Jerusalem. Memory sustains hope.
- *2 Timothy 1:1–14:* After beginning with a prayer, Paul thanks God for the sincerity of Timothy's faith and urges Timothy to keep before him the sound teaching he has had, and to live by faith and love that are ours in Jesus Christ.
- *Luke 17:5–10:* Jesus reminds the disciples of the tremendous strength and power of faith. He told them the story of a servant who works all day in the fields who should expect no reward. "We are worthless slaves; we have done only what we ought to have done."

ALTERNATIVE READINGS
- Habakkuk 1:1–4; 2:1–4
- Psalm 37:1–10

KEY WORDS, IDEAS, AND CONCEPTS TO EXPLORE
- Faith
- Hope
- Pastoral epistles (see Proper 19, Year C)
- Prayer
- Servanthood

STORIES TO TELL
- The ministry of Timothy.

CHRISTIAN PRACTICE AND LITURGICAL TRADITION

The duty of all Christians is to follow Christ; to come together week by week for corporate worship; and to work, pray, and give for the spread of the kingdom of God (BCP 856).

FORMATION IN BAPTISMAL DISCIPLESHIP

The Christian hope is to live with confidence in newness and fullness of life, and to await the coming of Christ in glory, and the completion of God's purpose for the world.

Proper 23, Year C (The Sunday Closest to October 12)

THEME OF THE LECTIONS

God is faithful. That is the word that must be proclaimed.
- *The Collect:* See Year A.
- *Jeremiah 29:1, 4–7:* The prophet tells how the exiles from Jerusalem should live while in exile in Babylon.
- *Psalm 66:1–11:* A communal song of thanksgiving for what God has done.
- *2 Timothy 2:8–15:* Paul writes from prison, reminding Timothy that even though he is wearing chains like a criminal, the word of God is free. He urges Timothy to continue to proclaim the glorious salvation in Christ Jesus and to work to be worthy of God's approval, and to be forthright in speaking the truth.
- *Luke 17:11–19:* Jesus heals ten lepers. One returns to offer thanks. Jesus tells him his faith has made him well.

ALTERNATIVE READINGS
- 2 Kings 5:1–3, 7–15c
- Psalm 111

KEY WORDS, IDEAS, AND CONCEPTS TO EXPLORE
- Word of God
- Faithfulness
- Eternal glory

STORIES TO TELL
- Jesus' healing of the ten lepers.

CHRISTIAN PRACTICE AND LITURGICAL TRADITION

The Book of Common Prayer offers a variety of prayers and litanies for giving thanks (BCP 836–841).

FORMATION IN BAPTISMAL DISCIPLESHIP

The congregation's prayers always include praise and thanksgiving. We become increasingly aware of God's power as we express thanks for what is happening in our lives and in the world.

Proper 24, Year C (The Sunday Closest to October 19)

THEME OF THE LECTIONS

We are to preach, teach, and live the faith. Because God loves us, it is all right to "pester" God with our prayers and petitions.

- *The Collect:* See Year A.
- *Jeremiah 31:27–34:* A new covenant will be given in which God will write on the people's hearts and "they shall be my people."
- *Psalm 119:97–104:* Love for God's instruction yields wisdom and understanding.
- *2 Timothy 3:14–4:5:* Paul tells Timothy to remember from whom he learned the truths of the faith, and to proclaim the message, to use every gift at his command, and to teach with the necessary patience. He must keep calm, face the hardships, and work for the spread of the gospel.
- *Luke 18:1–8:* In order to show his disciples that they were to keep on praying and never lose heart, Jesus told a parable about a persistent widow and a judge who didn't fear God and cared nothing for the people. The Righteous Judge will hear the prayers of his chosen.

ALTERNATIVE READINGS

- Genesis 32:22–31
- Psalm 121

KEY WORDS, IDEAS, AND CONCEPTS TO EXPLORE

- Petition
- Fervent prayer
- Role of scripture
- Scripture as inspired

STORIES TO TELL

- The persistent widow.

CHRISTIAN PRACTICE AND LITURGICAL TRADITION

- Scripture is read at every service of worship "for teaching, for reproof, for correction, and for training in righteousness" (2 Timothy 3:16).
- The service of Evening Prayer opens with the words of Psalm 70:1: "O God, make speed to save us. O Lord, make haste to help us" (BCP 117). In these and many other prayers we cry out to God for help and blessing.

FORMATION IN BAPTISMAL DISCIPLESHIP

Scripture must be at the heart of every aspect of congregational life. Dialogue about and study of the scriptures needs to be an integral part of meetings, educational events, and times of discernment.

Proper 25, Year C (The Sunday Closest to October 26)

THEME OF THE LECTIONS

One's prayer and faith in proclaiming the gospel is remembered by God.

- *The Collect:* See Year A.
- *Joel 2:23–32:* The outpouring of God's spirit on the land will follow the days of darkness and judgment.
- *Psalm 65:* A communal song of thanksgiving to God who answers prayer and cares for creation.
- *2 Timothy 4:6–8, 16–18:* Paul, imprisoned in Rome, is secure in the knowledge that his rewards are waiting for him. The Lord gave Paul strength to preach the gospel, and rescued him from the lion's jaws. The Lord will continue to be with Paul and keep him safe until the Lord's heavenly reign begins. Paul's faith in proclaiming the gospel is remembered.
- *Luke 18:9–14:* Jesus told a parable regarding self-righteousness. Everyone who exalts himself will be humbled, but the one who humbles himself will be exalted.

ALTERNATIVE READINGS

- Sirach 35:12–17
- Jeremiah 14:7–10, 19–22
- Psalm 84:1–6

KEY WORDS, IDEAS, AND CONCEPTS TO EXPLORE

- "That Day" (the day of Christ's return, judgment day, the Day of the Lord)
- Prayer
- Pharisees and tax collectors
- Sinner

CHRISTIAN PRACTICE AND LITURGICAL TRADITION

- Confession and penitence are a part of every worship service. Even when there is not a specific prayer of confession at the service, the Eucharistic prayers and other prayers of the prayer book include an acknowledgment of sin.
- The customs associated with Lent and Holy Week provide a time for the acknowledgment of sin and the need for repentance.

FORMATION IN BAPTISMAL DISCIPLESHIP

Congregational life is balanced between joy and praise on the one hand and a constant awareness of the need for repentance and renewal on the other. The congregation lives in the light of the coming day of judgment.

Proper 26, Year C (The Sunday Closest to November 2)

THEME OF THE LECTIONS

The covenant demands justice. Without justice, praise and sacrifice are empty acts that do not make God's people righteous.

- *The Collect:* See Year A.
- *Habakkuk 1:1–4; 2:1–4:* Habakkuk describes the breakdown in Judah's legal system, allowing for ruthless accumulation of wealth. He prophesies to the people that the righteous live by their faith, and God's rule is reliable.
- *Psalm 119:137–144:* God's righteousness.
- *2 Thessalonians 1:1–4, 11–12:* Paul, Sylvanus, and Timothy write to the congregation in Thessalonica, thanking God for their increasing faith and love in the face of the troubles they endure. The persecutions will prove them worthy of the kingdom of God, for which they are suffering. Christ is to be glorified through the witness of the church.
- *Luke 19:1–10:* Zacchaeus, the chief tax collector in Jericho, seeks out Jesus. His actions confirm that he too is heir to the promise of salvation.

ALTERNATIVE READINGS

- Isaiah 1:10–18
- Psalm 32:1–8

KEY WORDS, IDEAS, AND CONCEPTS TO EXPLORE

- Righteousness
- "Worthy of (God's) call"
- Tax collectors
- Justice as a right response to God
- Salvation is available to all

STORIES TO TELL

- The story of Zacchaeus.

CHRISTIAN PRACTICE AND LITURGICAL TRADITION

- Form IV of Prayers of the People include "Guide the people of this land, and of all the nations, in the ways of justice and peace; that we may honor one another and serve the common good" (BCP 388).
- The Book of Common Prayer contains "Historical Documents of the Church" including how the church has defined salvation through the Councils of the Church (BCP 863–878).

FORMATION IN BAPTISMAL DISCIPLESHIP

The Baptismal Covenant demands that the Christian be guided by the biblical call for justice.

Proper 27, Year C (The Sunday Closest to November 9)

THEME OF THE LECTIONS

The resurrection of the dead is proclaimed.

(Note: The themes of the season of Advent begin to be expressed this week, offering an opportunity to explore the rich heritage of Advent.)

- *The Collect:* See Year A.
- *Haggai 1:15b–2:9:* A vision of Judah's restoration and the reconstruction of the Temple in glory.
- *Psalm 145:1–5, 18–22:* A celebration of God's sovereignty and greatness OR *Psalm 98:* An enthronement psalm claiming victory and salvation with joyful noise.

- *2 Thessalonians 2:1–5, 13–17:* The Day of the Lord Jesus Christ will come unexpectedly. The church in Thessalonica should live in faith and love, knowing that God has not destined them for the terrors of his wrath but to receive salvation through Jesus Christ who died so that his true followers, alive or dead, may live in company with him.
- *Luke 20:27–38:* The Sadducees challenge Jesus regarding the existence of the resurrection. Jesus' response is that God is not God of the dead, but of the living. For him all are alive.

ALTERNATIVE READINGS

- Job 19:23–27a
- Psalm 17:1–9

KEY WORDS, IDEAS, AND CONCEPTS TO EXPLORE

- Salvation
- Resurrection
- Redeemer
- Sadducees

CHRISTIAN PRACTICE AND LITURGICAL TRADITION

- The Apostles' Creed and the Nicene Creed affirm the resurrection of the dead and the final judgment: "He will come again in glory to judge the living and the dead, and his kingdom will have no end" (BCP 359).
- "The Christian Hope" section of "An Outline of the Faith" (BCP 861–862) discusses the final things.
- The joy of the resurrection is reflected in the traditions of Christian burial. See the rubric that begins, "The liturgy for the dead is an Easter liturgy. It finds all its meaning in the resurrection. Because Jesus was raised from the dead, we, too, shall be raised" (BCP 507).

FORMATION IN BAPTISMAL DISCIPLESHIP

The congregation lives in the light of the resurrection and the final judgment. Hope and judgment characterize the outlook of the church as it proclaims Christ to the world.

Proper 28, Year C (The Sunday Closest to November 16)

THEME OF THE LECTIONS

The coming day of glory and judgment is ushered in by a time of frightening upheaval and persecution.

- *The Collect:* See Year A.
- *Isaiah 65:17–25:* God is still in control of human history. There is a promise of a new heaven and a new earth.
- *Canticle 9 (Isaiah 12:2–6):* The First Song of Isaiah; God is our salvation.
- *2 Thessalonians 3:6–13:* Because they believe that the age in which they live will not continue, and that they themselves are above ordinary obligations, some Christians are living in idleness. Paul appeals to them in the name of the Lord Jesus Christ to work quietly to earn their living, and he charges everyone never to tire of doing right.
- *Luke 21:5–19:* Jesus' words about the destruction of the Temple are reminiscent of previous prophecies about God's judgment, sharing what the cosmic signs of the end of the world will be like. Jesus urges his followers, "By your endurance you will gain your souls."

ALTERNATIVE READINGS

- Malachi 4:1–2a
- Psalm 98

KEY WORDS, IDEAS, AND CONCEPTS TO EXPLORE

- A new heaven and a new earth
- The coming of the Lord
- End times
- Judgment day

CHRISTIAN PRACTICE AND LITURGICAL TRADITION

See Proper 27, Year C, as well as general remarks in the chapter concerning the season of Advent.

FORMATION IN BAPTISMAL DISCIPLESHIP

See Proper 27, Year C, as well as general remarks in the chapter concerning the season of Advent.

Proper 29, Year C (The Sunday Closest to November 23)

THEME OF THE LECTIONS

This day is often referred to as Christ the King, or the Reign of Christ, Sunday. Christ's sovereignty is the major theme in the lections for all three years.

- *The Collect:* See Year A.
- *Jeremiah 23:1–6:* God promises restoration to kings, portrayed as the shepherd of their people.
- *Canticle 4 or Canticle 16* (The Song of Zechariah) OR *Psalm 46:* A song of Zion that proclaims God's cosmic sovereignty.
- *Colossians 1:11–20:* Christ is the image of the invisible God; all things were created through him or for him. He is the head of the body, the church, and its origin. God chose to reconcile all things to himself through Christ, making peace through the shedding of his blood on the cross.
- *Luke 23:33–43:* Luke links the royal titles Messiah of God and King of the Jews with Jesus' identity as the servant who suffers as the chosen one.

KEY WORDS, IDEAS, AND CONCEPTS TO EXPLORE

- Christ as king or sovereign
- The work of a shepherd
- Firstborn of all creation
- Messiah

CHRISTIAN PRACTICE AND LITURGICAL TRADITION

- Some of the traditions associated with worship in the Episcopal church have their origins in the royal court: for example, purple, the color for Advent and Lent, was the color associated with royalty and became linked to the coming of Christ as king.
- The psalms and prayers of the church are filled with imagery of the ruler.

FORMATION IN BAPTISMAL DISCIPLESHIP

"Jesus is Lord" (the earliest Christian creed) means that Jesus stands above all other earthly power and authority. All through history and into the present moment, choosing God above earthly authority has caused persecution and conflict in the life of the church. The congregation and wider church must witness always to the authority of Jesus Christ, realizing that there will be times when conflict will be the direct result of such a witness.

PART III:
KEYS TO TEACHING AND LEARNING

The Learning Process

Christ's promise to be present when two or three are gathered together in his name (Matthew 18:20) applies to education as well as prayer. The minute we sit down together, we are involved in education; every encounter, whether planned or unplanned, is an opportunity to teach and to learn. Creative and thoughtful planning, however, can enhance the process of learning.

Whenever we start to plan we must be in touch with others, asking if our ideas fit within the overall educational goals of the congregation. Sharing with one another in God's presence produces a synergy of ideas; choosing together among such ideas results in smoother, clearer, and more creative planning; seeking to fill in gaps and to avoid disjointed activities makes for a more cohesive and complete educational program. Whether our colleagues are those working at our side or the far-off writers of books to which we turn, we are never alone in the task of education.

THE ROLES OF TEACHERS AND LEARNERS

The role of the learner, as one on a quest, is to ask questions, and one of the teacher's responsibilities is to use questions carefully to stimulate and encourage the learner's reflection. The teacher must be a questioner as well, and certainly is in a position to accomplish the greatest learning. On the other hand, the role of the teacher cannot be that of someone with all the answers. Many people are reluctant to volunteer as teachers because they feel they "don't know enough," when actually the chief requirement is a willingness to search, while enabling and organizing the journey that the whole group takes together as co-learners.

The Teacher Is . . .

- *A listener* who is attentive enough to hear what the learners say, who is aware of what is unsaid, who responds without judgments that stifle, and who knows how to wait upon God.
- *A translator* who puts the words of the church into language that is understandable and images that are recognizable to the learners. "What is the meaning?" is the foremost question.
- *A custom designer* who tailors the curriculum for a specific moment to fit a specific group of learners by being aware of their interests, skills, and experiences, and by planning and organizing their time together.
- *A pacesetter* who provides a setting and an opportunity to learn within a trusting and respecting community of explorers that cares for and accepts one another, who presents something to pique the learners' curiosity and stir up their questions.

Questions Are Useful . . .

- *For information* to recall specific facts, to seek data, or to determine what has been understood. Some questions require correct answers, although the closed nature of such answers tends to limit discussion. At the same time, too many of such questions create a testing, competitive atmosphere where learners can be put on the defensive.
- *For analysis* to stimulate thinking further, to lead to conjectures, to dig for reasons, to evaluate a situation. These questions offer the possibility of several responses. Additional questions may follow naturally. "Why—?" and "What do you think—?" can initiate them. But if thoughts are belittled, judged, or contradicted by others in group, open expression becomes reluctant or stifled.
- *For personal reactions* to identify with, or to relate something to one's own life, as guides to discover values, to make decisions, to reflect. Answers will be interpretive, and might include "What would you have done—?", or "When have you ever felt—?" But it should be noted that many such questions do not contribute automatically to the learning of the whole group. To avoid invasion of privacy, reserve the learner's right to delay an answer or to be silent.

PLANNING AN EDUCATIONAL OFFERING

The Setting

Ask the questions: Who? Where? When?

- Who will be there? Whom do we hope to include? Although "education is for everyone," we must be aware of the needs of each specific group of learners.
- Where will it be? What space is available? In what places can learning occur? Recognize that learning can happen at all sorts of occasions (teenagers serving a church supper, a baptism, vestry planning time, stewardship programs). Comfortable space, lighting, and decor help set the atmosphere but are secondary to the people involved and to the message.
- What time is available? What time span is needed? Part of an hour? An evening? A weekend? Perhaps only a few minutes, recurring daily? A series of several weeks? A year-long event? A wide variety of time and space could be considered, but the choice must be right for the group and the topic. Examine and reexamine the situation over time.

The Purpose and Objectives

- Ask the questions: What do we hope to accomplish? Why are we doing it?
- Develop a purpose statement for the session or program that answers these two questions, such as "To do something in order that something might happen." Be specific as to what you are going to do and what you hope will happen.
- List the objectives you hope to accomplish. Objectives should be attainable and measurable.
- To avoid the frustration of an incomplete task, remember that the briefer the time available, the more pointed the focus must be.

The Leading Theme

Ask the question: About what main idea are we concerned?

- Considering a common theme can give unity and continuity to a congregation's several programs. Be sure the theme is inclusive enough and part of the church's mission.
- Looking at an idea within a theme from several viewpoints, in a variety of ways, gives unexpected insights and understandings.
- It is not necessary to teach all there is to know about a theme at one time. Search out the themes within themes. Focus on one point, then, God willing, tomorrow and next year will bring more opportunities.

- The church year provides a framework of themes, and the catechism in the Book of Common Prayer organizes the "Outline of the Faith" into eighteen topics. (See "A Seasonal Guide to An Outline of the Faith" later in this chapter for further ideas.)

The Ways and Means

Ask the questions: How will we learn? What are the alternatives? What are the resources available?

- Remember that "resources" are people and places, as well as books and activities.
- Explore different ways of learning: lecturing and reading aloud are often the least effective modes of teaching. Try reading together, viewing pictures and slides, doing skits and field trips. Reflecting upon firsthand experience is often the most valuable way to learn.
- A change of pace stimulates imagination and avoids overworking any one sort of activity.

Planning the Learning Event

- Ask the questions: Which activity will we choose? What are the learners going to do?
- Activities should actively involve most learners and call for creativity by the learners.
- Each activity should contribute directly to the focus and be appropriate to the age and skills of the learners.
- Choose activities that the leader has confidence in doing.
- Activities should fit into the time and space allowed.

The Procedure

Ask the questions: What is the schedule? Who has what responsibilities, before and during the event?

Stages to a learning event include:

- *Launching:* Mark the beginning, clarify the purpose, provide continuity with what has been done before.
- *Presentation:* May be done by teachers or by others.
- *Exploration:* Should always be done by the learners.
- *Creative Response:* Teachers should encourage learners to risk trying new things and responding in new ways.

- *Conclusion:* May give carry-over, link to next occasion, or be a "cliff-hanger," but be aware that the same people may not be in attendance each time the group meets.

Being aware of how long each activity should take helps avoid interruption or an unrealistic schedule.

- The teacher needs to know what the logical next step is and to be prepared to move on to a parallel activity, further exploration, or to summary reflection.
- The teacher should keep an overall time scheme in mind, yet remain flexible to extend or cut short the allotted time as responses require. Knowing the focus will help avoid being sidetracked while still acknowledging concerns and interests of the group.
- To backtrack or repeat simply for those who were absent previously denies the work of those who were present. If necessary, include latecomers briefly by having learners review for them.
- Responsibilities are best designated and shared as widely as possible by all those involved.

The Evaluation

Ask the question: How will we know we have reached our objectives?

Evaluation is a crucial aspect of any learning event. Evaluation enables us to learn from both our successes and our failures. As soon after the event as possible, stop to review what you did and how you did it.

- Take a short time at the end of a session to get the evaluation of the participants. Youth or adult participants can respond to a written evaluation form; children can be asked questions informally as you are wrapping up a session or after a session is over. The following are examples of the kinds of questions you may want to ask.
  - Our purpose for offering this program was [state the purpose]. How has this purpose been accomplished or not accomplished for you?
  - What in this program was most meaningful to you? Least meaningful?
  - If we could do this program again, what would you change? Add? Leave out?
  - What effect will this program have on you in the future? (Frame this question to fit your purpose statement. For example, if you have just offered a course on world hunger, ask how it will affect the participants' response to the crisis.)

- As part of your evaluation, analyze all the informal and formal sources of data available to you.
  - Think about how you and the participants felt about the session.
  - The "body language" of the participants can tell you more about how involved they felt during the session.
  - Attendance may be controlled by outside circumstances, but people will find ways to attend programs that are really important to them.
  - Where are the handouts and artwork done by the participants? If you find "take home" material left in the pew, take note: their impact probably was not felt.
  - Check with parents: what do their children talk about on the way home from church?
- What long-term effects do you see from the program? Are people who were considered "newcomers" becoming more active? If so, that is positive feedback for your planning group.

Sharing the Biblical Story

Basing Christian education on the biblical stories helps us connect to God in a personal and communal way. Sharing these stories week after week in the liturgy allows us to become part of the story. John Westerhoff states, "In the community's liturgy, story and action merge; in worship we remember and we act in symbolic ways which bring our sacred traditions and our lives together, providing with both meaning and motivation for our daily existence" (*Will Our Faith Have Children*, Morehouse, 2000). The liturgical Bible readings, the seasons and festivals of the church year, and the sacraments and other rites of the church mark the growing points in each person's life. Education programs that have the biblical story at its core will help all ages see their lives and their world through the eyes of God as revealed in the biblical story.

Using the lectionary as the primary emphasis for education comes from the school of "narrative theology." This does not look at doctrine and a conceptual understanding of the faith, as important as that is, but rather at the stories that led individuals and communities of people to confess the one true God. Something happened to those people thousands of years ago to respond to God, "Hear I am!" and "We believe!" Using the approach of narrative theology, stories are not used as illustrations to explain a theological concept. They are seen as the primary source of God's revelation. The preacher and teacher engage the listener through sermon and lesson plan. Participants are invited to step into the biblical drama, to experience the joy, the anguish, the tension, and the hope in each story as experienced through God's people. They are drawn into their own stories as they reflect how it intersects with the biblical story.

Telling the stories that come up in the lectionary week after week offers both teacher and preacher an effective way of helping children and adults engage in the study and appreciation of the scriptures. However, not every week has appointed texts that lend themselves to storytelling. Educators often call them "problem weeks" and find themselves at a loss with how to proceed. The key is to discover the story that lies behind the appointed lection. For example, when Paul's letter to the Philippians is the reading for the day, turn to the sixteenth chapter of the Acts of the Apostles and tell the story of Paul's captivity in the city of Philippi. After telling this story, read or paraphrase the appointed epistle. The text will then have meaning as it is put into the context of the community of which it was first written.

TELLING THE STORY

Before we can share the power of a Bible story, we ourselves must thoroughly understand the story. One of the basic approaches to understanding a story is to know the literary type to which it belongs. It will clarify what the author intended and what our ancestors had in mind when they repeated the story throughout the generations.

- *Myths* are traditional stories that originate in preliterate societies. They deal with supernatural beings, ancestors, and heroes as they sum up a people's cultural ideas and commonly felt emotions. Myths deal with ultimate origins, meanings, and values as they narrate a sacred history. They explain the unexplainable and establish for society the basis of understanding origins, codes of morality, and life values. Many of the stories in Genesis provided the Israelites with the theological understanding of their call to be Yahweh's people.
- *Legends* are unverified stories about the heroes of a people. They are passed down from generation to generation, and though they may be partly historical, they have taken on fanciful details. They are often an important part of the story of a nation. These stories are partly told to inspire the next generation and partly to explain the origins of traditions and the viewpoint of the people. Some of the accounts of Elijah and Elisha and other Old Testament heroes are of this nature.
- *Parables* are different than legends and myths in that they confront the accepted norms so as to open the hearer's mind to new understandings of truth and possibility. Parabolic religion, which Jesus represented, forces

us out of our safe systems of accepted knowledge and understanding and confronts us with uncertainty and confusion so that we can move into deeper realms of reality that God is always opening up to us. God is always calling us into deeper communion and mystery. Parables make room for the mystery and transcendence of God by throwing the doors wide open to new possibilities of truth. We do not tell parables to answer questions or to resolve issues; we tell them with the deliberate intention of raising questions and of forcing the hearers to reexamine their assumptions about life and truth.

Steps for Preparing to Tell the Story

1. Read the story you want to tell in its entirety.
2. Jot down on an index card the turning points and details that help shape the story.
3. Let your mind go; imagine yourself telling the story effectively to the group you will be sharing it with. Picture the kind of response you would want from them. In your mind, begin telling the story to the imagined group. Repeat the process until you can actually see the scene you are describing. Go over the story in your mind until you are ready to throw the index card away.
4. Tell the story!

TELLING THE STORY WITH YOUNG CHILDREN

Sitting on the floor with young children gives an intimacy, a feeling of being in the story together. If adults are included in the group, have them sit behind the children. When children receive a story, the parents will receive it too. If a child is blocked from receiving the story because of being too far away from the story-teller, the caregiver will be distracted by the child's inattention. This is true for the classroom as well as the sanctuary! Encourage families to sit "up front and close" to the action of the liturgy.

Felt boards, pictures, objects, and manipulatives have their place in helping the hearers respond to the story. Some teaching methods for storytelling are centered on the materials so that they become the focus, such as in *Godly Play, Catechesis of the Good Shepherd,* and *Beulahland.* However, we often want the hearers to picture the story in their minds. Visual aids will cause the listeners to see the picture we present rather than involving themselves in living into their own pictures.

Once the story has been told, we can sit back and listen to the hearer's responses. This is not the time to interpret the story for them or turn it into a teaching device. Key your remarks to their responses. Providing a means for the individual or group to respond to the story in an open-ended way helps integrate the story. Respond with art materials: clay, paint, pastels, tissue paper, and fabric. Dramatize the story and videotape it to present to others. Write a poem. Sing a song about the story. The possibilities are endless.

THE STORY THROUGH MUSIC AND DRAMA

"He (or she) who sings, prays twice" is a familiar quote from St. Augustine of Hippo. Most of our vivid memories of worship during childhood probably include a hymn or two in which we learned a Bible story or important element in the liturgy, often with hand motions. To sing is to include all of the brain—the left hemisphere for the verbal, the right hemisphere for the musical. Children up to the ages of seven or eight think symbolically and intuitively rather than conceptually. So many of the tenets of our faith are abstract, so dramatic play through singing, dancing, and moving are means to learn about the world and the deep meaning of the biblical story. Our faith tradition is full of song: Miriam singing at the shore of the Red Sea (Exodus 15:20–21), King David dancing in jubilation (2 Samuel 6:14–16), and Jesus with his disciples "when they had sung the hymn, they went out to the Mount of Olives." (Mark 14:26).

Everyone can participate musically, from playing an instrument to clapping, beating time on a drum or dancing and singing. Noted priest and author who teaches using movement and music, Nancy Roth, writes in *We Sing of God: A Hymnal for Children* (New York: Church Publishing, 1989), "The gift of listening, the gift of singing and of playing, the gift of moving and dancing and the gift of poetry and art, are given us by God in order to glorify the Creator." Take advantage of the many hymnals produced by and for the Episcopal Church. There are many songs that correspond to the lesson themes each Sunday in our lectionary that will enhance and make memories for all God's children.

REFLECTION AFTER WORSHIP

The following questions can be for personal reflection or else conversation within the family. It might also serve as an evaluation tool for those involved in planning the liturgy in a congregation.

- Which part of worship was most meaningful for you? Why?
- What detracted from your worship experience?
- What do you think the overall theme of this day's worship was?
- Say something about the music that was included in the worship today.
- On this particular day, how did worship make you feel?
- What did you see, hear, or smell at worship that caught your attention?
- Tell what one of the lessons was about.
- What was the sermon about? Name one story or example that the preacher used that you liked. How did the sermon make you feel? What is one way in which this sermon is different from other sermons you have heard?
- If you were the preacher, what message would you have given?
- How did the prayers make you feel?
- Was there any portion of the service in which you felt uncomfortable? Why do you think this occurred? What could have alleviated this, if anything?
- What is one thing you would like to take from this service to think about for the rest of the week?

BIBLE STUDY METHODS FOR HOME AND CHURCH

Reflecting on scripture can be done individually or within a group, including the family. A variety of methods can be used, with some being best for small groups. Reading or hearing the passage from a variety of biblical translations can also open up new insights. A study Bible that has footnotes or sidebars of explanation can enhance individual and group reading. Light a candle. Begin with prayer. Be comfortable in silence. Let the Spirit speak to you.

Lectio Divina

When we pray with the scriptures, we are engaged with God's word personally instead of academically. In praying scripture, the imagination is engaged and we dwell with the text instead of reflecting on the text. In the tradition of the church, the praying of scripture was known as *lectio divina*—the process of divine reading of scripture. John H. Westerhoff, III in *Living Faithfully as a Prayer Book People* (Harrisburg, PA: Morehouse Publishing, 2004) describes the process as follows:

- *Lectio* (to read): If a lesson is read in public, it should be read very slowly and clearly so that the listeners can fully hear it. If you read it alone, you may want to read it more than once aloud until you have made it your own.

- *Meditatio* (to meditate): Enter the passage fully. Be present to it, enter into it, and let it engage you completely and personally. Exercise your imagination and experience the text.
- *Oratio* (to pray): Converse with God about your experience. Reflect on this piece of scripture until God reveals to you some insights and implications for your life of faith.
- *Contemplatio* (to contemplate): Be silent before God, empty your conscious mind, and open yourself to receive the grace God desires to give you so that you might, with God's help, live out the implications of your conversation with God.

The Aural Method

This method and variations on it have been used throughout many parts of the world. It is a variation on the base community methods of South America, although many call it African Bible Study. Since that name reinforces Africa as a single country rather than a continent of many nations, the Aural Method name is preferred. *Time frame:* ½ – 1 hour.

Three important principles govern this method of experiencing scripture:

1. Confidentiality is always strictly observed. Whatever is said in the group of a personal nature is not to be repeated outside the group. It is not even a topic for subsequent conversation with the individual involved. "What is said here, stays here."
2. Participants are free to "pass" at any time if they cannot think of a response or do not wish to share it.
3. When a person is speaking to the group, the group simply listens with no response. No one is to discuss what someone else has said, though sometimes another person's response may trigger a similar thought.

STEPS FOR THE AURAL METHOD

1. A person appointed reads the passage slowly. Before the reading, allow a minute or so of silence as the leader reminds people to listen for the word or phrase that catches their attention.
2. Participants take a minute to recall in silence the word or phrase that caught their attention.
3. Beginning with the leader, each person says the word or phrase with the group (no more than just a word or phrase).
4. Someone else reads the passage (opposite sex of first reader).

5. Participants think about: "Where does this passage touch my life today?" (3–5 minutes of silence)

6. Each person shares these: "For me, . . . "

7. Someone else reads the passage out loud again.

8. Participants think about: "From what I have heard and shared, what does God want me to do or be this week? How does God invite me to change?" (3–5 minutes)

9. Each person to share these: "For me, . . . " The leader reminds the group that each person will pray for the person on their left, naming what they share in this step, so they will want to listen carefully and remember any specifics the person names.

10. Invite each person to pray for the person on their left, naming what was shared in Step 9, and to pray that prayer daily until the group meets again. (Or a general form prayer, for example, "Christ, may your blessing go with _____. Fill her/him with your love and grace.")

11. Say the Lord's Prayer together.

For variety, the following questions may be used:

- After the first reading, "What does this reading say to you about God?"
- After the second reading, "What does this reading say to you about who you are?"
- After the third reading, "What do you hear God asking you to do or be this week?"

Equipping the Saints

This approach by the late Verna Dozier, a pioneer Christian educator and biblical scholar, is taken from *Equipping the Saints* (Alban Institute, 1985) and uses more than one translation. It studies the Bible in significant segments—not verse by verse. Try to find several translations and encourage group members to bring one or more translations with them. Preferably each person will have at least two translations. You will also need at least one and preferably two or more commentaries. If a commentary or reflection by someone from another culture is available, it would be helpful to read as part of the discussion in Step 3. It would give one perspective on the passage that speaks to its meaning today; the group then would identify the passage's meaning for them. *Time frame:* 1½ – 2 hours.

STEPS FOR EQUIPPING THE SAINTS

1. Clarify what the passage is saying.
- What do the words in the passage mean?

- Why do certain translations use different words?
- What do commentaries say about any obscurities in the passage?
- What nuances do the words have that may not be apparent in English?
2. Clarify why the passage was preserved.
- What was the significance of this passage to the community that preserved it?
- What were the issues they were dealing with at the time?
- How did this passage speak to those issues?
3. Reflect on what the passage means for us today.
- What is the passage calling me/us to do?

Close the group meeting with prayer.

Listen for the Word

This method can be used in a family, between a parent and child, individually, or in a group setting. It lends itself to journaling or drawing as part of the reflection. The focal point is to listen for a word or phrase that touches your life. *Time frame:* 30–45 minutes.

READ THE GOSPEL

In silence, reflect on the word or phrase that touches your life, nothing else.

Question:
- Who are you in the story? (Name the character at this time in your life).

READ THE GOSPEL A SECOND TIME.

Use a journal to respond to the questions:
- Who are you in the story? Name one experience or relationship in your life that illustrates that for you.
- In your life this week, with your family, at your work, ministry, in your friendships, with neighbors, name one concrete way you are called to live this gospel message.
- If that is how you are called this week, what will it cost you to live that message?
- Are you willing to pay the price?

READ THE GOSPEL A THIRD TIME

Silent reflection.

Questions:
- Name some value or issue this gospel raises for you.

- Name one concrete way you feel the community of _____ is called to live this gospel message today.

CLOSING QUESTIONS
- Where have you been challenged or affirmed through this reflection?
- How can it help you this week?

Modern Application

This method is suited for families, youth, as well as small groups. It allows for connecting personal experiences, current events, and the biblical story. *Time frame:* 45 minutes.

STEPS FOR MODERN APPLICATION
1. Read the text.
2. As a group, decide upon a modern situation that is similar to the biblical one.
3. Individually write how you imagine the modern situation unfolding, if it were a scene you were observing.
4. Discuss your different scenes. What do the scenes say about what is important for you in the passage? What do the scenes say about how the biblical passage can be applied to life today?
5. Individually identify a scene from your own life (personal, school, work, social, or political) related to the scene you constructed.
6. Say how you will use what you have learned from the Bible passage.

Transforming Bible Study

Walter Wink explains this approach in his book *Transforming Bible Study* (Nashville: Abingdon Press, 1990—out of print, check your local Resource Center); it is also the basis of Patricia Van Ness's book *Transforming Bible Study with Children* (Nashville: Abingdon Press, 1991—also out of print). Both books would give additional help to the group leader. *Time frame:* 1½–2 hours.

This process requires careful planning and preparation by the group leader. The questions in steps 3 and 4 need to be thought out and formulated beforehand. If imaginative meditation is to be used, it needs to be developed before the meeting. If activities are planned, materials need to be obtained and set up. Someone inexperienced in doing this type of process may wish to seek a mentor to help design and guide the process until the group is used to it. Once it is familiar to everyone, group members can help plan and facilitate the process.

Ground rules for use of this approach are as follows:

- The text is the focus, not the leader. The leader poses questions that enable the participants to enter into dialogue with the meaning of the text at all levels.
- Everyone is invited to join the conversation. Each member of the group has a different perspective to offer that will increase understanding of the text and its application.
- Everyone is equal before the text. Both learned scholars and beginners have their own responses to the text.

STEPS FOR TRANSFORMING BIBLE STUDY

1. *Take time for silent centering.* Participants quietly explore the anxieties and expectations they have brought with them. They examine how willing they are to let something new happen and whether they can be open to the Spirit and to one another.
2. *Someone reads the passage from scripture.*
3. *The leader asks prepared questions about the context of the text.* The questions are designed to help the group identify the critical issues in the text and to understand the text in its own right. For example, they might consider working on the Sabbath (Matthew 12:1–8; Mark 2:23–28; Luke 6:1–5).

- What is the charge brought against Jesus? What significance do you attach to the fact that it is the disciples, not Jesus, who are accused? Is the issue religious or economic?
- What is Jesus' defense? Does it meet the Pharisees' objection? How does Matthew change it?
- Explain the absence (in Matthew and Luke) of verse 27 in Mark. What do you think is the original core of the narrative?
- What is the basis for action on the Sabbath? What was its purpose? Does Jesus make "man the measure of all things?" Does he make himself the measure? Why doesn't Jesus take up the comparison with David and conclude, "so the Son of David is lord even of the Sabbath?" Does Jesus appeal to his own authority or to a principle inherent in the situation? In the material that Matthew adds, is the appeal made to Jesus' authority or to a principle inherent in the situation?
- Is Jesus granting his followers license to do what they do? What attitude does Jesus take toward the Sabbath here?
- Who or what is the "son of man" here? Is it Jesus?
- What do you learn about Jesus here?

4. *The leader asks questions that help the group members explore the impact the text is making on them.* The group explores the linkages between the text and modern life. The leader may invite the group to enter imaginatively into one or more of the biblical characters and experience them in either their historical setting or in a modern context. The leader may ask the group to explore their emotional responses to the symbols and ideas, for example, the parable of the man with the withered hand (Mark 3:1–6; Matthew 12:9–14; Luke 6:6–11).

- The authorities do not understand Jesus' sense of justice in the scene. Why? At what point does the duty to comply with laws cease to be binding, in view of the need to help others or to oppose injustice? How is this liberating power manifesting itself in us today as we relate to the power structure of society?

- Now close your eyes and envision that you are:
  - Jesus coming into the synagogue on the Sabbath. You know that your opponents are present. You see a man with a deformed hand sitting in the congregation. Even though he asks nothing from you, you call him over and ask him to stretch out his hand. Then you heal him. Your enemies leave to plot against you.
  - One of the Pharisees, entering the synagogue right behind this Galilean rabbi, whom you distrust. You, too, see the crippled man. You know Jesus can heal him, but if he does, he will have broken the Sabbath law against work. Jesus reminds you that the importance of life supersedes the law and calls the man to him. The man exposes his crippled hand to Jesus, and Jesus makes it well in front of your eyes. You leave to plot against Jesus.
  - The crippled man, sitting in the synagogue and waiting for the service to begin. Your withered and useless hand is resting in your lap. Because of your hand, you can't do heavy work. Life is difficult. There is a commotion at the door, and a stranger comes in—followed by a group of Pharisees. They begin talking about healing on the Sabbath, and suddenly the stranger turns to you and calls you over to the group. You go to him. "Stretch out your hand," he says, "and show us your crippled limb." And suddenly your hand is no longer crippled.

- How did you feel as Jesus? As the Pharisee? As the crippled man? Which did you identify with most? Why?
- Why does Jesus make the man display his withered hand? Are there times when we have to display our withered parts in order to be healed?

5. *The group explores how the text can be applied.* Through music, movement, painting, sculpting, written dialogue, and small group discussion, each person allows the broken aspects of his or her life to be called forth into healing. For example, using the withered hand passage, distribute a piece of clay to each person. Have each person make the withered part within him- or herself. Share in the whole group or smaller groups.

6. *Close the group with prayer.* The activity (like the one described above) may elicit emotions; a quiet time of prayer during which people are free to offer prayers aloud if they wish is helpful in facilitating the transition from the group experience to leaving.

Reflection Beginning with Scripture

More than Bible study, this is a method of theological reflection that focuses on a selection from scripture and uses it as the starting point for reflection. Developed and used in the *Education for Ministry* (EfM) program from the University of the South, School of Theology in Sewanee, Tennessee (http://www.sewanee.edu/EFM/index.htm), this and other forms of theological reflection are the core aspects of this four-year adult formation program. The passage may come from the week, or the group may select a passage that is of special interest. *Time frame: 1½–2 hours.*

1. *Select a piece of scripture.*
   - A person in the group reads the selected passage of scripture.
   - Be silent for a couple of minutes.
2. *First responses.*
   - What word or phrase stands out for you? Share this in the group.
3. *Hear the passage again.*
   - Another person reads the selected passage again. Perhaps a different translation may be used. The group is silent for a couple of minutes.
4. *Examine the passage.*
   - What do you know about the meaning of the text or its original setting?
   - What is happening in the text? What is going on?
   - How have others interpreted this text? What kind of a text is this (sermon, parable, etc.)?
   - What might it mean today?
5. *Examine the scripture.*
   - What is the world like in this passage (creation)?
   - What human predicament in the world is revealed in this passage (sin)?
   - What indicates a change of mind, heart, or behavior (judgment)?
   - What gives rise to celebration in this world (redemption)?

6. *Making connections with our own experiences.*
- With whom do you identify in this passage?
- Can you recall a time in your life when you experienced an event or situation very similar to the one in the passage? What were your thoughts and feelings?
- What does that event or situation mean to you in light of this passage?
- In what way does the tradition support, inform, and/or challenge your experience?

7. *Look at the world (culture) around us.*
- What does the culture say about the world described in this passage? (Focus on one or two elements of culture. Remember that culture is not something bad.)

8. *What is my position?*
- Where do you stand?
- What do you believe about the matters or issues raised in the reflection?
- What is your position on these matters?

9. *Identify insights.*
- What new insights have emerged as a result of this reflection?
- What can you affirm or state that you have learned?

10. *Implications for the future.*
- Is there anything you intend to do differently as you live out your ministry?
- What help might you need to carry out your intentions?
- What are the consequences for others and for the future?

Reflection Based on Ubuntu and Indaba

This process deepens the theological realities of the Christian community, to accept the dignity of every person (transcending our great diversity) and to engage in our central mission—the work of reconciliation.

WHAT ARE UBUNTU AND INDABA?

The African concept of *Ubuntu*, from the Zulu word "humanity," is difficult to translate into English. According to Archbishop Desmond Tutu, the central idea of Ubuntu affirms that our humanity is inextricably mutual. Therefore, social harmony is the greatest good. In essence, Ubuntu asserts that we are created for community. It says, "a person is a person through other persons;" I am, because we are. In short, I am a person because you are a person.

At the heart of Ubuntu is forgiveness, forgiveness that leads to reconciliation. Archbishop Tutu writes in *No Future Without Forgiveness* (Doubleday, 1999), "to forgive is indeed the best form of self-interest, since anger, resentment, and revenge are corrosive of that *summum bonum*, that greatest good, communal harmony that enhances the humanity and personhood of all in the community." This echoes one of the main principles of our Baptismal Covenant—that we are all created in God's image and are to respect the dignity of every human being.

Indaba is a process based upon the Zulu and Xhosa ideal of purposeful discussion of the common concerns of our shared life. It is a method of engagement in dialogue. First and foremost, an Indaba acknowledges that there are issues that need to be addressed effectively in order to foster ongoing communal living.

The goal of an Indaba is to provide people (often from a variety of generations) with an opportunity to talk together, to share their stories, and to communicate their thoughts and ideas on a specific topic with an intentional focus on respect of all the participants' perspectives. The importance of being reconciled in community is held above all else. For Christians, that means to put Christ at the center of every discussion.

HOW DO YOU CONDUCT AN INDABA IN THE EPISCOPAL CHURCH?

Indaba depends upon dialogue. It is ideally suited to small groups. The Indaba should begin with Bible study and reflection—a sharing of stories based on the theme, on the topic that is affecting the community. The Indaba continues with face-to-face conversations that often include the exchange of conflicting perspectives and challenges to participants' various perspectives.

Each small group has an impartial listener, whose role is to capture the spirit of the face-to-face conversation. Each small group also has a facilitator, whose purpose is to gather the necessary resources, including (but not limited to) pertinent Bible passages, prayers from the Book of Common Prayer, and stories to share that enrich and challenge. It is the duty of the facilitator to invite the group into the process and to put closure on the process, as well.

Ubuntu should permeate an Indaba. Ubuntu, actualized into the Indaba process, strengthens participants by allowing them to hold forgiveness and reconciliation as the highest priority. In short, it allows them to understand that "who I am as a person depends on who you are as a person," that we are interconnected. This is the hoped-for objective to keep before the group during the Indaba.

PRAXIS OF THE PROCESS

The Process takes about two to two-and-a-half hours, with groups to be made up of no more than twenty-five people. It is strongly suggested that the facilitator schedule at least three meeting times, called sessions. Ideally, there should be eight sessions, two meeting times per week over a four-week time span. Invitations should be sent at least two to three months in advance.

This process can be used for many things in addition to discussing biblical passages. It can help prepare for diocesan conventions, vestry meetings, or General Convention. It can assist in making critical decisions about mission and ministry, to engage in a strategic planning process, or for basic congregational development, such as creating ministry with children.

THE INDABA PROCESS IN DETAIL

1. *Welcome, with introductions.*
2. *Name the topic.*

Topics can be anything that is challenging your congregation. This can include: financial struggles, mission work, ministry with children and young people, church schools, the environment, declining attendance, health and nutrition, healing of the past, and (of course) social justice issues such as human sexuality, racism, sexism, ageism, etc.

3. *Engage in Bible study.* Focus on a chosen scripture passage (The "I am" statements from the Gospel of John were used during the 2008 Lambeth Conference using Indaba.)
   - *Ask:* How is the Lord God speaking to us through the words of scripture?
   - *Pray:* That the participants can accept their different interpretations of scripture, setting aside self-interest and that the Holy Spirit is present with the group, to lead it into truth.
   - *Ask:* How does the scripture message offer hope to our world?
4. *Go deeper into the topic.* Some suggested ways to develop conversation about the topic include:
   - Show video clips of a variety of bishops or theologians speaking from their divergent perspectives.
   - Read stories reflecting on the topic, chosen to represent a variety of perspectives.
   - Use a video resource from a published curriculum, such as *Living the Questions* or *NOOMA.*
   - Listen to guest speakers who will share their own stories from a variety of perspectives.
5. *Reflect:*
   - What are we hearing as we listen or read the stories, how does what we are hearing in the stories impact or how is it indicative of the relationships and ministry of our community?
   - How does scripture inform what we are hearing in the stories?

- What is most important, or urgent for our time together; is there something or someone in need of forgiveness? What would be most important to reconcile for our ministry to go forward?
- When will we gather again to consider this depth of conversation?

6. *Send out.*
- To send folks out to continue to do the work of Ubuntu, you would want to set at least two more meeting times, if you have not as yet scheduled another gathering. You might need to do an Action Plan that names specific work/mission that needs to be accomplished, in a time frame, with accountability, i.e., who will follow through?

7. *Remember, conclude in prayer!*

> *Bless the Lord, O my Soul, and all that is within me, bless his holy Name.*
> *Bless the Lord, O my Soul, and forget not all his benefits.*
> (Psalm 103:1-2)

A Seasonal Guide to
"An Outline of the Faith"

"An Outline of the Faith commonly called the Catechism" (BCP 845–862) provides a brief review of the church's teaching that can be used as an outline for instruction. The following pages suggest links between the church's calendar of seasons and feast days and the various sections of the catechism that might be incorporated into an educational program, sermon, or discussion group offered during that season.

ADVENT

- *The Old Covenant (BCP 846–847):* The church looks back to the old covenant during Advent in order to understand the future promise of God.
- *God the Son (BCP 849–850):* Advent is a time of looking for Christ to come again.
- *The Christian Hope (BCP 861–862):* Advent points ahead to Christ's coming again and shares the vision of God's coming reign.

CHRISTMAS

- *God the Son (BCP 849–850):* Christmas celebrates the incarnation of God in Jesus.
- *The New Covenant (BCP 850–851):* Christmas proclaims that all people could know God "in the flesh" in Jesus. The New Covenant was established out of that encounter of "knowing the Lord" (Jeremiah 31:31–34).

EPIPHANY

- *The Ministry (BCP 855–856):* Epiphany and the Sundays after the Epiphany focus on the calling of the disciples and the nature of discipleship.
- *Holy Baptism (BCP 858–859)* One of the four "especially appropriate" times for baptism is Epiphany 1, the feast recalling the baptism of Jesus.

LENT

- *Human Nature (BCP 845):* Lent helps us see who we are in light of the gospel.
- *The Ten Commandments (BCP 847–848):* Lent focuses on the covenant made at baptism and renewed at every celebration of the Holy Eucharist. The Penitential Order often used during this season may include the reading of the Decalogue (BCP 317–318/350).
- *Sin and Redemption (BCP 848–849):* Lent deals directly with sin and redemption.
- *God the Son (BCP 849–850):* Lent reminds us of the role of Christ in bringing salvation.
- *The Holy Scriptures (BCP 853–854):* The lectionary readings during Lent provide a sweep of the biblical story recalled at the Easter Vigil.
- *Holy Baptism (BCP 858–859):* Lent is a season of preparation for baptisms at the Easter Vigil.
- *Other Sacramental Rites (BCP 860–861):* The rite of the Reconciliation of a Penitent (BCP 447–452) is especially appropriate during the Lenten season.

HOLY WEEK

- *Sin and Redemption (BCP 848–849):* Holy Week deals directly with redemption through Christ's death and resurrection.
- *God the Son (BCP 849–850):* Holy Week reminds us of the role of Christ in bringing salvation.
- *The Holy Eucharist (BCP 859–860):* Maundy Thursday remembers the institution of the Lord's Supper.

EASTER

- *God the Son (BCP 849–850):* Easter proclaims Christ's victory even over death.
- *The New Covenant (BCP 850–851):* A new covenant people was formed out of the resurrection of Christ.
- *The Holy Spirit (BCP 852–853):* The resurrection led to the gift of the Holy Spirit promised by Jesus before his death (John 15).
- *Holy Baptism (BCP 858–859):* Baptism into the new covenant of life in Christ is the primary focus of the Easter Vigil. The vigil is one of the four "most appropriate" days for baptisms.
- *The Holy Eucharist (BCP 859–860):* Every Sunday is a "little Easter," a day to proclaim that Christ has risen.
- *The Christian Hope (BCP 861–862):* Easter expresses the hope of resurrection.

ASCENSION DAY

- *God the Son (BCP 849–850):* The Feast of the Ascension points to the eternal role of Christ, seated at the right hand of God.

THE DAY OF PENTECOST

- *The New Covenant (BCP 850–851):* The new covenant established in Christ was written on the hearts of the people through the indwelling power of the Holy Spirit.
- *The Holy Spirit (BCP 852–853):* The Day of Pentecost marks the gift of the Holy Spirit to the church.
- *The Church (BCP 854–855):* On the first Pentecost the church was empowered to act in the name of Christ. This feast day is considered the "birthday" of the church.
- *The Ministry (BCP 855–856):* Christians are empowered for ministry by the Holy Spirit.
- *Holy Baptism (BCP 858–859):* The Day of Pentecost is one of the four "most appropriate" days for baptism in the church calendar. Pentecost recognizes the empowerment of the Holy Spirit at baptism and confirmation.

TRINITY SUNDAY

- *God the Father (BCP 846):* Trinity Sunday is a time to focus on the Trinity as a way of understanding God. God the Father has traditionally been known as the first person of the Trinity.
- *God the Son (BCP 849–850):* Trinity Sunday is a time to focus on the Trinity as a way of understanding God. God the Son has traditionally been known as the second person of the Trinity.
- *The Holy Spirit (BCP 852–853):* Trinity Sunday is a time to focus on the Trinity as a way of understanding God. God the Holy Spirit has traditionally been known as the third person of the Trinity.
- *The Creeds (BCP 851–852):* God the Trinity is described in the creeds of the church, including the Nicene Creed (BCP 326/358), the Apostles' Creed (BCP 53/96), and the Creed of Saint Athanasius (BCP 864).

THE SEASON AFTER PENTECOST

- *The Holy Scriptures (BCP 853–854):* The gospels and epistles are read semi-continuously for half of the year as a way of exploring the New Testament in depth.
- *The Ministry (BCP 855–856):* The lectionary readings during the weeks after Pentecost focus on the ministry of Jesus and the early disciples.

ALL SAINTS' DAY

- *The New Covenant (BCP 850–851):* The feast of All Saints recognizes the covenant community in this life and in the age to come.
- *The Church (BCP 854–855):* All Saints' Day celebrates the communion of saints that is the church throughout all ages.
- *Holy Baptism (BCP 858–859):* The feast of All Saints is one of the four "most appropriate" days for baptism in the church calendar. Those who are baptized are welcomed into the communion of the saints.
- *The Christian Hope (BCP 861–862):* All Saints' Day recognizes the hope of life to come in the communion of saints.

ALL DAYS AND SEASONS

- *Prayer and Worship (BCP 856–857):* Prayer and worship lie at the heart of the Christian faith and life.
- *The Sacraments (BCP 857–858):* The sacraments of God's grace are celebrated and lived out by Christians every day.
- *Other Sacramental Rites (BCP 860–861):* Other sacramental rites celebrated in the Episcopal Church throughout the church year include Confirmation, Ordination, Holy Matrimony, Reconciliation of a Penitent, and Ministration to the Sick.

Suggested References and Resources

THE LECTIONARY

Bartlett, David and Barbara Brown Taylor, editors. *Feasting on the Word: Preaching the Revised Common Lectionary, Year B, Volumes 1, 2, 3.* Louisville: Westminster/John Knox Press, 2008.

Borsch, Frederick Houk. *Introducing the Lessons of the Church Year.* New York: Church Publishing, 2009.

Lawrence, Kenneth T., editor. *Imaging the Word: An Arts and Lectionary Resource, Vol. 1.* Cleveland: Pilgrim Press, 1994.

_____. *Imaging the Word: An Arts and Lectionary Resource, Vol. 2.* Cleveland: Pilgrim Press, 1999.

_____. *Imaging the Word: An Arts and Lectionary Resource Vol. 3.* Cleveland: Pilgrim Press, 1996.

Milton, Ralph and Margaret Kyle. *Lectionary Story Bible: Year A.* Kelowna, British Columbia: Woodlake Books, 2007.

_____. *Lectionary Story Bible: Year B.* Kelowna, British Columbia: Woodlake Books, 2008.

_____. *Lectionary Story Bible: Year C.* Kelowna, British Columbia: Woodlake Books, 2009.

Plater, Ormonde. *Intercession: A Theological and Practical Guide.* Cambridge, Mass.: Cowley Publications, 1995.

Ramshaw, Gail. *A Three-Year Banquet: The Lectionary for the Assembly.* Minneapolis: Augsburg Fortress, 2004.

Ramshaw, Gail, ed. *Intercessions for the Christian People*. Collegeville, Minn.: Liturgical Press, 1999. (Prayers of the People reflecting the themes of the Propers are offered for every Sunday and Holy Day in the three-year lectionary.)

The Revised Common Lectionary. New York: Church Publishing, 2008.

Revised Common Lectionary Prayers: Proposed by the Consultation on Como Texts. Minneapolis: Augsburg Fortress, 2002.

Thompson, Katie. *The Complete Children's Liturgy Book: Liturgies of the Word for Years A, B, C*. Mystic, Conn.: Twenty-Third Publications, 2008.

Treasures Old and New: Images in the Lectionary. Minneapolis: Augsburg Fortress, 2002.

Texts for Preaching: A Lectionary Commentary Based on the NRSV. Louisville: Westminster/John Knox Press, 1995. (Separate volumes are available for Years A, B, and C.)

LITURGY AND WORSHIP

Atkinson, Clifford W. *A Lay Minister's Guide to the Book of Common Prayer*. Harrisburg, Pa.: Morehouse Publishing, 1988.

Black, Vicki K. *Welcome to the Bible*. New York: Church Publishing, 2007.

_____. *Welcome to the Book of Common Prayer*. New York: Church Publishing, 2005.

_____. *Welcome to the Church Year*. New York: Church Publishing, 2004.

Bock, Susan K. *Liturgy for the Whole Church: Multigenerational Resources for Worship*. New York: Church Publishing, 2008.

The Book of Occasional Services 2003. New York: Church Publishing, 2003.

Changes: Prayers and Service Honoring Rites of Passage. New York: Church Publishing, 2007.

Enriching Our Worship: Supplemental Liturgical Materials. New York: Church Publishing, 1997.

Giles, Richard. *Times and Seasons: Creating Transformative Worship Throughout the Year*. New York: Church Publishing, 2008.

The Book of Occasional Services. New York: Church Publishing, 2004.

Lesser Feasts and Fasts 2006. New York: Church Publishing, 2006.

Kitch, Anne E. *What We Do in Church: An Anglican Child's Activity Book.* Harrisburg, Pa.: Morehouse Publishing, 2004. (Spanish edition, 2008)

————. *What We Do in Advent: An Anglican Kid's Activity Book.* Harrisburg, Pa.: Morehouse Publishing, 2006.

————. *What We Do in Lent: A Child's Activity Book.* Harrisburg, Pa.: Morehouse Publishing, 2007.

Malloy, Patrick. *Celebrating Eucharist: A Practical Ceremonial Guide for Clergy and Other Liturgical Ministers.* New York: Church Publishing, 2007.

Micks, Marianne H. *Loving the Questions: An Exploration of the Nicene Creed.* New York: Seabury Classics, 2005.

Mitchell, Leonel L. *Praying Shapes Believing: A Theological Commentary on The Book of Common Prayer.* Harrisburg, Pa.: Morehouse Publishing, 1985.

Morris, Clayton L. *Holy Hospitality: Worship and the Baptismal Covenant.* New York: Church Publishing, 2006.

Nelson, Gertrud Mueller. *To Dance with God: Family Ritual and Community Celebration.* New York: Paulist Press, 1986.

Rowthorn, Jeffery W. *The Wideness of God's Mercy: Litanies to Enlarge Our Prayer.* New York: Church Publishing, 2007.

Webber, Christopher L. *Welcome to Sunday: An Introduction to Worship in the Episcopal Church.* New York: Church Publishing, 2002.

Westerhoff, John H. *Living Faithfully as a Prayer Book People.* Harrisburg, Pa.: Morehouse Publishing, 2004.

White, Steven J. *Intercessions: For Sundays, Holy Days, and Special Occasions, Year B.* New York: Church Publishing, 2008.

Learning Resources

Bailey, Julia Huttar and Ernesto Medina. *Awake My Soul.* New York: The Episcopal Church, 2000. http://www.episcopalchurch.org/documents/MYP_Awake_My_Soul.pdf

Battle, Michael. *Reconciliation: The Ubuntu Theology of Desmond Tutu.* Cleveland: Pilgrim Press, 1997.

Berryman, Jerome W. *Teaching Godly Play: The Sunday Morning Handbook, revised edition.* New York: Church Publishing, 2009.

Called to Teach and Learn: A Catechetical Guide for the Episcopal Church. New York: The Domestic and Foreign Missionary Society, PECUSA, 1994.

The Catechumenal Process: Adult Initiation and Formation for Christian Life and Ministry. New York: Church Hymnal Corporation, 1990.

The Children's Charter for the Church (The Episcopal Church). http://www.episcopalchurch.org/44385_48895_ENG_HTM.htm

Diehl, William E. *The Monday Connection: On Being an Authentic Christian in a Weekday World.* San Francisco: Harper San Francisco, 1991.

Dykstra, Craig. *Growing in the Life of Faith: Education and Christian Practices, 2nd edition.* Louisville: Westminster/John Knox Press, 2005.

Good, Deirdre. *Jesus' Family Values.* New York: Church Publishing, 2006.

Gordh, Bill. *Building a Children's Chapel: One Story at a Time.* New York: Church Publishing, 2008.

Halmo, Joan. *Celebrating the Church Year with Young Children.* Chicago: Liturgical Press, 1988.

Harris, Maria. *Fashion Me a People: Curriculum in the Church.* Louisville: Westminster/John Knox Press, 1989.

Kraus, Donald. *Choosing a Bible: For Worship, Teaching, Study, Preaching and Prayer.* New York: Church Publishing, 2007.

Love, Jean Floyd, Mickey Meyers, Sylvia Washer, and Sue Lou. *Get Ready! Get Set! Worship! A Resource for Including Children in Worship.* Louisville: Geneva Press, 1999.

Lucchese, K.M. *Folk Like Me.* New York: Church Publishing, 2008.

Mangan, Louise and Nancy Wyse. *Living the Christ Life: Rediscovering the Seasons of the Church Year.* Kelowna, British Columbia: Wood Lake Books, 2001.

May, Scottie, Beth Posterski, Catherine Stonehouse, and Linda Cannell. *Children Matter: Celebrating Their Place in the Church, Family and Community.* Grand Rapids: William B. Eerdmans, 2005.

McLaughlin, Nancy Ann. *Do You Believe? Living the Baptismal Covenant.* Harrisburg, Pa.: Morehouse Publishing, 2006.

Mercer, Joyce Ann. *Welcoming Children: A Practical Theology of Childhood.* St. Louis: Chalice Press, 2005.

Mick, Lawrence C. *Living Baptism Daily: A Guide for the Baptized.* Collegeville, Minn.: The Liturgical Press, 2004.

Mitchell, Leonel I. *Praying Shapes Believing: A Theological Commentary on the Book of Common Prayer.* Harrisburg, Pa.: Morehouse Publishing, 1991.

Morgan, Donn. *Fighting with the Bible: Why Scripture Divides Us and How It Can Bring Us Together.* New York: Church Publishing, 2007.

Morgan, Richard L. *Remembering Your Story: Creating Your Own Spiritual Autobiography.* Nashville: Upper Room Books, 2002.

Palmer, Parker. *Let Your Life Speak: Listening for the Voice of Vocation.* Chicago: Jossey-Bass, 1999.

Portaro, Sam. *Brightest and Best: A Companion to the Lesser Feasts and Fasts.* Boston: Cowley Publications, 2001.

Price, Charles P. and Louis Weil. *Liturgy for Living, Revised Edition.* Harrisburg, Pa.: Morehouse Publishing, 2000.

Pritchard, Gretchen Wolff. *Offering the Gospel to Children.* Cambridge, Mass.: Cowley Publications, 1992.

Russell, Joseph P. *Discovering Called to Teach and Learn* (The Episcopal Church). http://www.episcopalchurch.org/48931_59225_ENG_HTM.htm

Sandall, Elizabeth J. *Including Children in Worship: A Planning Guide for Congregations.* Minneapolis: Augsburg Fortress, 1992.

Schwab, A. Wayne. *When the Members are the Missionaries: An Extraordinary Calling for Ordinary People.* Essex, N.Y.: Member Mission Press, 2002.

Tammany, Klara. *Living Water: Baptism as a Way of Life.* New York: Church Publishing, 2002.

Tirabassi, Maren C. and Maria I. Tirabassi. *Before the Amen: Creative Resources for Worship.* Cleveland: Pilgrim Press, 2007.

Tye, Karen B. *Christian Education in the Small Membership Church.* Nashville: Abingdon Press, 2008.

Vest, Norvene. *Gathered in the Word: Praying the Scripture in Small Groups.* Nashville: Upper Room Books, 1997.

Wade, Frank. *Transforming Scripture.* New York: Church Publishing, 2008.

Watkins, Clare. *Living Baptism: Called Out of the Ordinary: Christian Discipleship in a Post-Christian World.* London: Darton, Longman, and Todd, 2006.

Webb-Mitchell, Brett P. *Christly Gestures: Learning to Be Members of the Body of Christ.* Grand Rapids: William B. Eerdmans, 2003.

Westerhoff, Caroline. *Calling: A Song for the Baptized.* New York: Seabury Classics, 2005. (Reflections on the meaning of baptism, using the Baptismal Covenant as a framework.)

Westerhoff, John H., III, *Will Our Children Have Faith? Revised edition.* Harrisburg, Pa.: Morehouse Publishing, 2000.

Wingate, Andrew, Kevin Ward, Carrie Pemberton, and Wilson Sitshebo, editors. *Anglicanism: A Global Communion.* New York: Church Publishing, 1998.

Music

Daw, Carl P. and Kevin R. Hackett. *A HymnTune Psalter: Book One and Book Two.* New York, Church Publishing, 2007.

Daw, Carl P. and Thomas Pavlechko, editors. *Liturgical Music for the Revised Common Lectionary, Year A, Year B, Year C.* New York: Church Publishing, 2007, 2008, 2009.

Hawthorne, Robert A. *Portland Psalter: Liturgical Years ABC (Book 1 and Book 2).* New York: Church Publishing, 2004.

Kucharski, Joseph, ed. *The Episcopal Musician's Handbook.* Living Church Foundation. Dated and spiral bound; published each year, incorporating all the hymns in the Episcopal hymnals according to the lectionary readings.

The Hymnal 1982. New York: Church Publishing, 1982.

Lift Every Voice and Sing II: An African American Hymnal. New York: Church Hymnal Corporation, 1993.

Roth, Nancy L. *A Closer Walk: Meditating on Hymns for Year A* New York: Church Publishing, 1998.

_____. *Awake, My Soul! Meditating on Hymns for Year B.* New York: Church Publishing, 1999.

_____. *New Every Morning: Meditating on Hymns for Year C.* New York: Church Publishing, 2000.

———. *Praise My Soul: Meditating on Hymns.* New York: Church Publishing, 2001.

Roth, Robert N. and Nancy L. Roth, editors. *We Sing of God: A Hymnal for Children* (Children's Hymnbook and Teacher's Guide). New York: Church Publishing, 1989.

Vidal-White, Fiona. *My Heart Sings Out* (Singer's Edition and Teacher's Guide). New York: Church Publishing, 2005.

Voices Found: Women in the Church's Song (Pew Edition and Leader's Guide). New York: Church Publishing, 2003.

Wonder, Love, and Praise: A Supplement to The Hymnal 1982. New York: Church Publishing, 1997.

BIBLES

Attridge, Harold W. and Society of Biblical Literature. *Harper Collins Study Bible, with the Apocryphal/Deuterocanonical Books: Fully Revised and Updated New Revised Standard Version.* New York: Harper Collins, 2006.

Birch, Bruce, Brian K. Blount, Thomas G. Long, Gail R. O'Day, and W. Sibley Towner, editors. *The Discipleship Study Bible: New Revised Standard Version with Apocrapha.* Louisville: Westminster/John Knox Press, 2008.

Coogan, Michael D., Marc Z. Brettler, Carol A Newson, and Pheme Perkins, editors. *The New Oxford Annotated Bible with the Aprocrypha, Augmented Third Edition, New Revised Standard Version.* New York: Oxford University Press, 2007.

Hastings, Selina. *The Children's Illustrated Bible.* New York: D.K. Children, 2005.

Harper Bibles. *The Green Bible.* New York: HarperOne, 2008.

Life Application Bible—New International Version Carol Stream, Ill.: Tyndale House Publishers, 1997.

O'Day, Gail R. and David Peterson, general editors. *The Access Bible: An Ecumenical Learning Resource for People of Faith, New Revised Standard Version with Apocrapha.* New York: Oxford University Press, 1999.

Peterson, Eugene H. *The Message: The Bible in Contemporary Language (New Testament with Psalms and Proverbs).* New York: New Press Publishing Group, 2004.

WEBSITES

Using the Revised Common Lectionary

Resources for congregations:
http://www.episcopalchurch.org/19625_21607_ENG_HTM.htm

The Episcopal Church and the RCL:
http://www.episcopalchurch.org/19625_19606_ENG_HTM.
htm?menupage=19605

Eucharistic Lectionary Psalms (from Grace Church, Newark, N.J.):
http://www.gracechurchinnewark.org/psalms.htm

Gospel Readings for Sundays and Holy Days (notated for singing) (from Grace Church, Newark, N.J.): http://www.gracechurchinnewark.org/Gospels.html

Prayers of the People (by Ormonde Plater):
http://members.cox.net/oplater/prayer.htm

The Anglican Gradual and Sacramentary (by David Allen White who explains it as "like the *Anglican Missal*, in that it provides the traditional anthems (sometimes called the minor propers) and special prayers and other texts, but it is designed to be used with the 1979 prayer book, *Lesser Feasts and Fasts*, and the *Book of Occasional Services*, and it provides not only traditional language but contemporary English and Spanish."): http://anglicangradual.stsams.org/

The Lectionary Page: http://www.io.com/~kellywp/index.html

The Lectionary: http://www.satucket.com/lectionary/

From the United Methodist Church:
http://www.gbod.org/worship/lectionary/default.asp

The Episcopal Church and The Book of Common Prayer

The Episcopal Church: http://www.episcopalchurch.org

An Episcopal Dictionary of the Church: A Glossary of Liturgical Terms: http://www.episcopalchurch.org/19625_19610_ENG_HTM.htm?menupage=19609

An Outline of the Faith (The Catechism):
http://www.episcopalchurch.org/19625_10898_ENG_HTM.
htm?menupage=72970